CAPITAL AND
TIME 307
53

CAPITAL AND TIME

A Neo-Austrian Theory

BY

JOHN HICKS

CLARENDON PRESS · OXFORD

1987

Oxford University Press, Walton Street, Oxford OX2 6DP
Oxford New York Toronto
Delhi Bombay Calcutta Madras Karachi
Petaling Jaya Singapore Hong Kong Tokyo
Nairobi Dar es Salaam Cape Town
Melbourne Auckland
and associated companies in
Beirut Berlin Ibadan Nicosia

Oxford is a trade mark of Oxford University Press

© *Oxford University Press 1973*

Reprinted (new as paperback) 1987

British Library Cataloguing in Publication Data
Hicks, John, 1904–
Capital and time: a neo-Austrian theory.
1. Capital
I. Title
332'.041   HB501
ISBN 0–19–877286–6

Library of Congress Cataloging in Publication Data
Hicks, John Richard, Sir, 1904–
Capital and time.
Reprint. Originally published: Oxford: Clarendon Press, 1973.
Includes bibliographies.
1. Capital—Mathematical models.   2. Austrian
school of economists.   I. Title.
HB501.H48 1987   332'.041   87-20233
ISBN 0–19–877286–6

PREFACE

THIS is the third book I have written about Capital. *Value and Capital* (1939); *Capital and Growth* (1965); *Capital and Time* (1973). They were not planned as a trilogy. I had no idea, when I finished the first, that I would write the second; when I finished the second, that I would write the third. Nor do the later volumes supersede the earlier, save in a few quite limited respects. Capital (I am not the first to discover) is a very large subject, with many aspects; wherever one starts, it is hard to bring more than a few of them into view. It is just as if one were making pictures of a building; though it is the same building, it looks quite different from different angles. As I now realize, I have been walking round my subject, taking different views of it. Though that which is presented here is just another view, it turns out to be quite useful in fitting the others together.

Value and Capital was a product of the Keynesian thirties. Though I began to write it before I had seen the *General Theory*, the 'capital' or 'dynamic' part of the book is deeply influenced by Keynes. The method, of course, being descended from Walras and Pareto, is quite un-Keynesian; but the problem to which it is applied, in the second part of the book, is similar to Keynes's problem. What determines the short-period equilibrium of a closed system, when that is conceived, not just in terms of tastes and resources but in terms of plans and expectations, oriented towards a future that is outside the period in question? In such *Temporary Equilibrium* analysis, the future plays its part, but it remains the future. We do not go ahead to later periods, when what was future becomes present.

By the time I wrote *Capital and Growth*, many others had gone ahead; a principal object in writing was to clear my own mind on what they had been doing. So *Capital and Growth* is critical and expository, rather than constructive. I was fully aware, by this time, of the variety of ways by which 'capital' could be approached, of the variety of angles from which the 'building' could be viewed. I had no desire to champion any one to the exclusion of others.

There was no reason in principle why the methods that were listed in *Capital and Growth* should be the only ones possible; and it was not long after I had finished writing when my attention was drawn to an important approach which I had overlooked. This is the approach that is developed in the present volume. It is descended, as I emphasize in my sub-title, from the 'Austrian' theory of Böhm-Bawerk and Hayek—a theory which had gone out of fashion, because of an obstacle which appeared to confine it to particular and practically unimportant applications. By developing an idea that was already present in *Value and Capital*, I was able to show that this obstacle could be overcome. There was something to be made of an 'Austrian' theory, after all.

The suggestion, which started my thinking in this direction, came (as will be explained) from Charles Kennedy[1]; but it soon became apparent, as I proceeded, that there were others, especially among Joan Robinson's circle at Cambridge, who were working on somewhat similar lines.[2] A first draft of my own work was published as 'A Neo-Austrian Growth Theory' in the *Economic Journal*, June 1970. The present version begins by covering the same ground (in what is, I hope, a simpler and more readable form) but afterwards pushes much further on. The whole of the discussion of the 'Full Employment path', which proves to be one of the most suggestive parts of the construction, is new to this book. So is most of Part III.

I have several times written on Measurement of Capital, but it has taken a long while (even with the aid of my new model) to clear the matter up. In the paper on that subject which I gave at the London meeting of the International Statistical Association in 1969 (and which appeared in their Proceedings) I saw a part of the truth, but only a part; the same is true of the paper on 'Value and Volume of Capital' which was published in the *Indian Economic Journal* in that same year. At the end of 1970 I lectured on Capital Measurement at the University of Manchester, but I did not publish those lectures, since I could see by that time that I was not ready. I am grateful to my friends at that University for allowing me to abstain from publication of those lectures as I gave them.

---

[1] See below, p. 5n.

[2] D. M. Nuti, 'Capitalism, Socialism and Steady Growth', *Economic Journal* (March 1970); A. Bhaduri, 'A Physical Analogue of the Re-Switching Problem' (Oxford Economic Papers, July 1970). I am, however, in closer agreement with Arrow and Levhari, 'Uniqueness of the International Rate of Return with Variable Life of Investment', *Economic Journal* (September 1969), from whom I take the term 'truncation'.

Such of their substance as was worth preserving is included in this book.

I am well aware, in concluding this book, that the task I set myself is by no means completed. Not only in Chapter XII ('Ways Ahead') but in several other places also, one catches sight of further questions which need to be examined. I am sure, however, that there are plenty of people who will want to examine them; it is time I called them in.

Oxford   J.R.H.
December 1972

CONTENTS

PART I

MODEL

PART II

TRAVERSE

PART III

CONTROVERSY

PART I

MODEL

I

GOODS AND PROCESSES

1. A CAPITAL good, it is commonly said (and I have said it myself), is one that 'can be used in any way to satisfy wants in subsequent periods'.[1] It is not ruled out, on this definition, that the same good may be both capital good and consumption good. The domestic car is usable this week, and will continue (one hopes) to be usable in subsequent weeks; it satisfies present wants and future wants *jointly*. The same is true of consumer capital goods generally. But it is not only the durable goods which are at present in the possession of the consumer which have this property of present–future *jointness*. For the same is true of the car that is hired, or rented, even one that is only rented for a particular occasion. It still serves, or is intended to serve, both present and future wants; but the present and the future wants are wants of different people.

Thus if one is thinking in terms of ownership, the capital good–consumption good line is drawn in one place; but if one is thinking in terms of want-satisfaction, it is drawn in another. Houses, of course, are the prime example of a good which may be owned outright by the current user, or may be rented. In some states of society, most houses are rented; in others, most are owned outright. But unless we are specially interested in questions of home ownership, we are usually prepared to reckon all houses as consumers' capital goods, because they satisfy (directly) both present and future wants. We may nevertheless be willing to take as our standard case that in which all houses are rented—reckoning the home owner as paying an 'imputed rent' to himself.

It remains the case, if we take the latter view, that the fundamental distinction among capital goods is between those which satisfy present and future wants jointly, and those which derive the whole of their value from the contribution which they are expected to make to the satisfaction of future wants. As has just been shown, this is not the same as the distinction in terms of

[1] *Social Framework*, 4th edn. (1971), p. 95.

ownership. Nor is it the same as another distinction, which is also a matter of jointness (or complementarity). There are goods which have utility in themselves, by themselves; and there are goods which are only useful in combination with something else. Most of the goods with future use only are prevented from being useful in the present because there is further work which must be done on them before they can become useful; their utility may thus be said to be *indirect*. There are nevertheless a few cases (such as the maturing of wine) where mere lapse of time confers utility; and there are many cases in which a good is useful in the present, when complementary labour is available, but in the absence of that labour would not be useful at all. 'Horizontal' complementarity of this sort is one thing; the 'vertical' complementarity, with which we shall be mainly concerned, is another.

2. We may set aside the question of ownership of consumer durables by supposing that all such are rented, not purchased outright. This is not so ferocious an assumption as it may appear. It does not oblige us to think of the consumer as paying rent for the clothes on his back. For the most important type of consumer durables, houses, it is easily acceptable. And since it is the practice of statisticians to treat all purchases by consumers as 'consumption' (except the purchase of houses), it may be claimed that it is quite in line with the facts, as presented to us by the statisticians; even if it is not in line with what, in a more critical mood, we might prefer to regard as the facts.

Consumers may then be regarded as buying just three sorts of things: (1) 'single-use' consumption goods, which are wholly consumed in the current period, and which have utility in themselves, without further work (or what counts as further work) being done on them; (2) direct labour services; (3) the services of such capital goods as are capable of providing services in the present, either by themselves, or in conjunction with current labour. All of these categories will be formally covered by the following analysis, but to the second—the direct labour services—I shall give little attention. In spite of the increasing importance of the so-called 'service industries', most of them (I believe) come into the third, not the second category. The prime example of direct hiring of labour, unaccompanied by hiring of capital goods, is domestic service. Though such hiring persists in some of the professions, in an advanced economy it is usually on the way out. The more typical case is the purchase of the railway ticket, when the consumer is buying the services of the railway equipment, and of the driver, jointly.

3. So, by our assumption all capital goods are producers' goods; all purchase and sale of capital goods is sale by one producer (or firm) to another. And all producers' goods are capital goods—so capital goods are simply stages in the process of production. The sales of capital goods, such as the sale by the firm which produces a raw material (or machine) to the firm which uses it, result from the *disintegration* of the productive process; in a (vertically) integrated process they would not occur. Now the extent of integration, in an actual economy, is a thing which can vary and does vary, very much, from time to time. It is necessary, when constructing a model, to make some particular assumption about integration. There are, so far as I can see, three main alternatives.

One, which at first sight is the most attractive (but proves treacherous), is the *Method of Sectoral Disintegration*. This admits just two kinds of 'firms': those which make capital goods, now identified as 'machines',[1] and those which use them. The accounting distinction between Consumption and Investment is converted into an industrial division. But the accounting division is not an industrial division. There is investment while the machine is being built, and there is disinvestment while it is being used. What, therefore, is liable to happen, if this Method is adopted, is that the time taken to make the machine is liable to be forgotten; and that depreciation, if dealt with at all, is dealt with in a very clumsy fashion. The value of the machine, when it is transferred from the one sector to the other, is made a basis for the valuation of capital in general—for this is the only point at which the price of a capital good becomes *visible*. But there are elements in the value of the capital stock (in both sectors) which this leaves out of account.[2]

Very much better is the *Method of von Neumann*.[3] This is to

---

[1] Or 'tractors', as I called them in *Capital and Growth* (1965).

[2] This is the substance of the criticism which was made (against my own use of the Sectoral Method, in some central chapters of *Capital and Growth*) by C. M. Kennedy ('Time, Interest and the Production Function' in *Value, Capital and Growth*, pp. 275–90). The work which has gone into the present book took its origin from reflection upon the consequences of the criticisms he there made.

[3] 'A Model of General Economic Equilibrium' (English translation in *Review*

admit a regular (and high) degree of disintegration. The productive process, in each 'firm', lasts just one period. All of the firm's inputs are acquired at the beginning of the period; and at the end it sells—all it has. There is then a regular market in capital goods (or producers' goods) at all stages of production (in the technical sense); a system of prices is set up, which reflects the state of the general process, at every stage. Since the length of the *period* is arbitrary, and may (if we desire) be infinitesimally short, the behaviour of the economy—the whole behaviour of the economy—both in quantity and in value terms, is kept under continuous observation. Logically, the scheme is *tight*; the Sectoral Method, in comparison, is quite flabby.

It is by no means my intention, in this book, to criticize the von Neumann method. It would be presumptuous to do so, and for my purpose it is unnecessary. The position of this method, on its own ground, is secure. It is superbly adapted for the application of modern mathematics; the principles to which it leads have great elegance, and—so far as they go—indisputable validity. Yet the categories with which it works are not very recognizable as economic categories; so to make economic sense of its propositions translation is required. One has got so far away from the regular economic concepts that the translation is not at all an easy matter.

4. Thus there should be room for a third method, expressible more naturally in economic terms. Such a method I hope to work out in this book. It is at the other extreme from the von Neumann method. The von Neumann method is the extreme of disintegration; there is a complete reference back to the market in every period, a period which can be made as short as we like. Ours, on the other hand, is the extreme of (vertical) integration. There is no 'intermediate' reference back to the market. The production process, over time, is taken as a whole.

I have elsewhere[1] called this method 'neo-Austrian'. It is recognizably descended from the 'Austrian theory of capital'—the theory of Böhm-Bawerk,[2] that was subsequently elaborated by

---

of Economic Studies, 1945–6). I gave my own version of the von Neumann model in *Capital and Growth*, Chs. XVIII–XIX.

[1] 'A Neo-Austrian Growth Theory' (*Econ. Jour.* 1970). I shall subsequently refer to this first sketch of the theory that is presented in this book, as NAGT.

[2] *Positive Theory of Capital* (1889).

Wicksell[1] and Hayek.[2] But it is not just Austrian, it is neo-Austrian; for it differs from the old Austrian theory in one essential respect.

Like Böhm-Bawerk (or Hayek) I think of the general productive process as being composed of a number (presumably a large number) of *separable elementary processes*. The separability is essential, and it is of course not wholly realistic. It is a leaving-out of one kind of complication, in the hope that by doing so we shall be able to see the rest of the problem more clearly. I think I shall show that it is a justified hope.

The elementary process, of the older Austrian theory, was of a simple, too simple, type. There was associated with a unit of output, forthcoming at a particular date, a sequence of units of input at particular previous dates. The sequence of inputs, and the single output, constituted the process.

There is a useful analogy with static 'Walrasian' theory. We are accustomed to think of a product being made by the combination of a number of factors, or inputs. A 'technique' is defined by a set[3] of input coefficients, the quantities of the factors that are needed to make a unit of some particular output. The Austrians, being more interested in time-structure than in qualitative differences between factors, thought of final output as being made by a combination of *previous* inputs, inputs of which the interesting characteristic was the date at which they were applied. A 'technique' for them was thus an elementary process, in which a series of *dated* input-quantities combined to produce the unit of output. There were no intermediate sales in the course of the process, no sales of producers' goods, no sales of capital goods. Inputs, accordingly, were *original* inputs; in Böhm-Bawerk labour only, in Wicksell labour and land.

It has nowadays become familiar that the *simple* Walrasian scheme, just defined, is not always sufficient, even for static analysis. It omits the case of joint supply. The technique which produces no more than one kind of product is only one kind of technique; the more general technique produces a range of products. It then becomes impossible to define the unit technique as one that produces a unit of output; we have to introduce an artificial unit—the *activity*.

---

[1] *Lectures on Political Economy*, Vol. 1 (1901).
[2] *Pure Theory of Capital* (1941) and earlier writings.   [3] Or 'vector'.

Even in static analysis the complication is serious; but the corresponding complication, in 'Austrian' theory, strikes deeper. For the only kind of capital-using production which will fit into the old Austrian scheme is production without fixed capital, production that uses working capital (or circulating capital) only. Fixed capital (plant and machinery) will not fit in. For fixed capital goods are 'durable-use goods'; their essential characteristic is that they contribute, not just to one unit of output, at one date, but to a sequence of units of output, at a sequence of dates. We cannot introduce them into an elementary process, in which they are to be *internal*, unless we reckon that process as producing a sequence of outputs—a sequence of outputs that are *jointly* produced.

The passage from the old Austrian theory to the 'neo-Austrian' is exactly analogous to the passage from old Walrasian theory to Activity Analysis. While the old Austrian theory was 'point-output' (its elementary process having a single dated output), we shall use an elementary process that converts a sequence (or stream) of inputs into a sequence of outputs. Our conception of capital-using production is thereby made much more general. The former difficulty of dealing with fixed capital is wholly overcome.

5. The consequences of the change are very considerable. We find, to begin with, that some very characteristic features of the old Austrian theory have to be abandoned.

To Böhm-Bawerk, who carried separability so far as to take as his elementary process the application of labour at one date and the appearance of the product at a later date (point input–point output), Production was a combination of Labour and Time. The Time that was taken in production was an identifiable figure— the degree of Roundaboutness. The capital employed in a process could only be increased, without the Labour employed being increased, if Roundaboutness was increased; so Roundaboutness was a measure of capital intensity. It was easy to show that a fall in the rate of interest would favour the adoption of techniques involving greater Roundaboutness—on this point input–point output assumption.

It was natural to take it that much the same would hold when the single input was replaced by a sequence of inputs. It did not appear that more needed to be done than to take the average of the intervals between the inputs and the single output—the Average degree of Roundaboutness, or the Average Period of Production.

So far all seemed well; but when we generalize the process, making a stream of inputs produce a stream of outputs, the whole notion collapses. This is most obvious if we take the case of an unterminating process, a process that goes on for ever; there is no reason why such a process should not be included. Except in the limiting case where the output is pure personal service, it will still be true that the stream of inputs must begin before the stream of outputs; nothing is produced from nothing. But the initial deferment, which may include a long period of pure experiment, has nothing to do with the capital-intensity of the process as a whole. For the determination of a Period of Production, we must be able to associate particular inputs with particular outputs; and it is in the very nature of the use of durable instruments that this cannot be done.[1]

Thus the neo-Austrian theory cannot look like the old Austrian theory. In fact, for a good part of the way, it has a closer resemblance to the growth theory, or growth theories, which have been evolved, using the other methods, during the last twenty-five years. That this is so should not be surprising. So long as we confine ourselves to the study of steady states, including the comparison of steady states, it matters little what system of integration or disintegration one assumes. Propositions may be differently phrased, but the formulations should be consistent with one another. The reader will in fact find, in most of Part I of this book,

[1] There remains the interesting question why Roundaboutness works, under Böhm-Bawerk's assumption, but not otherwise. The answer was given in my *Value and Capital* (1939), Ch. XVII.

On the point input–point output assumption, it is a condition of equilibrium that $wa = pR^{-t}$, where w is the wage of labour, a the labour coefficient, p the price of the product, and $R = 1 +$ the rate of interest. Differentiate logarithmically with respect to R, holding p constant. Then $-\mathrm{d}(\log w)/\mathrm{d}(\log R) = t$, so that t is the *elasticity* of the curve relating w to R. This elasticity, as we shall see, is an index which survives, and retains its importance, in the case of the generalized process. In Böhm-Bawerk's case, but in that case only, is it equal to t—the degree of Roundaboutness.

Though I had got so far as that, already in 1939, I did no more than put forward the argument as a criticism of the old Austrian theory. It was not until many years later that I perceived that I was in fact putting the theory into a much more useful form.

that he is being conducted, in a novel way, over familiar ground. The results that are reached are in substance those to which he is accustomed; but I think he will find that the route by which they are reached has some merit. The mathematics involved is rather simple[1]; the argument proceeds, rather strictly, in economic terms. Because, throughout, we are talking economics, there are a number of economic issues which arise by the way, on which the discussion throws light.

6. Part II of this book, by contrast, is a voyage of exploration. I launch out from the Steady State, and examine the paths, the possible paths, along which the model can adjust itself to new conditions. This is not just a matter of the 'stability of equilibrium'. Even if we are assured (as we may not be) that the model has a tendency to converge to a new equilibrium, it remains a matter of importance what happens on the way. It seems possible, on the method developed here, to make some progress towards answering these questions.

Something, of course, can be said by the other methods. I believe, however, that our method is the more penetrating. When one seeks to analyse the *Traverse* from one steady state equilibrium to another, by the Sectoral Disintegration method, its weaknesses show up. They are obscured in steady state theory, for there all the items that are included in the capital stock maintain their proportions; but it is impossible for these proportions to be maintained along a Traverse, so that there the reduction of Capital to 'Tractors' is bound to be misleading.[2] No such objection as this can be raised against the von Neumann method; the main achievement of that method in non-steady state economics (the Turnpike Theorem) stands perfectly firm. But the Turnpike Theorem belongs to Optimum theory, not to positive theory; it is in fact in Optimum theory that the von Neumann assumption de-

---

[1] There are 'Notes' to Chs. II and III with some heavier mathematics, but they are not essential to the argument.

It is indeed at first sight surprising that the admission of joint production, which obliges the static Activity Analyst to have recourse to matrix algebra, has no such effect in the present theory. The reason, I think, is that we are *helped* by Time. Static 'activities' are all on a par, so we have to search to find our way among them. But in the flow of Time there is only one *present*; it finds itself.

[2] I now regard the 'Traverse' chapter of *Capital and Growth* (Ch. XVI) as no more than a demonstration of the incompetence, in that field, of the Sectoral Disintegration Method.

velops its main strength. For it is characteristic of this assumption that it provides for continuous, or nearly continuous, changes in direction; that makes it better adapted for use in Optimum theory than for the determination of such paths as an actual economy, bound down by extensive *complementarities over time*, can reasonably be expected to follow. It is in fact here, when we leave the Steady State, that the assumption we make about integration or disintegration becomes so important. The von Neumann assumption makes the economy too flexible; by going to the other extreme we may well make it too inflexible; yet even so the possession of the alternative will give balance.

The issue, I think, is quite practical. There are in fact two ways in which an actual economy can react to technical change. It may, on the one hand, transfer appliances, which were acquired in the past to take part in production on one technique (and were designed to take part in production on that technique), applying them, as best it can, to serve as instruments for a purpose for which they were not designed. There is no doubt that this happens; and that quite often the transfer is fairly easy. Many capital goods are fairly non-specific; they can be turned to quite a variety of different uses. Transport equipment, perhaps, is the leading example; nothing is lost by the transfer of a truck from the carriage of one sort of package to the carriage of another. And when we remember that raw materials, being producers' goods, count on our classification as capital goods, the scope for such transfer, over the whole economic system, must be granted to be wide.

Alternatively, the funds which would have been used for replacement of capital goods of the old sort, or for investment in such capital goods, may be transferred to finance the production of capital goods of the new kind. There is again no question that this happens. Whether the adjustment is made more in the one way, or more in the other, is an empirical question: a question that may be differently answered for different adjustments, and differently answered at different places and times.[1]

So it is unwise to commit ourselves, finally, to the one route or

[1] The point was elegantly made many years ago, by Dennis Robertson: 'If the capitalist is to be allowed time and facilities for turning his spades into a steam-plough, it seems unreasonable not to allow him time and facilities for turning them into beer.' ('Wage-Grumbles', in *Economic Fragments*, 1931, p. 50.)

to the other. I may well be felt to have committed myself, in Part II, too firmly to the latter route; it is certainly the route which on the method adopted is the easier to explore. But that is just because Part II is a piece of exploration. I do not suppose that I have done all that can be done by this method; I am indeed rather sure that I have not. There is much that I leave to others. One of the things which I am (mainly) leaving to others is the extension of the analysis to incorporate 'malleability'—some degree of 'malleability'. I shall however show that there is no reason why this should not be done.

I have appended, to form Part III, a discussion of some controversial issues, on which the work which we shall have been doing may be found to throw some light.

NOTE TO CHAPTER I

THE HISTORY OF 'AUSTRIAN' THEORY

1. IN my sub-title, and in the text of Chapter I, I have proclaimed the 'Austrian' affiliation of my ideas; the tribute to Böhm-Bawerk, and to his followers, is a tribute that I am proud to make. I am writing in their tradition; yet I have realized, as my work has continued, that it is a wider and bigger tradition than at first appeared. The 'Austrians' were not a peculiar sect, out of the main stream; they were in the main stream; it was the others who were out of it.

The concept of production as a process in time, with capital (the *capital account*) as the 'report' that is made in the present on the state of that process, is not specifically 'Austrian'. It is just the same concept as underlies the work of the British classical economists, and it is indeed older still—older by far than Adam Smith. It is the typical business man's viewpoint, nowadays the accountant's viewpoint, in old days the merchant's viewpoint. It is the view which forced itself upon the merchant, as soon as he began to think about his business, to fit his activities into a rational scheme. There is curious evidence for this in a place where it is surprising to find it—in a passage in the Introduction to the *Decameron*, written about 1360. Boccacio is describing the impact on people's minds of the Great Plague at Florence, the expectation that they had not long to live. 'Instead of furthering the future products of their cattle and their land and their own past labour, they devoted all their attention to the consumption of present goods.'[1] Why does Boccacio write like Böhm-Bawerk? The reason surely is that he was trained as a merchant.

What Böhm-Bawerk did was to take the classical concept of capital, and to marry it with the theory of individual choice which he got from Menger. To his contemporaries (such as Marshall and Clark) who were already converted to a utility theory that was fairly similar, the latter aspect of his work was not particularly striking; they were much more impressed by his trenchant re-formulation of the classical concept of capital, which seemed to them quite outré, *because they themselves were rejecting it.* The principal reason why they rejected it was that it could not find a place in a static theory. The only capital which could find a place in a static theory was a capital that meant capital goods—'appliances', as Marshall likes to say. There are doubtless other reasons why they turned to 'Realism', as I am tempted to call it; we must have a name for that viewpoint once we have recognized it. But this, I think, is the main reason. From the Realist viewpoint the process is lost to sight.

For two generations, the times of Marshall and Pigou, Realism was (on the whole) dominant. The static method with which it was associated was a powerful method; for the purposes of that time, it seemed to serve. Keynes, of course, was brought up as a Realist; even the *General Theory* remains, for the most part, a Realist book. But the stimulus to Social Accounting, and then to Growth Models, which followed from Keynes, led to a reaction. One can deal with a 'short period' (Keynes's own preoccupation in the *General Theory*), even saving and investment in a short period, on Realist lines; but it is impossible to deal with a sequence of such periods, logically, without re-imposing accounting discipline. So it is that the present generation of economists has begun to turn away from Realism—returning to the Classical Tradition which the Austrians had kept alive.

That is how I have come to see the story; it does not fit well into conventional terms. Marshall and Pigou are called 'neo-classics'; but from the point of view of capital theory they were not neo-classics, they were anti-classics. It is the post-Keynesians who would better be called neo-classics; for it is they who, to their honour, have wrought a Classical Revival.

[1] 'Non d'aiutare i futuri frutti delle bestie e delle terre e delle loro passate fatiche, ma di consumare quegli che si trovavano presenti si sforzavano con ogni ingegno.'

II

THE PROCESS AND ITS PROFILES

1. WE are now to define a productive process as a scheme by which a flow of inputs is converted into a flow of outputs. A firm, when it is a producing unit, may itself be regarded as the embodiment of such a process; but there are many (perhaps most) actual firms which are combinations of several producing units, each of which may usefully be regarded as embodying a process. It will still be a process, in our sense, if it would be *possible* to carry it on in a single firm. We must be ready, at least, for that degree of sub-division.

The process may be regarded in two ways: ex-ante and ex-post. When it is regarded ex-ante, it is simply a plan[1]; it is the set of relations which underlies a forward budget. Regarded ex-post, it is the set that underlies the actual achievement, such as is recorded in 'historical' accounts. Both aspects will have to be considered, before we have done; but throughout this chapter (until we come to its last section) the process will be considered in the ex-ante sense.

We are not to think of the flows as steady flows, proceeding at a constant rate over time. Later on we may allow some constancy, for special purposes; but if we began with constancy we should be giving our analysis a static character even at the start. In the course of the process inputs and outputs must be allowed to change; and there is in general no reason why they should not change in composition as well as in amount. Changes in composition will nevertheless, in most of our work, be neglected. That can easily be done, for the moment, if we take it that the prices of inputs and outputs are given (and are the same whatever the date to which they refer); the inputs and outputs can then be made homogeneous by taking them in value terms. That is what we shall be doing in the present chapter.[2]

The process may then be expressed as a pair of flows, of inputs

---

[1] In exactly the same sense as was used in the 'planning' chapters of *Value and Capital* (1939), Chs. XV–XVII.

[2] I shall further assume that successive inputs are acquired independently, and successive outputs sold independently; there are no long-term contracts.

and outputs (measured in money) varying over time. Any process, so expressed, has a distinctive time-shape, or *time-profile*.
Consider (as an example, but no more than an example) a process
which consists in the construction of a plant, its operation over a
period of years and its ultimate dismantling. The input–output
profile of such a process is illustrated in Fig. 1. There is an initial
construction period, with large inputs but no final output; it is
followed by a *running-in period*, in which output rises from zero to
a normal level, while input falls to its normal level (constructional
labour being laid off while the labour force which is to work the
plant is being built up). There follows a period, probably a long

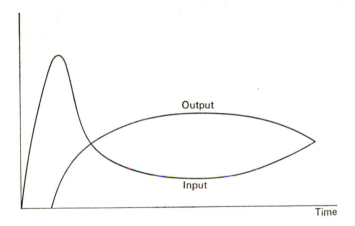

FIG. 1.

period, of *normal utilization*. Finally, as a result of a fall in the
output curve or of a rise in the input curve, the process comes to
an end.

   This is a fairly standard case, which it will be useful for the
reader to have in mind; but the analysis which follows is more
general. It applies to a process of this time-shape, and also to
processes of other time-shapes.[1] We have to examine what time-
shapes of processes are *viable*.

2. It may be taken for granted that every process must have a
beginning; but must it have an end? This is not a point on which

[1] It will of course apply to the elementary 'point input–point output' case of
traditional Austrian theory.

one needs to be dogmatic. It is perfectly possible (and realistically probable) that the process may not be *planned* to have an end; it is intended, when it is started, that it should go on indefinitely. It can certainly go on indefinitely if the plant, once constructed, needs no more than normal maintenance; for regular maintenance can of course be included among the flow of inputs required to work the plant. Even if it is clear that the time will come when the plant will require a more drastic replacement, we can still (if we like) reckon that replacement as internal to the process; we can put it in by introducing a second 'hump' into the input curve. So the making of a *permanent improvement* is to be reckoned as one kind of process. But it cannot be taken to be the only kind. There are processes, such as the working of mines, which quite certainly cannot go on for ever; in a general treatment they must be included. The common case, of the plant which after a time needs drastic replacement, may be looked at either way. We may regard the installation of the new plant as a continuation of the old process (after a second 'input hump') or we may regard it as the start of a new process. Economists (I think) have usually regarded it as continuation, so that the mine appears as the exceptional case; but either alternative is in principle open. I shall adopt the other alternative, of regarding the replacement as a new process; I believe that I can show that we gain a good deal by taking that course.

Our typical process, accordingly, will be *mortal*; it will have a terminus, or end, as well as a beginning. This, we shall find, leaves it open to us to accommodate the permanent improvement as a limiting case. It will fit in more easily than the mine would have done, if we had gone the other way.

3. We have now to consider what conditions must be satisfied *in general* by the time-profile of a process in order that it should be viable. By our assumption of given prices of inputs and outputs, we are already committed to a market economy; in such an economy there will also be a rate of interest.[1] The obvious test for the viability of a process is that it should yield the market rate of interest, *at least* the market rate of interest. But what exactly does that mean?

We may take it (at this stage) that the rate of interest is expected

---

[1] What determines that rate of interest we shall see later, in Chapter V.

to remain unchanged (as the prices of inputs and outputs are expected to remain unchanged) during the course of the process. Thus whenever at any date there is *net input* (an excess of the value of input over the value of output), funds will have to be borrowed, or drawn in some other way from outside the process; and on those funds interest will have to be paid. Any *net output* (excess of output over input) can similarly be invested outside the process, or used to repay past debts, which comes to the same thing. If at the end all borrowings, with interest due on them, have been or can be repaid, the process is viable.

When the test is expressed in this form, it leads at once to the familiar *discounted value* formula. Any payment (or receipt) can be moved to a later date by adding interest to it; or to an earlier date by discounting it. If we *capitalize* in this manner to the start of the process, we must discount the later payments and receipts according to the deferment; if we capitalize to the end of the process we must add interest. But whatever is the date for which we make the calculation, the test may be expressed by saying that the capitalized value of the output flow must be at least as great as the capitalized value of the flow of inputs. If we agree to reckon net inputs as negative net outputs, this comes to the same thing as saying that the capitalized value of the flow of net outputs must be non-negative. It is usually convenient to take the beginning as the reference date; so it will be the *discounted* value of the flow of net outputs which is to be non-negative.

4. I have taken a little trouble with this familiar condition, since we shall be using it a great deal, and in ways that are by no means so familiar. It is often supposed that it is the only condition for viability; but that is not so. It is a necessary condition, but not a sufficient condition. It would indeed be a sufficient condition if it were taken for granted that the process must go for ever; but why should that be assumed? Even if the process is technically interminable, it will be possible that it should be terminated. If it is not to be terminated, other conditions are necessary.

Consider the case of a process which (technically) could go on for ever, but which in fact is to be terminated, because it is profitable to terminate it, after a length of time (from the start) which we will mark by the letter at the end of the Greek alphabet, omega or Ω. How is Ω determined? It is determined, of course, in the usual economic manner. It must be more profitable to carry on up to Ω than to carry on for any other period (shorter or longer). And the test of profitability is the same discounted value formula. The capitalized value of the process at its beginning (time o) must be greater than its capitalized value would be if it were carried on for any other duration.

Suppose we consider the alternative of an earlier termination, at time t_1, where $t_1 < \Omega$. The capitalized value of the process, terminating at Ω, must be greater than the capitalized value with termination at t_1. But the difference between these is the capitalized value (at time o) of the 'tail' of the process from t_1 to Ω. If Ω is to be the most profitable duration, this capitalized value must be positive. But the capitalized value of the 'tail', at time o, is the capitalized value at t_1 discounted back to zero. If one is positive, the other must be positive. So if Ω is the optimum duration, the capitalized value of the process (what is left of the process) at any time before Ω must be positive.

Similarly, if we consider the alternative of a later termination, of extending the process to a date t_2, where $t_2 > \Omega$, we shall find that the capitalized value, at time Ω, of the 'tail' of the process beyond Ω, must be negative. These are necessary properties of the optimum duration.

It is accordingly suggested that we should associate with any process, not simply its profile of inputs and outputs (as illustrated in Fig. 1) but also a profile of capital values. This will express the value of the remainder of the process at each date in its course. This, it should be understood, is not a market value, for (as explained above[1]) we assume no market in capital goods, intermediate products, or unfinished processes; it is no more than a value that is implied in planning. It remains, even as such, of central economic importance.

We now have a firm rule about the behaviour of this capital value profile (Fig. 2). At every point, during the duration of the process, the capital value must be positive.[2] It may go up and down (there is no reason why it should have no more than a single peak) but it must remain positive; for at the point where

---

[1] p. 6.

[2] Some may prefer to say *non-negative*—in order to accommodate the possibility that the capital value curve touches the horizontal axis at some point, and then recovers into positive values. I would think it better, in such a case, to treat the revived process as a new process.

the curve intersects the horizontal axis the process will be terminated. (It will be seen at once that we can accommodate the case of the unterminating process without infringing our rule. The process can continue as long as the capital value curve remains above the horizontal axis; if it does so indefinitely, the process can continue indefinitely.)

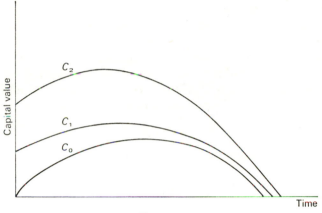

FIG. 2.

5. The capital value profile, unlike the input–output profile, depends on the rate of interest. How is it affected when the rate of of interest changes? We have, on this point a Fundamental Theorem.

Save in a limiting case (which we have in fact already decided to exclude from attention) it is always true that a fall in the rate of interest will raise the capital value curve of any process—will raise it throughout—while a rise in the rate of interest will lower it. That is the Theorem; it can be proved in various ways, but the following, I believe, is the most expeditious.

For this proof we need a device, which will often be useful to us in other connections. As the profiles have been drawn (Figs. 1 and 2) they have been shown as continuous curves; and that, very often, is how we shall want to regard them. But it is often more convenient to think of time as divided into periods ('weeks'), such that variations in input and output within the week can be neglected. The length of the week is quite arbitrary; by reducing it, we can approximate the continuous profile as closely as we like.

Suppose that the whole duration from o to Ω is divided into $(n + 1)$ weeks. Then we may express the input–output profile as $(a_0, a_1, a_2, \ldots, a_n; b_0, b_1, b_2, \ldots, b_n)$ in which a's are inputs, b's outputs. Write q's for net outputs (positive or negative), so that for any t (o to n), $q_t = b_t - a_t$.

Let us further suppose that all the payments 'of' the week (either way) are made at the beginning of the week. The counting-house, say, is only open on Mondays; it is on Mondays that both inputs and outputs are paid for. Let k_t be the capital value of the process (the remainder of the process) at the beginning of week t; at the moment, that is, when the counting-house opens.

Let r be the rate of interest for one week, and write $R = 1 + r$. So R is the interest multiplier for one week, and R^{-1} is the discount factor. Then (by the discounted value formula)

$$k_t = q_t + q_{t+1}R^{-1} + q_{t+2}R^{-2} + \cdots + q_nR^{-(n-t)}.$$

From this, and from the corresponding formula for k_{t+1}, we have at once

$$k_t = q_t + k_{t+1}R^{-1}. \tag{2.1}$$

The capital value at the beginning of week t equals the net output of week t (undiscounted, because it comes in immediately) plus the capital value at the end of the week, discounted for that one week.

Our Fundamental Theorem now follows directly. For suppose that the q's are unchanged but that r falls, so that the discount factor rises. We see at once from (2.1) that k_t is bound to rise, provided that k_{t+1} is positive, and provided that k_{t+1} is not reduced by the fall in interest. But a similar argument applies to k_{t+1}. Thus we may go on repeating, up to the end of the process, where $k_n = q_n$. Thus k_n is unaffected by the fall in r; so k_{n-1} must be raised, and therefore k_{n-2} must be raised; and so on, back to k_t. So long as all the k_t's are positive (as we have seen that they must be, in order that the process should be viable), every k_t (o to $n - 1$) must be raised by the fall in interest.

Into this argument, however, there has slipped an unnecessary assumption, which should be removed. We have taken it for granted that the duration of the process remains at $(n + 1)$ weeks, even though the rate of interest falls. But it is immediately clear that even if the duration is variable, it cannot be shortened.

For since we have shown that with unchanged duration, every k_t ($t < n$) will be *raised*, it must still be advantageous to go on for at least the same duration, at the lower rate of interest. All that is possible is that the process may be lengthened.

But the process will only be lengthened if k_{n+1} (which was zero at the higher rate of interest) becomes positive at the lower. That can happen, if the lengthening requires some net input (repairs, for instance, which only become profitable when the rate of interest falls). If it happens, however, all earlier k_t must be raised, *a fortiori*. So the Theorem continues to hold when duration is variable.

6. What we have found is illustrated in Fig. 2 (reverting, for the diagram, to continuous time). A fall in the rate of interest will shift the capital value curve, of a given process, from a form such as C_1 to a form such as C_2, raising it throughout, and (possibly though not necessarily) lengthening it. Just the same will hold for a process which at the higher rate of interest is not terminated; its curve must be raised, so it will still be unterminated at the lower rate. (It is of course quite possible that it will be unterminated at the lower, but terminated at the higher rate.)

Now in all this we have simply been comparing the capital value curves of the same process (with possibly variable terminus) at different rates of interest; so we can use the same diagram to show what happens when the rate of interest rises. When there is a rise in the rate of interest, there will be a fall in the curve (as from C_2 to C_1) and may be a shortening. If the rate of interest rises further, there may just be a further fall and a further shortening; and it may look as if this would continue until the process had vanished away! But consider what this means in terms of our 'weeks'. At the final step, when the process is reduced to week 0, week 0 alone, $k_1 = 0$ (since otherwise the process would be extended to week 1) but k_0 is positive. But

$$k_0 = q_0 + k_1 R^{-1}$$

so if k_1 is zero and k_0 is positive, q_0 must be positive. But $q_0 = b_0 - a_0$, so output is greater than input, in a process which consists of nothing but these terms. They are attributed to the beginning of their week (it will be remembered); so input produces output instantaneously! There is only one case in which this makes sense, the case of pure personal services, which are both input and output; but this we decided (in Chapter I) to put on one side. It is the limiting case, in which capital value is unaffected by the change in interest. Hereafter I shall leave it out.

There is then only one thing that can happen. A sufficient rise in the rate of interest must reduce k_0 to zero, while some of the later k's remain positive. The capital value curve then takes the form that is shown as C_0. At the rate of interest that corresponds to this the process can just be carried on (for a minimum duration). At lower rates it will of course be still more profitable, having capital value curves such as C_1 or C_2. At a higher rate of interest it will not be profitable to carry it on at all.

The rate of interest which is thus identified is (of course) what is commonly called the *yield* of the process, or the *internal rate of return*. It is the rate of interest which belongs to the process. The yield must be greater than the market rate of interest, if the process is to be viable. We have confirmed that familiar rule; but by establishing it in this manner, we have deepened our understanding of it.

For we have shown, quite strictly, that (excepting in the degenerate case of instantaneous production) such a yield must exist, for any process which could possibly be viable. And we have shown that the yield is unique. For a fall in the rate of interest, below the yield, must increase k_0. So it is impossible for k_0 to become zero again at a lower rate of interest. The yield, of a given process, with given prices of inputs and outputs, is unique —so long as we keep the condition that the process is to be carried on for the optimum duration.

7. By using this method of identifying the yield, we have also identified a curve (our curve C_0) which is associated with it. Since capitalization is here performed at the rate of interest which belongs to the process, we may call it the *proper* capital value curve of the process. The capital value must begin at zero, and thereafter be positive; so it must begin by rising. If the process terminates, the capital value must end by falling. Subject, however, to these conditions, there may be all sorts of 'humps' and 'dips' on the way.

A simple process such as was illustrated in Fig. 1 (with a single constructional period, followed by a single operational period) will have a simple capital value curve with a single hump, such as is shown by C_0 in Fig. 2. But there are many other sorts of processes which can be almost as easily accommodated. Take for instance the 'circulating capital model'—the maturing of wine or the growing of trees, the cases so much beloved by the older Austrians. What happens in that case is that the curve rises all the way from the start until the last 'week'—when the product is sold. There is a long rise and then a sudden fall. This may be contrasted with the case in which a manufacturing plant is purchased, at the start, in full working order, so that it appears as an input in the first 'week'; the curve is then humped the other way.

8. It is already suggested, by these illustrations, that the capital value curve can also be used to show the *capital invested* in the process. Along the proper curve, that is correct.

For it follows from the discounted value formula that (for any t between o and n)

$$k_0 = q_0 + q_1 R^{-1} + q_2 R^{-2} + \cdots + q_{t-1} R^{-(t-1)} + k_t R^{-t}$$

(as appears by substituting the formula for k_t that was given above). Therefore, if $k_0 = o$,

$$k_t = (-q_0)R^t + (-q_1)R^{t-1} + \cdots + (-q_{t-1})R \quad (2.2)$$

so that k_t is the sum of the $(-q)$, which are *net inputs*, from o to $t-1$, *accumulated* by interest up to week t. This evidently measures the capital invested up to week t. (It is obvious sense that at time o, before the process begins, the capital invested in it should be zero.)

Thus we have the further principle, still got (as throughout this chapter) from the study of the single process, taken in isolation, that if capitalization is performed at the rate of interest which belongs to the process—but only if it is performed at the rate of interest which belongs to the process—the forward measure of capital, got by discounting future net outputs, and the backward measure, got by accumulating net inputs, are the same. But if, on the other hand, we consider a process with yield that is greater than the market rate of interest—and if, as will be natural, we do the discounting (and accumulating) at the market rate of interest —the value of capital, measured forward, will be greater than the backward (or cost) measure, *at every stage of the process*. It will be greater, even at the beginning, when capital invested is zero. A value, dependent only on expectations, seems then to be conjured from the air!

We should nevertheless remember that the values, so far considered, are not market values. They are values implied in planning; no more. Capital invested, indeed, is something more solid; being backward-looking, it is based on fact, on what, at its date, is realized fact. When the process is considered ex-post, the capital invested in it will still appear. If the process is successful, being carried out as planned, and if its yield is greater than the market rate of interest, a capital gain will accrue, notionally at each stage of the process, but more than notionally at the end of the process. And there will be a similar discrepancy if, for some reason of our own, we discount (and accumulate) at a rate which is other than the yield of the process. We shall have to look out.

NOTE TO CHAPTER II

THE FUNDAMENTAL THEOREM IN CONTINUOUS TIME

I HAVE proved the Fundamental Theorem, in the text of Chapter II, in two steps: first on the supposition that time is divided into discrete intervals (weeks), inputs and outputs being acquired and sold at the beginnings of the weeks; secondly reformulating it for continuous time by a limiting process. I am inclined to think that this is the best way of proving it; it may however be felt that a direct proof for continuous time should be given. The direct proof is more difficult, but it does bring out some interesting points.

We still take inputs and outputs in value terms (as in the text) but t is now a continuous variable. So the process is $[a(t), b(t)]$, defined from o to Ω, with $q(t) = b(t) - a(t)$. The capital value of the process at time θ (o $< \theta < \Omega$) is

$$k(\theta) = \int_{\theta}^{\Omega} q(t)\, e^{-\rho(t-\theta)}\, dt$$

where ρ is the *instantaneous* rate of interest. It is sufficient, for the present purpose, to assume that $k(\theta)$ is a continuous function of θ, such that all differentiations and integrations that we require are permissible.

Put $\qquad \hat{k}(\theta) = k(\theta)\, e^{-\rho\theta} = \int_0^\Omega q(t)\, e^{-\rho t}\, dt$

so that $\hat{k}(\theta)$ is the capital value at time θ discounted back to time o. Then, differentiating with respect to θ,

$$\hat{k}'(\theta) = -q(\theta)\, e^{-\rho\theta}$$
$$= k'(\theta)\, e^{-\rho\theta} - \rho k(\theta)\, e^{-\rho\theta}$$

so that $\qquad k'(\theta) = \rho k(\theta) - q(\theta) \qquad\qquad (2.1')$

which corresponds to (2.1) in the text.

We have now to find $(d/d\rho)k(\theta)$ for given θ. As in the text we begin by supposing that Ω is unaffected by the change in ρ. Then

$$(d/d\rho)k(\theta) = \int_\theta^\Omega (\theta - t)q(t)\, e^{-\rho(t-\theta)}\, dt$$

$$= \theta k(\theta) - e^{\rho\theta} \int_\theta^\Omega tq(t)\, e^{-\rho t}\, dt$$

$$= \theta k(\theta) + e^{\rho\theta} \int_\theta^\Omega t\hat{k}'(t)\, dt \qquad\text{(by the above)}$$

$$= \theta k(\theta) + e^{\rho\theta}\, [t\hat{k}(t)]_\theta^\Omega - e^{\rho\theta} \int_\theta^\Omega \hat{k}(t)\, dt$$
$$\text{(integrating by parts)}$$

$$= e^{\rho\theta}\, [t\hat{k}(t)]^{t=\Omega} - \int_\theta^\Omega k(t)\, e^{-\rho(t-\theta)}\, dt. \qquad (2.2')$$

We know, by the truncation property, that all $k(t)$, for $0 < t < \Omega$, are positive. Thus the integral in (2.2') is positive, for every θ. If we can take it that the term in square brackets is zero, the theorem (for given Ω) is proved.

With a terminating process (Ω finite), $k(\Omega)$ must be zero, so the condition is satisfied. Having proved the theorem for given Ω, we can go on to extend it to the case of Ω variable, as in the text. (Nothing appears to be gained by a re-statement of this part of the argument in symbolic form.) But there remains the case of the unterminating process (Ω infinite). Here there does seem to be something to be added.

It will be necessary, if the theorem is to be true in this case, that the limit of $t\hat{k}(t)$ should be zero, when t increases without limit. This, it is fairly obvious, will not be true without restriction; but it is true provided that $k(t)$—the capital value of the process at time t, *not* discounted back—always remains finite. For if $k(t)$ remains finite, however large is t, it must have an upper bound; call this k^*. Then for all t, $t\hat{k}(t) < k^*\, (t\, e^{-\rho t})$; and $t\, e^{-\rho t}\, (\rho > 0)$ tends to zero as t increases.

The condition, it will be noticed, is economically significant. Any unterminating sequence of q's, in which all q's after a certain date are positive, will indeed have all k_t's after that date infinite, if the rate of interest is zero; while if these later q's have a positive growth rate, a rate of interest greater than that growth rate will be needed to keep k_t's finite. There will, in general, be some positive rate of interest which is just sufficient to keep capital values finite; and it is obvious that only for rates of interest that are greater than that critical level will our theorem make sense. For rates of interest above that level, we now see, the theorem holds.

III

SOCIAL ACCOUNTING

1. A WORD must be said, before going further, on the question of scale. This is a question which in the preceding chapter we were able to avoid. We were solely concerned with the capitalization of a *given* process; so we did not need to attend to the effects of 'horizontal' changes in size. What would happen if all (a_t, b_t), all inputs and outputs, were increased in the same proportion? Would the process still be viable?

It would obviously be a great convenience if we could permit ourselves to say that it did not matter, if we allowed ourselves to introduce, at this point, the well-tried assumption of constant returns to scale. For by that assumption the scale of production and the technique of production are separated. The (a_t, b_t) which we have been considering can then be regarded as determining a process of given technique and of unit size. We can vary size, without varying technique, by multiplying these *coefficients* (as they will have become) by a scale factor (x). Or, what comes to the same thing, processes of various sizes can be regarded as combinations of x unit processes. Can we venture to allow ourselves this simplification?

I think it may be justified, up to a point, in the following manner. Suppose we admit that there is a certain size of process that is the most economic. If an attempt were made to carry on the process at a little less, or a little more, than this optimum size, the inputs (proportionately increased) would not suffice to produce the outputs (increased in the same proportion). Then we must take the economic size as the size of the unit process. It will only be possible to vary size, without varying technique, by adding whole units.

This, I think, is by no means unreasonable. It does indeed exclude the possibility that there is no economic size: that as output is increased *at all dates* in the same proportion, the inputs *at all dates* that are required to produce them can be increased in what, for some at least, are smaller proportions. That, I suppose, is conceivable; but it may be doubted whether it is what even the strongest partisans of unlimited increasing returns have had in mind. We can on the other hand admit an economic size to any given process, and yet admit the possibility that there may be unterminating processes which are such that the ratio of output to input (b_t/a_t) can grow indefinitely as t increases. I shall not in fact take account of this possibility; but it is well to observe that it is not excluded by constant returns to scale, as here interpreted.

There remains, of course, the major difficulty: that our unit process ought in strictness to be taken as being of very considerable size. There must therefore be problems of fitting supply to demand—to a demand which will not fit a whole number of efficient unit processes. There are doubtless many problems, in the real world, which must be classified as being of this type; and there are branches of economics (such as the theory of Monopolistic Competition) which pay particular attention to them. What we do, if we allow ourselves to go so far as to assume *continuous* constant returns to scale, is to put these things on one side. That, in effect, is what I shall be doing here; and I can do so with a better conscience since there are some quite similar problems which I shall be able to treat, even though I permit myself the simplification of treating x (the scale factor) as a continuous variable.

2. With that objection dismissed, I proceed to construct a model of an economy, in terms of its productive processes.

I begin with the simplest case, of an economy which uses no more than a single kind of process, or single technique. All of its unit processes are identical, and all are carried through as planned. We will take it that this single process is a terminating process, with a capital value curve such as was illustrated in Fig. 2 above. Since old processes are being terminated, the economy can only be kept going if new processes are continually, or frequently, being started. The activity of the economy is governed by the rate of starts, for which we may use our variable x. If x were constant over time, the (single-process) economy would be in a stationary state; if it had a constant growth rate, the whole economy would be in a steady state, with that constant growth rate. But we do not need to confine ourselves to such steady states, which the present model can readily transcend.

At any moment of time, there will be many processes in

existence, some just started, some well under way, some nearly finished. Thus there is a population of processes, very like a human population, save that if all the processes have the same time-profile, the 'life' of every process is the same. The 'death-rate' of the population of processes is thus a reflection of its 'birth-rate' $(n + 1)$ weeks ago. Just as in the case of the human population, the size and rate of change of the present population of processes is in part a reflection of the way in which starts have moved in the past.

A process which was started t weeks ago will have input a_t and output b_t in the current week. If we use T to denote the current week,[1] the rate of starts t weeks ago can be written x_{T-t}. So the part of current input which is due to the starts t weeks ago, is $x_{T-t}a_t$. The part which is due to current starts is $x_T a_0$. So total current input, which I shall call A_T, is

$$x_T a_0 + x_{T-1} a_1 + \cdots + x_{T-n} a_n = \sum_0^n x_{T-t} a_t$$

for processes started before week $T - n$ are *dead*. Current output, in the same way, is $B_T = \sum_0^n x_{T-t} b_t$; current net output, $Q_T = B_T - A_T = \sum_0^n x_{T-t} q_t$; while for the current value of capital,

$$K_T = \sum_0^n x_{T-t} k_t.$$

3. What is the relation between these 'macro-economic' magnitudes? It makes a difference, we shall find, according as we measure capital in the forward-looking manner, which is what we did in the greater part of the preceding chapter, or in the backward-looking manner, which was introduced at the end. Let us begin, in this place, with the forward-looking measure.

We know, it will be remembered, that for every t (from 0 to $n - 1$)

$$k_t - k_{t+1} R^{-1} = q_t \qquad (2.1)$$

while since the process terminates after week n, $k_n = q_n$. How

---

[1] I shall always use capital T to indicate calender time.

should this be translated into macro-economic terms? It is at once suggested that we should calculate

$$K_T - K_{T+1}R^{-1}$$
$$= (x_T k_0 + \cdots + x_{T-n}k_n) - (x_{T+1}k_0 + \cdots + x_{T-n+1}k_n)R^{-1}$$
$$= -x_{T+1}k_0 R^{-1} + x_T(k_0 - k_1 R^{-1}) + \cdots$$
$$\qquad\qquad + x_{T-n+1}(k_{n-1} - k_n R^{-1}) + x_{T-n}k_n$$
$$= -x_{T+1}k_0 R^{-1} + (x_T q_0 + x_{T-1}q_1 + \cdots + x_{T-n}q_n)$$
$$= -x_{T+1}k_0 R^{-1} + Q_T.$$

Now *if we are discounting at the proper rate* (*or yield*) *of the process*, $k_0 = 0$, so that the first term, which I shall call the Discrepancy, vanishes. Under this condition, therefore

$$K_T - K_{T+1}R^{-1} = Q_T \qquad (3.1)$$

the natural analogue of (2.1).

Multiply up by R, which is $(1 + r)$. Then

$$rK_T - (K_{T+1} - K_T) = (1 + r)Q_T.$$

Now the appearance of the interest multiplier before the Q_T is the principal place where we suffer from our peculiar device of the 'week' and the counting-house open only on Monday; for we find, as a result of this device, that interest on the net input of the week (since it was paid for on the Monday) is included in the capital at the end of the week; that is what the term rQ_T shows. If we had worked with continuous time, this interest would have disappeared. By shrinking the week, we can cause it to disappear, thus making (3.1) approach

$$rK_T = (K_{T+1} - K_T) + Q_T \qquad (3.2)$$

as nearly as we like.[1]

4. Now this equation (3.2)—in form at least—is very familiar. It is nothing else but the *Social Accounting Equation*. rK_T is profits; $K_{T+1} - K_T$ is net investment; Q_T is net output, the difference between value of output and value of input—the *Take-Out*, as in the macro-economic application it will be convenient to call it. For consider the simplest application, to a completely integrated

[1] A direct proof, which works throughout with continuous time, is given in the note at the end of this Chapter.

economy, in which every process goes right through to a final output of consumption goods, and the only input is labour. Then final output *is* consumption (for stocks of consumption goods can only be accumulated within the process—it is not until the goods have passed into final consumption that the process is completed). So the Take-Out is the difference between final consumption and the wage-bill. So (3.2) gives

Wages + Profits = Consumption + Net Investment

directly. But the validity of the reduction is wider than that.

If some part of the output is used again as input, such intermediate goods will appear as output and as input, so the Take-Out again reduces to Consumption − Wages. If there are *original factors* other than labour (such as land) the rents on such factors will survive in A_T. The only characteristic of labour that has been used is that it is input and not output; so the rents will have to be treated, for this Social Accounting purpose, as if they were wages. Otherwise the Equation holds.

5. But what have we been doing? The Social Accounting Equation is usually reckoned to be an identity; yet we have 'proved' it. One cannot prove an identity; it is simply a matter of definition. What (so regarded) does it define? I think it is best to regard it as a definition of *profits*. The total *income* of the economy is defined as consumption + net investment; profits are then defined as income − wages (or minus wages and rents). What we have proved is more than that. What we have proved is that under appropriate conditions, profit is rK_T; profit is interest on value of capital. This is a proposition that may or may not be true. We have proved it in a special case, but only in a special case. How far can it be extended?

It has been shown to be necessary, even in our single-technique economy, for the proposition to be true, that $k_0 = 0$. The rate of interest, which is applied to K_T, and which has been used in the calculation of K_T, must be equal to the yield on the technique. Now this is a condition which in the single technique economy, it is fairly reasonable to impose.

For new processes, of the given kind, are continually being started. They will not be started unless it is profitable to start them—so their k_0 cannot be negative. But if it were positive, there would be a capital gain, to be got for nothing, on the starting of new processes. Thus it would seem to be a condition of equilibrium, in the market for funds, that the rate of interest should be such as to make $k_0 = 0$. 'Nothing is got for nothing.' I shall regularly assume, in the rest of this book, that the market for funds is at all times in equilibrium, in this sense. For the purposes of the investigations which we shall be making, I think it is a fair assumption. (I am sure, however, that there are other purposes for which it would be much less appropriate.) It is sufficient, by itself, to ensure that the Social Accounting Equation (interpreted as we have been interpreting it) will hold—in the single-technique economy.

And it is in fact sufficient for much more than that. For now suppose that there are many kinds of process (a_t, b_t) that are simultaneously in use. The fact that a process is in use does not imply that it would now be profitable to start it. When it was started, it appeared to be profitable, but conditions have changed. Either because of new invention, or because of changes in prices, its profitability has gone; so the starting of new processes of that kind would no longer be payable. It may nevertheless be profitable to carry on the remainder of such a process (either its full remainder, or a shortened remainder, it does not matter which). We may call such processes *obsolescent* processes, contrasting them with such processes as are still being started, which we will call *modern*.

The total input, at time T, is the sum of the inputs, at time T, over all *living* processes, both modern and obsolescent. Total output and total capital are similarly the sums of output and capital over all processes. Now so far as the modern processes are concerned, the argument we have been using for the single-process economy holds without qualification. Their k_0 is zero; so for each of these processes its $K_T - K_{T+1}R^{-1}$ = its Q_T.

What, however, of the obsolescent processes? They are not now being started; so that at the prices (and technical knowledge) of time T their k_0 must be negative. (If it was not negative, they would be started, so they would not be obsolescent.) But it is only for a modern process, that is now being started, that we have to use $k_0 = 0$ to get the Social Accounting Equation. For the Discrepancy is $-x_{T+1}k_0R^{-1}$; and this will vanish if $k_0 = 0$, *or if* $x_{T+1} = 0$. The first of these holds for modern processes; the second for obsolescent processes.[1] So the Social Accounting Equation holds for all processes; and therefore for the whole economy.

6. I turn to the consideration of the backward-looking measure of capital, where the position is distinctly different. It will make for clarity if we now use c_t for *capital invested* at the beginning of week t from the start of the individual process, so that, from (2.2),

$$c_t = (-q_0)R^t + (-q_1)R^{t-1} + \cdots + (-q_{t-1})R$$

in general. The relation (2.1) still holds for the c's, as may be readily verified:

$$c_t - c_{t+1}R^{-1} = q_t \qquad (3.3)$$

(capital invested at the end of the week equals capital invested at the beginning minus net output—or plus net input—on the Monday, the whole being accumulated for the week by the interest multiplier).

Using C_T for the total of capital invested, the reduction of $C_T - C_{T+1}R^{-1}$ can then proceed as for K_T, in all the middle terms. But now it is *necessary* that $c_0 = 0$; for there is inevitably, at the start of the process, no capital invested. And now it is not necessary that c_{n+1} should be zero. It will be zero if interest is applied at the rate which is proper to the process; for at the proper rate of interest forward and backward measures are the same throughout. But if interest is not applied at the rate which is proper to the process, we cannot assume that c_{n+1} is zero.

Thus to make the reduction for capital invested, we must put $c_0 = 0$, and apply (3.3) to all t from 0 to n (including n). So

$$C_T - C_{T+1}R^{-1} = x_T q_0 + \cdots + x_{T-n}(q_n + c_{n+1}R^{-1})$$
$$= Q_T + x_{T-n}c_{n+1}R^{-1}.$$

Now

$$c_{n+1} = (-q_0)R^{n+1} + (-q_1)R^n + \cdots + (-q_n)R = -k_0 R^{n+1}$$

so finally

$$C_T - C_{T+1}R^{-1} = Q_T - x_{T-n}k_0 R^n. \qquad (3.4)$$

---

[1] If we had worked with continuous time (as shown in the note to this Chapter) the Discrepancy would have reduced to $-x(T)k_0$; for the length of the 'week' would have been reduced to vanishing.

If interest is not applied at the proper rate, there will be the Discrepancy $x_{T-n}k_0R^n$.

The trouble, as before, is with obsolescent processes; for there is no reason why interest should not still be applied at the proper rate in modern processes (modern processes being currently begun, and modern processes that have been begun in the past). There is no Discrepancy on the modern processes, but on obsolescent processes there may be a Discrepancy. And here there is no reason why the Discrepancy should disappear.

An obsolescent process, by definition, is one that it would now not pay to start; its k_0 is negative. That is to say, the value of its outputs, at present prices, when capitalized at the present rate of interest, is less than the value of its inputs, similarly capitalized. And it is clear that such valuation at present prices is the valuation which is appropriate to get the capital invested in the obsolescent processes; we are not concerned with 'historical cost' in the accounting sense. If the capital invested in the obsolescent processes is consistently valued in this manner, there must be a deficit on them—a deficit which will finally be revealed when the processes terminate. Now at the present time (our time T) there will be obsolescent processes which are currently being terminated; for each type of process that is being terminated, the number of terminating processes will be given by the number of starts n weeks ago (x_{T-n}). These x's will not be zero, and with obsolescent processes k_0 will be negative, so the Discrepancy, as shown in (3.4), will be positive. Thus $C_T - C_{T+1}R^{-1} > Q_T$, or $C_{T+1} < (C_T - Q_T)R$. From this, if we shrink the week, so as to avoid interest on Q_T, we have $rC_T > (C_{T+1} - C_T) + Q_T$. The Social Accounting Equation does not hold.

Profit may still be defined as Consumption + Investment − Wages; but profit, so defined, will be less than interest on capital invested. The modern processes will be earning the market rate of interest on the capital invested in them; but the obsolescent processes have a lower rate of return, and that brings down the rate of return on *capital invested* as a whole.

7. This is an important result; but we should be careful how we take it. Practical measures of capital (as we shall see[1]) are almost inevitably backward-looking measures; for the data from which

[1] In Chapter XIII below.

they are derived belong to the past. It is only on what has happened in the past that we have *information*. But if capital is measured in this way, as capital invested, then (as we have just seen) there will be a *Discrepancy*; but if that is so, how is it that we get on as well as we do? The reason, it is fairly obvious, is that the data we use already incorporate an attempt to obviate the Discrepancy—by allowances for obsolescence. Now the obsolescence allowance, though it is incorporated in past data, is itself forward-looking. It is based upon an estimate of the capital loss which is expected to occur in the future—which would occur, that is to say, if no allowance for obsolescence were made. The loss is taken in advance, so as to ensure that it does not have to be borne all at once. This is intelligible in practice; and it is equally intelligible in the light of our present construction.

We are already beginning to draw some advantages from our model. We have been able to draw a clear distinction between the 'ideal' social accounting system, such as it is natural to use in theory, and the practical system which inevitably stands proxy for it in applied economics. The former is based upon a forward-looking valuation of capital; the latter upon a backward-looking valuation. The former is self-consistent, automatically; the latter is not automatically self-consistent. It is only made approximately self-consistent by the introduction of an obsolescence allowance, and it depends upon the accuracy of that allowance for the achievement of such consistency as it does achieve. The two are not identical; we need to exercise considerable care if we are to allow ourselves to substitute one for the other.

The bearing of this upon recent controversy will be rather obvious. We shall return to consider it in that context in Chapter XIV below.

NOTE TO CHAPTER III

THE SOCIAL ACCOUNTING EQUATION IN CONTINUOUS TIME

WHEN we work with continuous time, the Social Accounting reduction comes out rather more neatly.

I confine attention to the economy that is using one single kind of process (or single technique); since, as shown in the text, generalization from that is easy. We then have, with continuous time,

$$K(T) = \int_0^{\Omega} x(T - t)k(t)\,\mathrm{d}t.$$

Differentiating with respect to T,

$$K'(T) = \int_0^{\Omega} x'(T - t)k(t)\,\mathrm{d}t$$

$$= -[x(T - t)k(t)]_0^{\Omega} + \int_0^{\Omega} x(T - t)k'(t)\,\mathrm{d}t \qquad (3.1')$$

(integrating by parts). Now it was shown in the Note to Chapter II that

$$k'(t) = \rho k(t) - q(t). \qquad (2.1')$$

When this is substituted in $(3.1')$, we find that the integral term reduces to

$$\rho K(T) - Q(T).$$

Thus the Social Accounting Equation holds, provided that $[x(T - t)k(t)]$ vanishes at its limits. If $k(0) = 0$ and $k(\Omega) = 0$, the condition is obviously satisfied. If however we are discounting (or accumulating) at a rate of interest for which one or both of these are not true, we must make a correction, putting

$$K'(T) = x(T)k(0) - x(T - \Omega)k(\Omega) + \rho K(T) - Q(T) \quad (3.2')$$

which is the general statement of the Social Accounting Equation.

IV

TECHNIQUE AND TECHNOLOGY

1. In social accounting we are only concerned with values; we are not concerned with the quantities which these values represent, nor (in consequence) with price per unit of quantity. Thus we could deal with the accounting matters, which were our sole concern in the preceding Chapter, without making any assumption about physical homogeneity. Physically, there could be many inputs and many outputs; by confining attention to their values we made them homogeneous, whatever their physical character. When we pass to the more strictly economic application, we lose that advantage.

In this Chapter, and in most of those that follow it, I shall be trying to set the model to work. I am unable to do that without simplifying further. It is thus at this point that I shall introduce the standard simplifications of modern growth theory—taking the price-system, in particular, in the simplest possible terms. We have already allowed ourselves *one* rate of interest; we shall now allow ourselves just one other price, one non-intertemporal price. All 'original' inputs are taken to be homogeneous, and all final outputs homogeneous; so there is just one non-intertemporal price, the input–output price-ratio. It is natural, having made this simplification, to call the homogeneous input Labour; but we must be clear that no characteristic of actual labour comes into the argument, except that it is an input into the productive process, and not an output. If, at a later stage, we should feel the need to introduce a second original input (Land?), it would come in on exactly the same footing. No more than this is implied when we call the original input Labour.

There is no similarly acceptable term for a homogeneous final output, but it will make for convenience to have one. It is to be thought of as standing for 'consumption goods in general'; so I shall just call it *goods*. (I do not think this will cause any confusion since we shall have no producers' goods that are separately traded.) Our single non-intertemporal price-ratio will accordingly appear as the 'wage' of 'labour' into terms of 'goods'—the real wage of labour. I shall denote it by w.

By expressing it in this way, we in effect decide to take *goods* as our standard of value. It would indeed have been equally possible to have taken the value of goods in terms of labour as our fundamental price-ratio, making labour the standard of value instead of goods. That is to say, we might have decided to work in terms of wage-units, in Keynes's manner. Identically the same theory could be expressed either way. The wage-unit form has the advantage that it leads one to interpret a fall in *w* as a rise in money prices relatively to money wages; and that is in fact how we shall often want to interpret it. I have however decided against it, for the following reason. By taking *goods* as standard, we commit ourselves to taking the rate of interest to be a *goods* rate of interest. If (as before) $R = 1 + r$, then R is the value of goods, to be delivered at the beginning of the week, in terms of goods to be delivered at the end of the week. So r is a *real* rate of interest, in what is now a familiar sense. If we had taken labour as standard, the rate of interest would have to have been a labour rate of interest in the same sense; and I think the reader will feel, as I do, that this is a more awkward concept. (We cannot have a money rate of interest until we have introduced money.) So I just lay it down that the rate of interest is a real rate of interest—a goods rate of interest.[1]

2. We can now set to work. Since we are working with goods as standard, b_t can be used, either to represent the quantity of the goods that are produced in week t of a unit process, or the value of those goods; for these come to the same thing. But if, as will now be convenient, we use a_t to denote the *quantity* of the labour input, the value of that input, in terms of goods, is wa_t. So the net output (positive or negative) which we shall still call q_t, is $b_t - wa_t$. The (initial) capital value of the unit process

$$k_0 = \sum_0^n q_t R^{-t} = \sum_0^n (b_t - wa_t) R^{-t}$$

now depends on w.

---

[1] A labour standard, in the sense that is used in this paragraph, is quite a different matter from the 'labour embodied' standard that was invented by Ricardo, adopted by Marx, and developed by contemporary economists, in particular by Sraffa and by Joan Robinson. That also will find a place in our work, later on (see below, p. 72n.).

It is at once apparent that k_0 diminishes when w increases (r being constant). For the a's (labour inputs) are non-negative, and some at least must be positive. It is of course possible that the rise in w may shorten the duration of the process; but this cannot prevent the fall in k_0. It may moderate the fall; but that is all. Thus if we start from a combination of wages and interest (w and r) which make $k_0 = 0$ for a given process, a rise in w, without change in r, must make $k_0 < 0$. It can only be returned to zero, so that the process again becomes viable, by a fall in interest—which, by the Fundamental Theorem of Chapter II, must (by itself) raise k_0. It follows that for a given process there is a functional relation between the values of w and r which make it *just* viable ($k_0 = 0$). This relation may be drawn out as a curve, which we have now proved to be a downward-sloping curve. The curve may also be interpreted as showing the rate of return on the given process for various levels of w.

This is of course none other than the wage-interest curve, or wage-curve, which is familiar in other forms of growth theory. But though it has been so much used, it lacks a satisfactory name. We shall find, as we go on, that to describe it as a wage-interest curve[1] is inadequate; for it has other important properties, which this description fails to bring out. It is in fact nothing less than the translation of the *technique* (which, when originally defined as a sequence of inputs and outputs, is a purely technical relationship) into economic terms. It is the economic expression of the technique. So I have decided to describe it, in this book, as the *efficiency curve* of the technique. The suitability of this description will, I think, become clear as we go on.

3. We can now proceed to use the efficiency curve, in the manner that has become conventional, to give a theory of *choice of technique*. The principle of this need not detain us, since it is exactly the same as in other versions.

We are to suppose that there are alternative techniques which are available 'within the technology'. Each of these techniques will have an efficiency curve, constructed on the principle just described.

---

[1] It is still less appropriate, on the present approach, to describe it as a 'factor–price curve' or 'factor–price frontier'. In an 'Austrian' theory, the rate of interest is not the price of a 'factor'.

Take first the case in which there are just two alternative techniques, the efficiency curves of which are shown as AA' and BB' on Fig. 3. If there is a free choice between them, that technique will be chosen which has the higher rate of return. It might be that 'B' had a higher rate of return than 'A', whatever w; but what is here the more interesting case is that illustrated, in which 'B' has a higher rate of return for some w, while for other w it is the other way about. BPA' is then the outer frontier, the *efficiency curve of the technology*, which not only indicates the

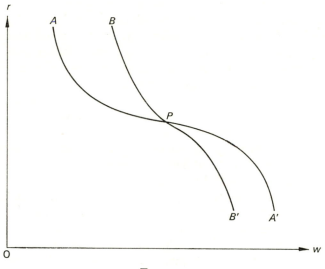

FIG. 3.

maximum rate of return available at each value of w, but also shows what technique must be adopted to get that maximum rate of return.

When there are many available techniques, the outer frontier is built up in the same manner, by taking the outer portions of the particular technique curves. Mathematically, the outer frontier is the envelope of the particular technique curves.

So much is very simple, and (I think) non-controversial. But from it one proceeds to an issue on which there has been active controversy—the question of 're-switching'.

It has been pointed out (at considerable length in the course of the controversy) that the mere rule of downward slope, established (in one way or another) for the efficiency curves of particular techniques, gives us no reason to suppose that the curves belonging to two techniques (such as AA' and BB' on Fig. 3) may not intersect more than once. For all that has been said, that must apply here. Nothing has been said which would lead one to suppose that the curves are straight lines (which could not intersect more than once); and it is in fact inconceivable, on our interpretation, that they could be straight lines. For we have assumed that 'labour' is the only input ('labour' is the name we have given to the only input); so we may take it that with $w = 0$, so that all q's are non-negative (some positive), there would be some value left in the process however high the rate of interest. The upper end of the curve (defined by $k_0 = 0$) must therefore be asymptotic to a vertical line. At the other end it must intersect the horizontal axis, for there must be some wage which would swallow up the whole proceeds (making $r = 0$). A *straight* line which would satisfy these conditions cannot possibly be drawn.

But this by no means shows that re-switching must occur; only that on the simplest test it is not ruled out. It may still be ruled out for other reasons. Some further analysis is surely required.

4. I begin by showing that there is a simple, but important, case in which it can be proved that re-switching cannot occur.

Suppose that each of the techniques that are in question are of the following *simple* form. There is a construction period, lasting m weeks, in which labour is applied at a constant rate but in which there is no final output. It is followed by a utilization period, lasting a further n weeks, in which labour is applied at a constant (but different) rate, and in which final output appears at a constant rate. I shall describe this form as a *Simple Profile*. We shall subsequently make much use of it, as an instrument of exploration; we can use it to great advantage, provided we recognize its limitations.

We may choose the constant rate of output as unit of quantity; so the Simple Profile may be written:

weeks	0 to $m - 1$	m to $m + n - 1$
inputs	a_c	a_u
outputs	0	1

There are four parameters to determine the technique: the input-coefficients, a_c and a_u, and the durations, m and n.

The efficiency curve of this technique has the equation

$$k_0 = -wa_c \sum_0^{m-1} R^{-t} + (1 - wa_c)R^{-m} \sum_0^{n-1} R^{-t} = 0$$

which is evidently non-linear.

Now suppose that the other technique (to be of the same general form) has different input-coefficients (a_c^* and a_u^*), but the same duration parameters (m and n). Its efficiency equation must then be

$$-wa_c^* \sum_0^{m-1} R^{-t} + (1 - wa_u^*)R^{-m} \sum_0^{n-1} R^{-t} = 0.$$

But here, in order to determine an intersection of the curves, we can eliminate R (for the discountings are all the same), getting

$$\frac{a_c}{a_c^*} = \frac{1 - wa_u}{1 - wa_u^*}$$

which determines w *uniquely*. (For suitable values of the input-coefficients, w will be positive.) Since both of the curves are downward-sloping, there is a unique r which corresponds to the unique w. There can only be one intersection.

5. But let us now see what happens when one of the duration parameters also varies. I shall take the case in which the construction periods are different; and, for simplicity, I shall assume that the processes are unterminating, so that for each of them n is infinite. Then $\sum_0^{n-1} R^{-t} = 1/(1 - R^{-1})$; so the equation of the efficiency curve may be written

$$-wa_c(1 - R^{-1}) \sum_0^{m-1} R^{-t} + (1 - wa_u)R^{-m} = 0.$$

or $\qquad\qquad -wa_c(1 - R^{-m}) + (1 - wa_u)R^{-m} = 0$

or $\qquad\qquad\qquad (1/w) = a_u + a_c(R^m - 1).$

Here then, at a point of intersection, we must have

$$a_u + a_c(R^m - 1) = a_u^* + a_c^*(R^{m*} - 1).$$

We have to see whether it is possible that this equation may have more than one solution (with $R > 1$).

We may choose the starred technique so that $m > m^*$; and we may then choose a time-unit so that $m^* = 1$. The equation to be investigated may then be written

$$a_c[(1 + r)^m - 1] = a_u^* - a_u + a_c^* r.$$

The properties of this equation may readily be studied graphically.

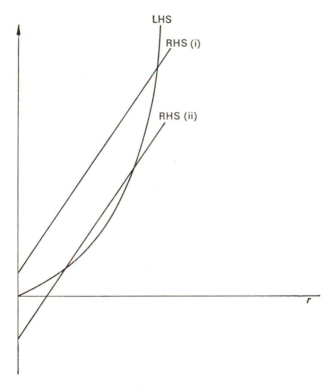

LHS

RHS (i)

RHS (ii)

r

FIG. 4.

Consider Fig. 4, in which the left-hand and right-hand sides of this equation are graphed as functions of r. All the input-coefficients are positive, so the right-hand side appears as an upward-sloping straight line. We have taken $m > 1$, so the left-hand side appears as a curve, which passes through the origin ($r = 0$), and thereafter has a continually increasing slope.

It is at once apparent that what happens depends on the

intercept on the vertical axis $(a_u^* - a_u)$. If this is positive, there will always be an intersection in the positive quadrant $(r > 0)$; but there can only be *one* intersection. No re-switching is possible. If on the other hand, the intercept is negative, then either there will be no intersection, or there will be two intersections. So the condition for re-switching is a negative intercept; but one that must not be too large.

What does this mean? A switch from starred to unstarred is a switch to a technique with a longer construction period; we now find that (for re-switching to occur) it must also be a switch to a technique with higher *operating cost* $(a_u > a_u^*)$. As we find, such a switch will ordinarily not be profitable. It could only be profitable (at some w) if there was an economy in construction cost *per week* (a_c) which offset the *double* disadvantage. That could happen; but it looks like being on the edge of the things that could happen.

6. This is no more than an illustration; but it is highly suggestive. Re-switching, in itself, is no more than a *curiosum*; if it is taken literally, it hardly seems to be deserving of the attention it has received. But its importance is not on its own account; it is for the much more substantial issue that lies behind it.

Why was it that we got no re-switching when $m = m^*$, but that it became a possibility when m and m^* were different? In the former case, the only difference between the techniques was in their input-coefficients a_c and a_u. Here, since at a point of intersection (or switch-point) total costs must be the same, the two techniques could be adequately distinguished by the ratio of a_c to a_u—a single parameter. If the change in technique, along the technological frontier of the economy, was always of this type, the change could be adequately described as a substitution of constructional labour for operational labour—the ratio between them would continually increase as one moved along the curve. Or, if one liked to describe the constructional cost as 'capital cost', the change could be described as a substitution of capital for labour.

As soon as we permitted a variation in m, this ceased to be possible. For the techniques were no longer capable of being distinguished by a single parameter. In our example, there would be just two parameters; but in general, of course, there may be many. There will be many 'directions' in which adjustments are made. A switch from one technique to another may be motivated by the saving that is made in one of these directions; but in order to secure that saving, it may well be necessary—technically necessary—in some other directions to incur some extra expense. The switch will nevertheless be profitable if the saving outweighs the expense. But the balance between this saving and this expense itself depends upon prices (represented, in the present model, by w); if prices were different it might go the other way. That is what produces the 're-switching' possibility.

One may not be greatly impressed by that possibility; it would indeed seem natural that at the stage when the reversal occurred, it would be some quite different technical switch which would be in question. One must nevertheless accept (1) that the movement along the technological frontier is a matter of choice between *technically given* alternatives; (2) that some at least of the switches will be a matter of balance between advantages and disadvantages, a balance which itself is affected by prices; (3) that it is therefore impossible, in general, for the movement to be representable in terms of any *single* technically given parameter. This is the important result which emerges.

The argument applies to any technically describable parameter. So it does not only apply against the representation of the effect of a rise in the real wage as a substitution of capital for labour, in the sense above described; it also applies against the alternative representation, that due to the older Austrians, where the effect appears as a 'lengthening of the period of production'.[1] Both are special cases, in which the differences between the techniques are reduced to differences in a single parameter. Neither, in general, is admissible.

It is of course true that whenever a rise in the wage induces a change in technique, the change must always be such that, at the switch-point, the new efficiency curve has the greater slope.[2]

---

[1] I did in fact make the point, in criticism of Böhm-Bawerk, in Chapter XVIII of *Value and Capital*. It is the same point as I am making here.

[2] It was this which I endeavoured to express, in the chapter of *Value and Capital* just cited, in terms of a 'period of production' that was weighted by discounted values. There is nothing wrong with that treatment; but, except for its particular purpose, of criticizing the 'old' Austrian theory, it is not very useful. It is better to go straight to the slopes (or elasticities) of the efficiency curves.

That is unaffected; and there are many purposes for which it is all that is required.[1]

[1] It can be shown, in much the same way, that we get the same complication when we abandon our assumption that labour is the sole input into the constructional stage of an (otherwise) Simple Process.

If we are to keep our single non-intertemporal price-ratio, the new input must be taken to be 'goods' (final product) 'fed back' into the process. If b is the amount thus fed back, per unit of final product, the efficiency equation becomes

$$(-b - wa_c) \sum_0^{m-1} R^{-t} + (1 - wa_u)R^{-m} \sum_0^{n-1} R^{-t} = 0$$

or
$$(b + wa_c)r_{m,n} + wa_u = 1$$

where $r_{m,n}$ (the *gross* rate of return) depends on r, m and n only.

Consider the possibility of switching to a technique with the same m and n, but different a_c, a_u and b. With w and $r_{m,n}$ taken as co-ordinates, each efficiency equation appears as a branch of a rectangular hyperbola, having asymptotes outside the positive quadrant. Two such curves may have (i) no intersection in the positive quadrant, (ii) one such intersection, or (iii) two intersections, but not more than two. Since their intercepts on the axes are $w = (1/a_u)$ and $w = (1/a_u^*)$, $r_{m,n} = (1/b)$ and $r_{m,n} = (1/b^*)$, it is necessary, if $a_u - a_u^*$ and $b - b^*$ have opposite signs, that there should be one intersection and no more. If these differences have the same sign, there must either be no intersection or two intersections. But if there is any intersection while they have the same sign, it is directly evident, from a comparison of the efficiency equations, that $a_c - a_c^*$ must have the opposite sign. So the 're-switching' case is that in which there is a substitution of constructional for utilizational labour, which carries with it an economy in 'feedback'. Complementarity again!

This, I think is substantially what happens in conventional *sectoralized* theory (such as that which I used in Part III of *Capital and Growth*). The 'feedback' there appears as employment of *machines* as well as labour in the *machine-making* industry.

V

FULL PERFORMANCE AND FULL EMPLOYMENT

1. IT would be perfectly possible, at the point we have now reached, to go forward on the well-beaten path of modern growth theory: using the relations, which are already at our disposal, so as to establish the conditions for the model economy to be in a *steady state*. As will be shown in the following chapter, we are ourselves on the way to a steady state theory, which is not substantially different from that which has become conventional; for in the steady state, where the structure of the economy is the same in every time-period, time has been so nearly abolished that the passage from the assumption of a 'sectoralized' technique to our assumption of a technique that is time-articulated cannot make much difference. So in our steady state theory we shall do little more than confirm well-established results. I wish, however, to present those results in a new way; and for that I need some additional preparation.

The steady state, in this book, will be no more than a means to an end—to the study of an economy which is *not* expanding uniformly, an economy in which things actually happen. Now for the study of a non-steady state path more assumptions are needed than for the study of a steady state path; more assumptions, and more distinctions. It will be useful, before we pass to the formal theory of a steady state, to examine these distinctions. For when we have them, we shall find ourselves able to take the steady state theory itself in a more fruitful way.

2. I begin with a distinction that is already present in steady state theory; for it will help in the setting-out of what follows. All we have got from the efficiency frontier (of the given technology) is the determination of the rate of interest (and the most profitable technique) when the wage is given—or, alternatively, of the wage and the corresponding technique when the rate of interest is given—so that, even for the determination of the *price*-system, something more is required. This can be found, as is well known, in two ways. We may, on the one hand, make the 'classical', or Ricardian, assumption that the wage is given exogenously—being determined in some way outside the model. The price-system is then complete, but the corresponding quantity system, and in particular its rate of growth, remain to be determined. It can however be determined in a fairly simple way, by reference to saving propensities, which (on these assumptions) determine the rate of accumulation. The whole steady state model is then complete. But a steady growth, at constant wage and constant technique, requires a steady expansion in the employment of labour. A perfectly elastic supply of labour, at the given wage, must therefore be included in the assumptions.

We may alternatively take it that the rate of expansion of the labour supply is given, and that the whole of the given labour force is to be kept fully employed. We have then to begin with the quantity-system. In a steady state, the general growth rate is governed by the rate of increase of the labour supply; the rate of capital accumulation must be set to match. If it is the case that the rate of accumulation depends solely upon the rate of interest (and this, on some hypotheses about saving, does actually happen), we can determine the rate of interest as that which is needed to call forth the required rate of saving. The technological frontier will then determine the rate of wages, and the technique that corresponds. So we here determine the quantity-system and then determine the price-system from it. But the hypothesis on saving, which has this convenient result, is rather special. More generally, it may be expected that the rate of accumulation will be influenced by the technique adopted; the price-system and the quantity-system will then need to be simultaneously determined.

This is no more than the baldest summary of steady state theory; I shall fill in the details later. My present purpose is merely to remind the reader that steady state theory, in the conventional form, divides into these two branches. There is (1) the *Fixwage* theory, as I shall call it, in which w (the *real* wage) is given but employment is variable, and (2) the *Full Employment* theory, where there is full employment of a labour supply the movement of which is given exogenously. The same distinction, we shall find, carries over into the more general analysis. Whether or not our economy is to be in a steady state, we shall find it convenient to analyse its performance, first on the one assumption and then on the other.

The first part of this chapter will deal with the Fixwage theory. It may well be felt that to give it so much attention needs justification; I think that the justification can be provided, on several levels. Theoretically, it is justified as being much the simpler assumption; for with w given, the dominant technique (the technique that will be used for new processes) is directly determined from the technology; if the technology does not vary, the dominant technique will not change. That is an immense convenience; it is, for this reason alone, a useful case with which to start. So regarded, it is no more than a stepping-stone; but I think it is more than that. We need not put much weight on the fact that it was Ricardo's assumption—justified, so he thought, on the Malthusian ground that wages approximated to some level of subsistence, physiologically (or perhaps culturally) but not economically determined. It is more to the point that it has been found[1] to be a useful assumption for the study of 'underdeveloped' countries. We may regard our model economy as a representation of the 'developed' sector of such a country, there being a subsistence sector outside it. Labour can be drawn from the subsistence sector, and will be drawn from it quite freely, as soon as the wage that is offered in the developed sector is marginally above what can be earned in the subsistence sector. The presence of the subsistence sector prevents the wage in the developed sector from rising above this basic level; so, to the developed sector, the supply of labour is perfectly elastic. This is no doubt an over-simplification of what actually happens in any actual economy; but it is near enough to what sometimes happens to be of some interest.

There are several other ways in which we shall need the Fixwage assumption; they will come to our notice as we go along.

3. On the Fixwage assumption, as already indicated, the dominant technique, and the rate of return on that technique, are determined from the technology frontier. Whether or not the economy is in a steady state, the new processes that are being started will use that technique; and so long as any new processes are being

---

[1] As for instance by Sir Arthur Lewis. See his *Economic Development with Unlimited Labour* (Manchester School, 1954).

started, the rate of return on that technique (in the perfect capital market which we are assuming) will equal the rate of interest. For if the rate of interest were higher than this return, no new processes could be started; and if it were lower, there would be a capital gain to be got for nothing, on the mere announcement of the intention to start a process. So the rate of interest is determined; and on the price-side, there is nothing more to be said.

What however determines the volume of employment? This, in general, will change from week to week; so we have to begin by examining what determines employment in a particular week (week T).

We may readily suppose that the processes started in week T produce no output in week T (their $b_0 = 0$). So B_T (the output of week T) depends entirely upon processes that have been started in the past, and of the techniques that are used in those processes (which, as we have seen, may be different from the technique that is now dominant). If we take our stand at week T, and are firm in our adherence to the Jevonian principle that 'bygones are bygones', then B_T is already determined. But the employment of labour (A_T), though it is largely determined in the same way, as a consequence of decisions made in the past, is not wholly so determined. For though the initial output in the new processes is taken to be zero, the corresponding input (a_0) cannot be taken to be zero; for if both a_0 and b_0 were zero, the new processes would not have been started. So A_T does depend, to some extent, on x_T —on the number of new unit processes started in week T.

What determines x_T? It is quite tempting, and is well in accordance with the view that is held by many (Keynesian or even Schumpeterian) economists, to say that x_T also should be taken as being exogeneous—for this is the same thing as saying that investment depends upon the optimism, or 'animal spirits' of entrepreneurs. But can we say that—within our model? Let us try to say it and observe the consequences.

B_T is then determined (from the past); A_T is determined (from the given x_T); and w is given. So Q_T ($= B_T - wA_T$) is also determined. It is determined *on the supply side*; but nothing has so far been said which will ensure a demand, that will take over that supply. In the simple case of 'no saving out of wages', Q_T must be equal to what 'capitalists' *want* to consume out of profits, if the market for final output is to be in equilibrium. (More generally,

B_T must be equal to what 'capitalists' and 'workers' together want to consume.) Nothing has so far been said which ensures that equality.

We suddenly find ourselves brought up against a central issue of Keynesian (and post-Keynesian[1]) controversy. It is an issue that far transcends our particular model; but it is a virtue of our model that in it this issue comes up so sharply. To sharpen it yet further, let us make an extra assumption—that the final output is non-storable; if it is not required in the current week, it will go to waste. (It will be useful to begin by making this assumption, since the notion of disequilibrium in the market is then quite unambiguous.)

If, under these assumptions, the rate of starts is taken to be exogenous, it can only be by chance that the market for final output can be in equilibrium. But must it be in equilibrium? A 'classical' economist—to use that term, for once, in Keynes's sense—would, I believe, insist that it must be in equilibrium; it would be brought into equilibrium by reactions that we have been leaving out. Current output, he would say, would not be allowed to go to waste, for there is something that can be done with it, even in terms of our model; it can be *lent*. Any attempt to lend it will exert a downward pressure on the rate of interest (the *real* rate of interest which is all that comes into the model); but any fall in the rate of interest will give the opportunity of a capital gain in the starting of a new process. That will ensure that sufficient new processes are started to absorb the surplus output. So there is no disequilibrium, after all.

It may naturally be objected that a great deal has to happen in the single 'week' (even on the single 'Monday') if this equilibration is to be carried through; but we have been unfair to our 'classical' economist in talking about 'weeks'. He must surely have been thinking of an equilibration that is spread over a longer period. But any such longer period is a succession of shorter periods; what is to happen, on his principles, in the shorter periods? In the shorter periods, output (if non-storable) must be going to waste—if there is insufficient demand for it. If that situation continues, over a number of shorter periods (or 'weeks'),

[1] See especially R. W. Clower, 'The Keynesian Counter-Revolution' in *The Theory of Interest Rates* (I.E.A. volume, 1965); also Leijonhufvud, *On Keynesian Economics and the Economics of Keynes* (1968).

then it is possible that in the end the 'classical' equilibration may operate; but that is the most that can be claimed for it.

We started with an exogenously given rate of starts, which engendered a volume of employment (and hence of Effective Demand) that was insufficient to absorb the current output. The economy would thus be in a state of *over-production*; and the natural reaction, to a state of over-production, is to *reduce* the rate of starts. But that exacerbates the disequilibrium. If this reaction is dominant, we have the downward instability, which to the followers of Keynes (and of Harrod) is very familiar. Unless this reaction is denied, and it is hard to deny it, the most that can be claimed by our 'classical' economist is that his relieving force *may* come on the scene in time to overcome it.

4. Even if the rate of starts is exogenous, it cannot vary indefinitely. It has a lower limit of zero; there can be no negative starts. Even if the rate of starts is zero, employment is not zero; for employment still continues on the uncompleted processes. But of course if the rate of starts continues at zero, the economy will gradually come to a stop. There is, on the other hand, a clear upper limit, so long as the rate of real wages is given. For while there can be excess supply (output going to waste) there can be no excess demand, for how should that excess demand be met (output being still taken as unstorable)? So the equilibrium of the market for final output sets an upper limit to the rate of starts.

We accordingly find that even in the Fixwage model, in which there is no question of the Full Employment of labour, there is something that corresponds. Let us call it Full Performance. At Full Performance the rate of starts is at its maximum—at the maximum permitted by the share of current output that is not absorbed by consumption out of wages paid to labour engaged on old processes, and not absorbed in consumption of other kinds. So at Full Performance activity is limited by saving—just as the older economists (*classical* economists in the usual sense, not specifically in Keynes's sense) supposed it to be. We can keep in touch with their theory, regarding it as a theory of Full Performance. We can nevertheless accept that an economy may run at less than Full Performance; and if confidence is insufficient, that is what it will do.

The point has now been reached at which we can abandon our non-storability hypothesis. If excess supplies are storable, they need not go to waste; they can pile up in surplus stocks. The first of the differences which this makes is that the economy can temporarily run above what we have called its Full Performance level of activity; the rate of starts may for a while be greater than that which we have just defined as its maximum—during the time while surplus stocks, previously accumulated, are being absorbed. Thus there can be a greater than 'normal' rate of growth during a phase of recovery from depression; a well-known phenomenon that fits in.

The question may nevertheless be asked: given that surplus stocks are technically storable, why should they be stored? The holding of stocks is itself an economic activity; it is itself a process, which will not be undertaken unless it is profitable to undertake it. Now it would seem at first sight that under the assumptions of our model (in which, it will be remembered, *goods* —that are themselves the product of the productive process—are the standard of value) there can be no advantage from stock-holding. The unit of goods is one unit now, and it will still be one unit in the future; so the rate of return on stock-holding must be zero. But this is false. The stocks which we are supposing to be carried forward are *surplus*. If they are not carried forward they will go to waste. This is the only alternative use for them which exists (for the time which would be needed for the 'classical' reaction to occur is not allowed); so in the alternative use their value is zero. So it will *always* be advantageous to carry them forward if the cost of carrying them forward can be neglected; and it will often be advantageous to carry them forward, so long as the costs of doing so are moderate—provided that there is an assurance that the condition of excess supply will not last indefinitely. But on this interpretation the carry-forward is a sign of disequilibrium—though if the whole of the surplus is carried forward the disequilibrium is *suppressed*. It is only because the system is on the edge of disequilibrium that the surplus can be carried forward.

It thus appears that we can take some account of stock-holding without making much change in our 'non-storability' analysis. Full Performance, in which there is no disequilibrium—no question of disequilibrium—retains its pre-eminence. The catastrophic possibility, a total failure of nerve, with no hope of recovery from the current disequilibrium, is still not excluded. (The stock-holding model would then work in the same way as the non-storability model, for no stocks would be held, since there would be no advantage in holding them.) But much more important is the possibility of temporary failures, from which there is an expectation of recovery; the stocks that are accumulated in such a 'depression' will then permit a temporary expansion, when the recovery comes, that goes beyond the Full Performance level. This may be granted; but it does not deprive Full Performance of its significance. The Full Performance path still shows the highest level of activity that can be *maintained*.

5. I may indeed digress, at this point, to make some remarks on the wider significance of the Full Performance concept; for though it has been thrown up by our particular model, it is rather obvious that it can be taken more widely. We cannot however use it, in more general application, without attention to questions of risk—questions which in this book are generally neglected, as for most of the problems with which we have been (and shall be) concerned seems fairly harmless. Here it is certainly not harmless. In a world in which prices were expected to remain unchanged, and expected with certainty to remain unchanged, the carry-over of stocks,[1] as we have seen, would be a sign of disequilibrium. But in a world of uncertain expectations this is by no means so. The carrying of stocks is then a means to liquidity; so some carriage of stocks is perfectly *normal*. We must suppose that *normal* stocks are carried all along the Full Performance path.

Even so, it would be possible for the economy to 'under-function'; when there was a deficiency of Effective Demand stocks would become greater than *normal*. But it would also be possible for it to 'over-function', stocks becoming less than *normal*; but this 'over-functioning' would be a condition that could not be maintained. We know all about this over-functioning in the case of a particular nation; the easiest stocks to run down are those of foreign exchange, so the over-functioning shows itself in a balance-of-payments crisis. A closed economy has no

---

[1] I neglect the minimum carry-over, necessitated by the need for avoidance of the extra costs of small orders.

such foreign exchange to run down; so over-functioning must be reflected in physical stocks. Both under- and over-functioning may nevertheless occur. The Full Performance path, on which neither occurs, retains its significance.

It has become very clear, from our analysis, that Full Performance is quite different from Full Employment. In our Fixwage model, with its perfectly elastic supply of labour, there is no Full Employment. Yet there is a limit to activity, in any but the very short run, which is set by Full Performance. Do we not see this in practice? Is it not one reason why developing countries, that have no scarcity of labour, yet seek to borrow abroad?

It has also become clear, from our analysis, that Full Performance has nothing necessarily to do with the monetary system. In our model there is no money; yet we have seen that it can under-function. What we have constructed is as near as can be to what a long line of eminent economists have described as a 'barter' system—a system which (they often supposed) would work quite smoothly if it were not for monetary disturbances. That, we can now see, is quite invalid. It was only because their conception of the barter system was too simple—too static—that they could bring themselves to endow it with such virtue. Money is not the cause of fluctuations; it is a complication, but no more than that.

6. I return to my formal analysis, proceeding (for the rest of this chapter) to leave Fixwage theory, and turning to that which we have seen to be its companion. Instead of taking the wage to be fixed and employment variable, we are to examine the conditions for the maintenance of Full Employment of an exogenously given supply of labour, the wage (the real wage) being allowed to be variable. We need not suppose that the supply of labour is constant over time; it may vary over time, but it varies exogenously. It may thus be expected that, excepting in a steady state, the wage will actually vary.

This at once presents a difficulty—a formidable difficulty. For in our way of determining the dominant technique (which may now be no more than the technique that is chosen for the new processes, that are currently being started), we supposed it to be chosen from those that were available within the technology, as being that which was the most profitable *at the current wage*. But in supposing that the current wage played this part in the choice of technique, we implicitly assumed that the wage was expected to remain unchanged, for the duration of the process. In Fixwage theory that caused no trouble; but in Full Employment theory, where changes in wages (over time) must undoubtedly be allowed for, the trouble it causes is very serious indeed.

There are, I think, two possible ways of dealing with it. One, which has in fact been abundantly explored by many writers, is to look for the path which would be determined by *correct* expectations; by expectations (of the course of wages) which are such that along the Full Employment path they can be fulfilled. The wages that are to rule, along the whole path, must then be simultaneously determined. The theory which emerges is not a sequential theory, of the kind we are here endeavouring to construct; past and future are all on a level. What emerges, in fact, is an optimum theory, of von Neumann, Turnpike or suchlike type; but that is not the kind of theory we are looking for here. It is necessary, for us, to choose the other alternative.

This is to suppose that expected wages are determined in some *given* manner. The simplest of such assumptions is the assumption of 'static expectations'—that, when the decision to adopt a particular technique for *new* processes is taken, the current wage is expected to remain unchanged.[1] It will not in fact remain unchanged, so the process that is chosen will not be an optimum process; the path that is followed will not, to this extent, be an optimum path. I shall nevertheless make use of the 'static expectations' assumption, since it probably throws as much light on actual processes of development as we can expect to get from our general approach. It provides, at the least, a foundation, a standard case. Other assumptions on the formation of expectations, if we like to make them, may well be best considered as deviations from it.

7. How then, on a Full Employment path, with static expectations, is the wage to be determined? It is tempting to argue as follows. Suppose that the wage is (provisionally) fixed at a particular level. Then, at that wage, Fixwage theory will apply. The

---

[1] I had better insist that it is the *real* wage that is expected to be unchanged. We know very well, in these days, that plans are often made on the assumption of rising *money* wages; but that is quite a different matter.

technique that is used in the new processes will be determined; B_T (as usual) will be given by the past, and Q_T by saving propensities; so there will be a particular rate of starts which will give Full Performance. This will determine a particular employment of labour (A_T). If this A_T is less than Full Employment, the wage will have to be adjusted, so as to yield Full Employment. But in which direction will it have to be adjusted? Up or down?

One is naturally inclined to jump to the conclusion that it is a fall in wages that is called for. But that, on our assumptions, does not unambiguously follow; it certainly does not easily follow. A fall in w will lead, in general, to a change in technique; but nothing has been said that makes it inevitable that the change should be such as will lead to a rise in the demand for labour *in the current period*. It is the whole sequence of a's and b's that will change, when the one technique is substituted for the other. The new technique must be such that it is the more profitable at the lower wage, though it was less profitable at the higher; but that says *nothing* about the relation between the initial inputs (a_0). It is by no means ruled out that, looking only at the current week, a rise in wages might introduce the right substitution. So it appears that on this route one gets no firm answer.

There is however another route on which the answer seems clearer. We always have the Social Accounting Equation: $B_T - wA_T = Q_T$. So if B_T is given, and A_T is given (Full Employment), w depends directly on Q_T. If there is no saving out of wages,[1] Q_T is consumption out of profits; and while we may make that consumption a function of current profits (say a constant proportion of current profits) we do not have to do so. In fact, when the 'week' is short, it is actually more reasonable to make consumption out of profits depend on the average of profits over many weeks (most of which are in the past) which the current week's profits will affect very little.[2] But that means that the current Q_T (bygones being bygones) may, at least approximately, be taken as an independent variable.

w is then determined, independently of any question of technique; the technique adopted (for new processes) will be determined as a consequence of this w. And x_T (the rate of starts) is also determined; it is the rate of starts which, with this technique,

---

[1] See note on following page.
[2] Compare the 'permanent income hypothesis' of Professor Milton Friedman.

gives Full Employment. So if Q_T is given the model is closed, and is rather easy to work with.[1]

8. This may well appear to the reader as something of a trick; the direction of causation seems to be taken backwards. To use the Social Accounting Equation in the way we have just been using it implies Full Performance; but while it is intelligible to vary the rate of starts so as to give Full Performance (for the rate of starts is our main index of Activity), variation of the rate of wages so as to give Full Performance is much harder to accept. Full Performance is however the key. If there is to be Full Employment *and* Full Performance, the Social Accounting Equation, as we have written it, must hold; and it is itself sufficient (with given Q_T) to determine the rate of wages. But this says nothing at all about what happens when there is not Full Performance.

We find ourselves, once again, in a position to throw new light upon major controversy. The determination of the wage rate, in the manner just indicated, is nothing else but the Wage Fund theory; a theory which was by no means killed by John Stuart Mill's 'recantation', but which has re-appeared, more or less surreptitiously, in the work of later economists.[2] The case of Mill is however by far the most interesting. His changes of attitude are clearly marked, and in terms of the present construction they fit into their places. We can elucidate Mill, and advance understanding of the present model, at one and the same time.

There are *three* of Mill's writings that are relevant. The first is the early essay 'On the Influence of Consumption on Production' probably written about 1830, but published in the *Essays on Unsettled Questions* (1844). This is actually, to modern taste, the deepest of all Mill's writings on the subject; it is one of the finest

---

[1] There is no difficulty in dealing with saving out of wages, if one supposes that consumption out of wages is a fixed proportion of wages. (This is a more reasonable assumption in the case of wages, in the very short-run, than the corresponding assumption about profits.) Let s be the fraction of the wage-bill that is saved. Then if C_T is consumption out of profits (which must now be distinguished from Q_T)

$$C_T = B_T - (1 - s)wA_T$$

and w is still determined, at $(B_T - C_T)/(1 - s)A_T$, which reduces to $(B_T - C_T)/A_T$ when s is zero.

[2] As in Pigou, *Theory of Unemployment* (1933), and in Kaldor, 'Alternative Theories of Distribution' (*R. Econ. Studies*, 1955; reprinted in *Essays in Value and Distribution*, 1960).

productions of Classical Economics. There is implied, in that essay, something which is very near to our concept of Full Performance.[1] Mill is perfectly aware, and indeed insists, that a condition in which the national economy is less than Fully Performing is perfectly possible, and must indeed be expected to occur from time to time. He is aware that lapses from Full Performance are associated with accumulation of stocks; but that the carrying of normal stocks is no sign of a lapse. All this, as we have seen, we may accept.

In the *Principles* (1848) there are passages that are linked to the essay. 'Because industry is limited by capital, we are not to infer that it always reaches that limit.'[2] But the discussion of lapses is almost entirely confined to the chapters that deal with credit; in those that deal with capital and wages Full Performance is nearly always taken for granted. Now if Full Performance is taken for granted, the famous Four Propositions about Capital are quite defensible; and the Wage Fund, in the sense above enunciated, appears as a corollary. The use which Mill makes of the Wage Fund in the *Principles* is indeed, for the most part, unobjectionable. He is mainly concerned with its bearing on the problem of population; the difficulty of increasing the Fund fast enough to employ (at constant real wages) a rapidly increasing population was his principal theme. (It is a theme with which, in these days, we are not unfamiliar.) He is perfectly clear that the Fund will increase more rapidly if there is more saving; and he is aware that 'improvements in production' will make that accumulation easier.[3] $B_T - Q_T$ may be increased by a fall in Q_T *or* by a rise in B_T.

Why then did Mill, twenty years later, 'abandon' the Wage Fund? The article,[4] in which the recantation occurs, is not one of Mill's better economic writings; one suspects that by 1868 he was much less interested in economics than he had been as a younger man. When one looks for the theoretical change, it is hard to find it. He is dissociating himself from the uses that others have made of the Wage Fund; and for that reason he (naturally enough) prefers a different expression. There is a change in emphasis, since

---

[1] It is called Full Employment, but it is Full Employment of Capital of which he is thinking. The association of Employment (and Unemployment) with Labour was a development that had not yet come about.

[2] Book I, ch. 5, sect. 2.   [3] See, for instance, Bk IV, ch. 4, sect. 6.

[4] Review of W. T. Thornton, *On Labour*.

the problems to which the theory is to be applied are different; but (so far as I can see) the substance remains the same. More stress is laid (than in the *Principles*) upon the effects of improvements in production (B_T); and much more stress upon the possibility of diminishing unproductive consumption (Q_T). But that is all.

We might well have expected more. Nothing is said about the Full Performance assumption, on which Mill himself had at one time been so clear. And nothing is said about the reasons which in fact led most of the next generation of economists (the so-called 'neo-classics') to *abandon the wage-fund*. These also have their place in our present discussion, and to them I now turn.

9. It should never have been supposed that the Wage Fund (however carefully qualified) was a *complete* theory of wages; it does no more, at the best, than explain how the wage is determined in the current 'week', the past course of the economy being given. It is a very short-run theory; it needs to be completed by the consideration of longer-run effects.

Our method of dealing with longer-run effects will be developed in later chapters; we shall try to exhibit them *sequentially*. This, if we can manage it, is surely the right way of dealing with them. The older economists, however, though they were conscious of the problem, did not attempt to deal with it sequentially; they *classified*. They distinguished (at the most) four phases: (i) ultrashort-period, (ii) short-period, (iii) long-period, (iv) ultra-long-period; the effects under these heads were treated *separately*. It is only in Marshall that all the phases appear; in Mill there are only two, the first and the last. His (i) is that which we have been discussing; his (iv) is his Stationary State. (It had to be a Stationary State, since he was insisting that production was ultimately limited by the fixed supply of Land.) Now to the neo-classics the Stationary State seemed much further away than it had seemed to Mill; they were readier to conceive of 'progress' going on indefinitely. So (iv) disappeared from view; they concentrated their attention on (ii) and (iii). These, in Marshall, are clearly distinguished—not so clearly in his contemporaries. But the focus of attention is the same.

Since effects under (ii) and (iii) were to be treated separately, there could be no genuinely sequential relation between them.

Marshall's 'short-period' is distinguished from his 'long-period' solely in terms of the constraints under which producers are supposed to operate. In the short-period, he says, 'producers have to adjust their supply to the demand as best they can with the appliances already at their disposal'.[1] Now how does this distinction—this famous and important distinction—fit into our present model? Can we find a place for it?

Only by removing an assumption, which we have hitherto been making—an assumption which may well have been causing trouble to the reader, but which I have deliberately not stressed, since it was only at the point now reached that I wanted to call attention to it. I have hitherto assumed that a process, once started, must be carried through on the original plan; though it may be cut short (or truncated), or it may be prolonged (in a manner which is implied in the original plan), if it proves to be profitable, when the time comes, to truncate it or to prolong it. These are the only *subsequent* adjustments of which we have taken account. It would however have been more realistic (it would at least have been a step towards realism) if we had admitted the possibility of subsequent adjustments of other kinds. Marshall's 'short-period' is a matter of such subsequent adjustments. His processes have alternative 'tails'; according to the state of the market (at a point where a switch is possible) one 'tail' or another will be adopted.

Since the technique of production is defined by the series of (a, b) coefficients, a *subsequent adjustment* is to be reckoned as a change of technique. The two techniques have the same coefficients, up to the point of adjustment; only afterwards is there a divergence. We shall need a name for changes of technique of this character; I shall call them *minor switches*. A major switch is one that can only be made at the start of a process; but a minor switch can be made to a process that has already been started.

The admission of minor switches makes no formal difference to the Wage Fund, as we have interpreted it. It will still be true that (at Full Performance) B_T is determined from the past, and Q_T is determined in the way that has been indicated. The only way in which the previous discussion must be modified, when minor switches are admitted, is that the labour employed *on the old processes* in week T is no longer pre-determined. In a model

[1] Marshall, *Principles*, p. 376.

without minor switches, additional labour could only be employed in the starting of new processes; but when minor switches are admitted, it is possible that additional labour may be employed on the old processes also. This, we shall find, makes little formal difference. It does however mean that additional output may be forthcoming, from the additional labour, more quickly than it would be forthcoming if there were no minor switches. The 'ultra-short-period' therefore appears to lose its importance; it is tempting to run on to the *short-period* (in Marshall's sense) when the additional labour is already producing some additional output. This (we can now see) is effectively what Marshall—and Keynes after him—did. They abandoned the wage fund because it seemed to them to be of little importance.

Our position is different, because we seek to establish a sequence. As an element in the determination of the sequence—no more than that—the Wage Fund comes back into its own. We shall see, in later chapters, that there are quite interesting things that one can do with it.

VI

STEADY STATES

1. THE general nature of the enquiry that lies before us is now becoming apparent. The one-week relations, which we were discussing in the last chapter, determine the course of the model in week T, when everything that has happened before week T is taken as given. Having determined the course in week T, we can then proceed to week $T + 1$, applying similar relations, but with the performance of week T now forming part of the past. And so on, and so on. The path of the economy, over any number of successive weeks, can thus be determined.

Any of the determining elements—technology, consumption propensities and so on—may of course be changing from week to week; but we shall make most progress in understanding the working of the system if we keep these determining elements constant, in some sense or other. For it will be a path that is constructed on this plan which will best exhibit the short-run and long-run effects of a particular cause. Such a path will begin from an initial position that is taken as a datum; its course, near the beginning, and perhaps long after, will be deeply affected by the nature of the initial position from which it has started. It is however possible (though, as we shall see, far from certain) that a point will finally be reached when the particular characteristics of the initial position cease to have much effect upon the path— when it comes to be determined (at least in some respects) by the *current* determining elements only. If this happens we may say that the model has reached a steady state.

A simple (but important) example of this proceeding is to be found in the application to the Fixwage economy, previously discussed. Suppose that a new technique, more profitable than any previously available, is introduced at time 0, when the sequence starts; but, during the period to be considered, there is no further 'invention'. All processes started after time 0 will use this 'modern' technique; but in the initial position there will still be old processes, using techniques that have become obsolescent, that are uncompleted. Gradually, as time goes on, these obsolescent processes will be completed, so that more and more of the processes that are 'alive' will be modern processes. A point must ultimately be reached when all of the processes that are alive are modern processes. One of the conditions for a steady state will then have been realized.

But it is not the only condition. For consider the state of the economy at the point when the last of the old processes has come to an end. All the processes which are then alive will be modern processes; but the product which is emerging from those processes, and the employment of labour on those processes, will depend on the rates of starts during the process of replacement. These may well be affected by the nature of the initial equipment (which is here to be understood as consisting of unfinished old processes, as they were in the initial position). Thus, at the point when the last of the old processes is completed, the effect of the initial equipment has not necessarily worn off. Before a steady state can be reached, further adjustments may still be called for.

Similar (but more complex) problems arise in other forms of the model. We must never take it for granted that there will be a regular convergence to a steady state. That is an issue which (as we shall see) must always be given attention.

2. I shall nevertheless confine myself, in this chapter, to an examination of the properties of steady states, postponing the question of convergence. Most of the familiar properties, as we shall see, remain valid in the present model.

I shall confine attention to the usual kind of steady state—defined by the condition that the composition of the capital stock, its proportional division into various categories—remains unchanged over time. The capital goods that exist at the time T are representative of processes that have been started at various dates in the past; so it is necessary, if these proportions are to remain unchanged (1) that the same technique should be used in all processes, (2) that the rate of starts should have a constant growth rate. The first condition is necessary in order that each capital good, as it passes along its own process, should have a successor in the process started just after it; the second is necessary, in order that the growth rate of each kind of capital good should be the same. This constant growth rate, of the rate of starts, is then the general growth rate of the system, which I shall denote by g.

If we write G for the growth multiplier, so that $G = 1 + g$ (analogously with $R = 1 + r$), then $x_T = x_0 G^T$, where x_0 is constant.

We already know that in an economy such as this, where only one technique is used, the employment of labour is given by $A_T = \sum_0^n x_{T-t} a_t$. So in the steady state

$$A_T = \sum_0^n x_0 G^{T-t} a_t = x_0 \left(\sum_0^n a_t G^{-t} \right) G^T$$

which has the same constant growth rate, as we should expect. In the same way

$$B_T = x_0 \left(\sum_0^n b_t G^{-t} \right) G^T$$

so that the (final) product has the same growth rate. Their ratio (B_T/A_T) is unchanged over time. It depends on the technique, and on the growth rate, but on nothing else.

This ratio—product per unit of labour (in the steady state)—may evidently be regarded as another expression of the *efficiency* of the technique; it is closely related to that which we have before encountered. For if $k_0 = 0$ (from which we derived the efficiency curve of Chapter IV) is written in full, it gives

$$w = \left(\sum_0^n b_t R^{-t} \right) \Big/ \left(\sum_0^n a_t R^{-t} \right)$$

while we have just found that

$$(B_T/A_T) = \left(\sum_0^n b_t G^{-t} \right) \Big/ \left(\sum_0^n a_t G^{-t} \right).$$

So (B/A) is the same function of G as w is of R—or the same function of g as w is of r. The same efficiency curve (and the reader will now see why I called it an *efficiency curve*) will, so it appears, express either relation.

That consumption per unit of labour (in the steady state) is the same function of the growth rate as the wage of the rate of interest, is a theorem which emerges in many growth models; it may be claimed that the deduction of it, which has just been given, brings out its point rather clearly. But though simple, it is somewhat treacherous. Before we can use it (and the uses we shall be able to make of it are quite extensive) we must examine it further.

3. The use of the efficiency curve that was made in Chapter IV (on choice of techniques) depended on the Fundamental Theorem of Chapter II. It was from that theorem that we concluded that the efficiency curve was downward-sloping. Does that apply here? Strictly speaking, I am afraid, it does not.

It will be remembered that our former proof was based on the possibility of *truncation*; the unit process, which embodied the technique, was taken to be of variable *duration*. That does not apply here. The technique (a, b) which enters into the formulae for w as a function of r, and for (B/A) as a function of g, extends for the same duration (to week n, as I have been careful to write it). The efficiency curve which expresses these relations is not the same as the efficiency curve with which we were previously concerned. In order to distinguish, I shall call the new curve a *restricted* efficiency curve.

The relation between the two curves is shown in Fig. 5. If

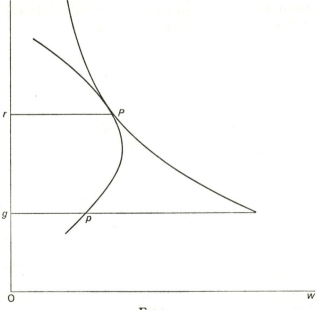

FIG. 5.

duration varies as we go along the *unrestricted* curve (our former efficiency curve) there will be a restricted curve corresponding to each duration. Duration is chosen so as to maximize the rate of return; so the unrestricted curve is the envelope of the restricted curves. (It is related to them in the same way as the frontier is related to the particular technique curves from which it is built up.) The particular restricted curve (of the steady state technique) will accordingly touch the unrestricted curve at the point P, the point which represents the actual combination of wage and interest that rules in the steady state. Otherwise it must lie within the unrestricted curve; for at any other wage, duration being variable, to follow the unrestricted curve would be more profitable.

Even along the restricted curve w is a one-valued function of r; so it is impossible for the restricted curve to turn 'upwards'. But it does not seem to be excluded that it should turn backwards (as drawn in Fig. 5). Can it turn so far backward as to make $(B/A) < w$, while $r > g$? No; in a steady state that is impossible, for another reason.

The Social Accounts would not come out right. In a steady state, in which prices do not change over time, profit is rK and net investment is gK. Wages + Profits = Consumption + Net Investment; so $wA + rK = B + gK$, whence $B - wA = (r - g)K$, and

$$(K/A) = \frac{(B/A) - w}{r - g}.$$

The latter is the slope of the efficiency curve (on the average between the levels of r and g); while the ratio of factor-shares (rK/wA) is its arc-elasticity. So it is necessary, if K is to be positive, that the efficiency curve, on the average between these levels, should be downward-sloping.

This, it must be emphasized, is simply a property of steady states. A technique, which had a restricted efficiency curve that did not satisfy this condition, could not be used in a steady state, but it might be used elsewhere. For the study of steady states, even for the comparative study of steady states, we can suppose that the only techniques available are such as to have restricted curves that in this sense are 'well-behaved'; others will just not appear. But when we come to the study of non-steady states, it may be wise to be more careful.

4. I shall accordingly assume, in the rest of this chapter, that the only techniques to be considered are 'well-behaved', having downward-sloping restricted efficiency curves.[1] The whole of the steady state theory can then be represented on a diagram (Fig. 6) in a very simple manner.

We need not now attend to the *unrestricted* curves. For the present purpose, a technique can be understood in the restricted

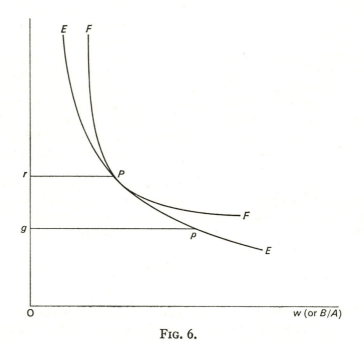

Fig. 6.

sense, so that the corresponding process has a fixed duration. We previously built up the technological frontier as the envelope of the unrestricted curves; but we have just built up the unrestricted as envelopes of the restricted. We can now omit the intermediate stage, and consider the frontier as an envelope of the restricted curves directly.

On Fig. 6, *FF* is the frontier (the efficiency curve of the technology), *EE* is the efficiency curve of the particular technique

---

[1] A backward-turning section of the curve, which did not affect the relation between (B/A) and w, would not affect the argument, so we need pay no attention to it.

(in the restricted sense) which is the actual technique in the steady state. It is chosen, out of the various techniques available, so as to maximize profit at the ruling rate of wages; so (as we saw in Chapter IV) EE touches FF at a point P, whose co-ordinates are w and r, the ruling wage and ruling rate of interest. Og being the growth rate, gp (with p on EE) is (B/A). (We are needing a name for this important magnitude; *steady state productivity*, I shall allow myself to call it—productivity of final output, that is, per unit of labour, in the steady state.)

All we need is one further condition, to establish a relation between the two 'levels'—between r and g, or between w and (B/A)—and the model, the steady state model, is complete.

As in other growth models, the simplest condition that will serve is to suppose that saving is a fixed proportion of profits. (It will be sufficient, in this chapter, to confine ourselves to that supposition; for it will only be used as an illustration.) Then, if $gK = s(rK)$, g/r is given. With that additional condition, the whole of the steady state system can be read off from the diagram.

It can evidently be read either way. If we make the Fixwage assumption (with its elastic supply of labour), the given w determines the technique (EE) and with it the rate of interest. The rate of interest then determines the growth rate; from which, and from EE, the steady state productivity is determined. The steady state productivity will be lower the higher is the growth rate; but that makes sense, since with higher saving consumption should be lower. (It will be remembered that it is a Full Performance path that is being determined.)

If, on the other hand, we make the Full Employment assumption, g is given (by the growth rate of the labour force which, in a steady state, must be constant). $g = sr$ then determines the rate of interest. The point P (whose co-ordinates are w and r) is then at the point where the horizontal through r intersects the frontier. EE is the particular technique curve which touches the frontier at P. Steady state productivity is gp, where p is on EE. We see that in this case the wage will be higher (because the rate of interest is lower) the greater is the saving propensity (s); but by a change in that propensity the choice of technique will also be affected.

This is the basis of the proposition which has been called by

Professor E. S. Phelps the 'Golden Rule'.[1] Consider Fig. 7, in which the frontier is shown as the envelope of a number of particular *EE* curves. (The *EE* curves are drawn as straight lines, for ease of drawing; but the linearity plays no part in the argument.) The growth rate is supposed to be given, as the exogenously given rate of the labour supply.

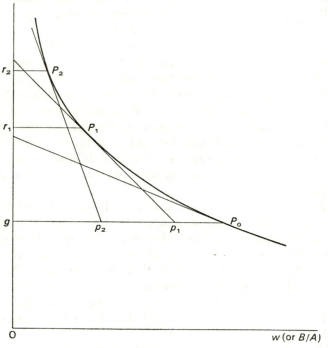

FIG. 7.

If the rate of interest is at or_2, the wage is at r_2P_2 and steady state productivity is at gp_2. When the rate of interest falls to or_1, the wage rises to r_1P_1 and steady state productivity rises to gp_1. When the rate of interest has fallen to og, the wage is equal to the steady state productivity; both are shown as gP_0.

We see at once that the maximum steady state productivity that is attainable with the given technology will be attained at the point where $r = g$, so that $B = wA$; the wage-bill is equal to the whole (consumable) product. As r falls towards g, steady state

[1] 'The Golden Rule of Accumulation' (*AER*, 1961).

productivity increases, up to gP_0. It cannot be further increased, with the given growth rate; it cannot be increased by a further fall in interest, or rise in wages. (Such additional wages, it is clear, could not be consumed; they would have to be saved.) For if the rate of interest fell further, below og, the particular technique curve, of the technique which it would then be most profitable to adopt, would touch the envelope below P_0 and would lie within the envelope; it must therefore intersect gP_0 to the left of P_0. Steady state productivity would be diminished.

This, I think, is the important aspect of the 'Golden Rule'. A condition in which $r < g$, so that $B < wA$, is not wholly fanciful. It does not necessarily imply that consumption out of profits is zero, or even negative! What is necessary is that saving out of wages should be greater than consumption out of profits. It might be surprising if that occurred when saving (out of wages or out of profits) was wholly voluntary; but nothing has been said which obliges us to assume that it is voluntary. Many modern countries enforce very large compulsory savings out of wages— by contributions to pension funds, social insurance and the like. One has the impression that there have indeed been some cases, when this has gone so far—only no doubt for short periods, and within national boundaries—as to make it reasonable to interpret the statistics as showing $B - wA$ negative.[1]

Technique will then be chosen on the basis of an artificial wage—a 'real' wage which is greater than anything that could possibly be consumed. What the 'Golden Rule' seems to show is that the technique which is chosen in this manner will not make for maximum productivity; it will economize in labour to a more-than-socially-desirable extent. This may well be so; but it must be emphasized that it is only for the Steady State that the 'Golden Rule' proposition has been demonstrated. gP_0 (on Fig. 7) is the maximum output per unit of labour that is attainable within the existing technology (and at the given growth rate); but that cannot be attained until the existing technology has been generalized—until all the processes that are 'alive' are *modern* processes. From an actual position, in which only a few of the processes that are alive are modern processes, such a position is unattainable immediately—whatever the rate of interest, or rate

---

[1] The most likely case that is known to the present author is that of (Western) Germany in the early nineteen-sixties.

of wages, or rate of saving. The path that is followed, or the paths that may be followed, from such a position, need a different and (as we shall see in Part II) a more complex investigation.[1]

5. We are almost ready to begin that investigation; but it will be useful, before we do so, to go one step further in the theory of steady states. For this is a convenient way of introducing a distinction, which will be of much importance later on.

Suppose we have an economy which is initially in a steady state, using a particular technique. Then, at time o, a new technique is introduced, which is more profitable than the old; so for processes started after time o, the new technique is adopted. It will take much time before the new technique is generalized, and further time before the system reaches a steady state under the new technique, if indeed that ever happens. But suppose it does ultimately happen. What can be said about the relation between the new equilibrium (or steady state) and the old?[2]

Take the Full Employment case which is here the more interesting. Since in this case the wage is flexible and must be expected to change during the transition, a full discussion should allow for changes in technique in the course of the transition, in response to the changing wage. But for that we are not yet ready. I shall therefore take it (in the rest of this chapter) that the new technique, introduced at time o, remains the most profitable technique, in spite of (possibly) changing wages. It remains the most profitable technique, even in the ultimate steady state.

The problem can then be analysed by a comparison of the efficiency curves of the two techniques—old and new. E^*E^* (Fig. 8) is the efficiency curve of the old technique, EE of the new. If P^* is the point on the old curve which represents the old

---

[1] The reader will doubtless have noticed that if we had taken our steady state to be a stationary state ($g = o$) in the manner of Mill or Ricardo, steady state productivity would have appeared as $\sum b_t / \sum a_t$ (undiscounted) which is a fair representation of what used to be called the 'whole product of labour'. We might then have re-drawn our diagram, taking the *whole product* (for each technique) as one unit, so that every efficiency curve passed through the same point on the horizontal axis; the wage would then be represented by the fraction of the whole product accruing to labour—which is very much what Ricardo meant by the 'wage'. There may well be something to be gained by this re-formulation, if distribution, rather than production, is the centre of our interest; but it seems to me to be much less convenient.

[2] It will be noticed that this is different from the usual 'comparative dynamics' problem, in which we compare two steady states that are not successive.

equilibrium (its co-ordinates, w^* and r^*, are the old rates of wages and interest), it is necessary, if the change-over is to be profitable, that P^* should lie *inside* the new curve. For this en- sures that at the old rate of wages, the rate of return on the new technique is higher. But it also ensures (*EE* being downward- sloping) that if the rate of interest were the same, the rate of wages would be higher.

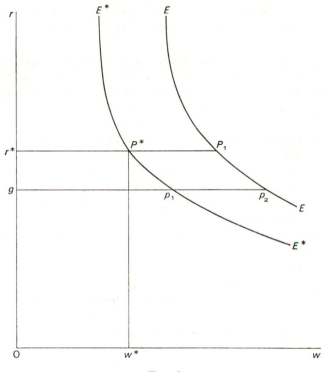

Fig. 8.

Now if we assume (as formerly) that saving is a given propor- tion of profits, we have $g = sr$ in the new equilibrium, as in the old, and s is unchanged. g (in equilibrium) is the rate of increase of the labour supply; and that (in the Full Employment case) may also be taken to be unchanged. It follows that r is unchanged. So the new equilibrium is represented on the diagram by the point P_1, where the horizontal through P^* cuts *EE*. The proportional rise in the wage (from the one equilibrium to the other) is shown as the ratio r^*P_1/r^*P^*.

Since g is the same in the two equilibria, the proportional rise in steady state productivity is shown as the ratio gp_1/gp^*. There is clearly no reason why these ratios should be the same. If they are to be the same, the curves must be related in a particular manner; they must have the same elasticity—or rather (and this is important) the same arc-elasticity. Only if the curves have the same arc-elasticity will the proportional change in (B/A) be the same as the proportional change in w, so that (B/wA) is unchanged.

We have reached this result under the assumption that $s\,(= gK/rK)$ is constant. But $B - wA = rK - gK = (1 - s)rK$, from the Social Accounting equation. It follows that constancy in (B/wA) implies constancy in (rK/wA); there is unchanged distribution between profits and wages. So 'equal elasticity' is the condition for unchanged distribution (between one steady state and the other).

The reader will doubtless be suspecting that our 'equal elasticity' corresponds to Harrod's *neutrality*. And so, up to a point, it does. Though the assumption we have made about saving is not the same as Harrod's, in the particular case of neutrality they come to the same thing. For if the ratio of profits to wages is unchanged, and the ratio of saving to profits is unchanged, the ratio of saving to total income (wages + profits) is unchanged. We might have made Harrod's assumption that the ratio of saving to total income is unchanged, and we should have got the same result.

Yet, though there is this correspondence, the classification to which we have come (in terms of the arc-elasticities of the curves) is not the same as his. For they are not concerned with the same thing. His is concerned with the effect of a change in technology (the whole spectrum of techniques) on the distribution of income; it is necessary (as we have seen), in order that there should be a simple answer to that question, that the change should be taken as a change from one steady state to another, as we have made it. But that, in our analysis, is only a particular application. A relation between the efficiency curves of two techniques (not two technologies) has no necessary relevance to the comparison of steady states; so it is available for use much more generally.

We shall see, in later chapters, how extensive is the use that can be made of it.

Let us see how it looks when taken in this manner. It is no more, we shall find, than an extension of a concept that is itself very easily intelligible.

6. What matters, we have come to see, is the horizontal ratio between the efficiency curves of the two techniques. This, when the efficiency curve was regarded as a wage-curve, was the ratio of the wages associated with a particular level of interest: $w(r)/w^*(r)$. But now it is to be regarded more generally, as an Index of Improvement in Efficiency, *in one sense or another*. It is a function of the rate of interest, so I shall denote it by $I(r)$. If r^* is the old rate of interest, $I(r^*) > 1$ is the condition for the *initial profitability* of the change. $I(g)$ is the ultimate (proportional) rise in productivity; the rise in productivity in the ultimate steady state.

Now we know from the efficiency equation that

$$w(r) = \sum_0^n b_t R^{-t} \Big/ \sum_0^n a_t R^{-t}$$

so

$$I(r) = \frac{\sum_0^n b_t R^{-t}}{\sum_0^n a_t R^{-t}} \Big/ \frac{\sum_0^{n*} b_t^* R^{-t}}{\sum_0^{n*} a_t^* R^{-t}}$$

where (a_t, b_t) are the input–output coefficients of the new technique, (a_t^*, b_t^*) of the old. Let us now make the simplifications of assuming that the lengths of the two processes are the same ($n = n^*$); and that the *output streams* are the same ($b_t = b_t^*$ for all t). These, I think it will be accepted, are modest simplifications; we simply regard the techniques as alternative ways of producing a *given* output stream.

$I(r)$ will then reduce to $\sum_0^n a_t^* R^{-t}/\sum_0^n a_t R^{-t}$, for the numerators cancel out. But this is the same as

$$w \sum_0^n a_t^* R^{n-t} \Big/ w \sum_0^n a_t R^{n-t}$$

which is simply the ratio of the cost of producing the given output stream, on the one technique and on the other, at wage w and rate of interest r. So $I(r^*)$ is a measure of the initial cost-saving, at initial prices (wages and interest). It is an index of Improvement in Efficiency, in that particular sense. By estimating it at other rates of interest, we get Improvement Indexes in other senses.

It is at once suggested that we should classify Improvements, according to the effect on the Index, when the rate of interest varies. We find no difficulty in saying that an Improvement is *neutral*, if a change in the interest rate has no effect on the Index; that, as we have seen, is in line with Harrod. But when there are effects, it is not *necessary* that they should be simple effects; it is possible, for instance, that a fall in interest from 10 to 9 per cent might raise the index, while a further fall from 5 to 4 per cent might lower it. (This, in another way, is what the re-switching controversy is about.) But perhaps the reader will be willing to accept that *most* technical changes are not infected by this difficulty. It is usually possible to give a straight answer to the question: would such and such an improvement offer a larger, or a smaller, saving in cost if the rate of interest were lower? An answer that does not depend on the size of the reduction, nor on the level of the rate of interest from which it is made. This may not be so; but the cases in which it is so are surely sufficiently important for us to need a classification which applies to them.

How then do we describe improvements which are biased one way or the other? There are several alternatives. The traditional 'labour-saving capital-saving' terminology is surely inappropriate. For (looking at the case where the output streams are the same) every improvement must be labour-saving somewhere; it is impossible that $I(r)$ should be greater than 1 for any r unless some $a_t < a_t^*$. Besides, we are comparing techniques; not considering the general effect of a change in the spectrum of techniques (the technology).

It would be more appropriate to say that when $I(r)$ rises with a fall in r, the change is to a technique which is more capital-intensive. In the comparison of steady states this is quite permissible. For we have seen that the capital–labour ratio (K/A), in the steady state, is reflected in the slope of the efficiency curve; so when $I(r)$ rises with a fall in r, the steady state capital–labour ratio increases. But it is not our intention here to confine attention to steady states; a description which emphasizes the respective characteristics of the techniques themselves, without special reference to their steady state properties, will therefore be more convenient.

Looking again at the case in which the output streams are the same, we see that $I(r)$ rises with a fall in r when the main cost-saving comes *late*; when the later sectoral ratios (a_t^*/a_t) are systematically larger than the earlier. It would then seem appropriate to say that the improvement is *forward-biased*. Similarly, when a fall in r lowers $I(r)$, I shall say that the improvement is *backward-biased*. Though the names are derived from the case in which the output streams are the same, they will serve us well as general descriptions. We shall make much use of them in what follows.

PART II

TRAVERSE

VII

THE STANDARD CASE AND THE SIMPLE PROFILE

1. THE problem with which we shall be concerned, in the whole of this Second Part, has already been described. It is the determination of the path of our model economy (the Full Performance or maintainable path) when the economy is not in a steady state. Such a path must have a definite time-reference; for, out of the steady state, one point of time is not like another. In particular, it must have a beginning. The path which follows from that beginning is what we have to determine; so the state of the economy at the beginning (and its previous history, in so far as that is relevant) must be taken as given. One would like to assume that this initial state is itself a mixed state, itself the result of a transition which is still incomplete; but a state of that sort we do not yet understand. So it seems inevitable that we should begin from what we do understand—that we should begin with an economy which is in a steady state, and should proceed to trace out the path which will be followed when the steady state is subjected to some kind of disturbance.

That is why I propose to consider the problem as one of 'Traverse'. We begin with an economy which is in a steady state, under an 'old' technique; then, at time o, there is an 'invention', the introduction of what, in some respects at least, is a new technology. Among the new techniques which thus become available, there is one which, at the initial rate of wages, is the most profitable; so, for processes started at time o (or immediately after time o) it is adopted. The new technique is adopted for new processes, but the old processes are continued, so long as it is profitable for them to be continued. However, in the course of the adjustment which follows, the rate of wages may change; and, as the result of the change in wages, without any further change in technology, a third technique becomes dominant. New processes then use the third technique, while the first and second (it may be) are still in operation. This is the kind of sequence, involving changes in wages and interest, in production and in employment, which we have to work out.

It cannot be taken for granted that the sequence, generated in this manner, will tend to a new equilibrium. It may or it may not. In most of the cases which we shall examine there will prove to be a tendency to equilibrium; so that our sequence can properly be considered as a *Traverse* from one steady state to another. But, as we shall see, it is far from clear that this is generally true. There are other possibilities.

The task thus outlined is formidable. I do not pretend that I have been able to complete it. Most of what I can offer[1] is no more than a fairly full solution for a quite Special Case, which I shall call the Standard Case. Even that, we shall find, gives a good deal of trouble.

It may well be felt that this Standard Case is so special as to be uninteresting. It is indeed true that it excludes complications, which have received much attention, and to which attention has been given in the earlier chapters of this book. It is a narrow front on which to advance. It may nevertheless be claimed that on that narrow front we can advance a long way. As a general theory, it is clearly inadequate; but as an instrument of exploration, it will serve.

2. The mark of the Standard Case is that it confines attention to techniques that have processes of a particular form—that which we called the Simple Profile. We have usually, in Part I, been able to take our techniques much more generally; the Simple Profile retains the vital distinction between construction and utilization—but almost nothing else. As we previously[2] defined it, it had the form

weeks	0 to $m-1$	m to $m+n-1$
inputs	a_c	a_u
outputs	0	1

a constant rate of input during the construction period, and a constant (but different) rate of input during the utilization period; zero output in the construction period, and a constant rate of output during the utilization period (one unit per week). In the

---

[1] All I offer in Chapters VII–X.   [2] Above, p. 41.

Standard Case, we assume that every technique (old or new) that is in question has this *Simple* form.

And that is not all. I shall also assume that the time-parameters, or *durations*, of the techniques (their m and n) are the same for each. It is only their input coefficients (their a_c and a_u) that are different. So the input coefficients suffice to determine the technique.

These are drastic simplifications; we should notice their consequences. They do not only mean that (as shown in Chapter IV) re-switching is excluded; they also mean that truncation is excluded. For once a process has reached the utilizational stage, its net outputs, in successive weeks, are all the same $(1 - wa_u)$. Thus, so long as w is low enough for $1 - wa_u$ to be positive, it will pay to carry the process to its appointed conclusion, whatever the rate of interest. And if w rose so high that $1 - wa_u$ became negative, it would pay to stop, whatever the 'age' of the process.

It will further be shown (in the Appendix[1]) that under these Standard assumptions we can expect a convergence to a new steady state. This does not merely mean that in this case we are justified in regarding the path as a *Traverse*; it will give us some direct help, in the following way. There is a distinction, in each of the applications which we shall be making, between what I shall call the Early Phase of the path and the Late Phase. The Early Phase extends from time 0, when the new technology is introduced, up to the point when the last of the old processes (those begun in the old steady state) is terminated. (By our assumption of equal durations, this is effectively the same as the point at which the first of the new processes is terminated—the point at which the first of the new 'machines' comes to be replaced.) The Late Phase is after that. We shall find that to calculate the path during the Early Phase is relatively easy; we can work it out in detail. To calculate the path in the Late Phase is much harder.[2] If however we know that the Late Phase will ultimately converge on a steady state equilibrium, we can use steady state theory to give us knowledge of that equilibrium; so if we know where the

---

[1] Sects. 7 and 8.

[2] The reason is that the Early Phase path is determined by a first-order difference equation, which is easily solved; but the Late Phase path is determined by a difference equation of higher order.

system will have reached at the end of its Early Phase, we do at least know the start of the Late Phase and where it is tending. We might like to know more, but this is something to know about the Late Phase of the path.

The final equilibrium may itself be far away—and it is absurd to suppose that there will have been in the meantime no new disturbance. The 'ultimate' steady state is not of much interest in itself, but as a help in determining the path that leads to it it can be used.

3. Our Standard Case assumptions are not yet quite complete. There is a further assumption, much less important than the others, chiefly introduced as a matter of convenience.

I shall assume that the length of the utilizational period is an integral multiple of the length of the construction period. Thus if the construction period of the 'machine' is one year, the same (by previous assumption) for all techniques, the machine will last for exactly so many years. This does not, I think, do more than avoid a 'raggedness' to which it is hard to attach much economic importance. But it does simplify things a great deal.

For it enables us to take the 'year' as our unit of time. Processes, we continue to suppose, are being started continuously (or every 'week') within the year; but that does not matter. The new technology becomes dominant at the beginning of year 0, so all the processes started in year 0 use the new technique. None of these processes produces any final output in year 0; but all of them produce some final output during year 1. Similarly, if the utilizational stage lasts for n years, all of the processes started in year 0 will terminate during year $n + 1$. So the processes started in a year can be taken together. We can use the 'year' as our period.[1]

The Simple Profile then takes the still simpler form (which we shall henceforward use)

years	0	1 to n
inputs	a_0	a_1
outputs	0	1

(Input is a_1 in each of the years 1 to n.) Net outputs are $q_0 = -wa_0$ and $q_1 = 1 - wa_1$.

---

[1] For further discussion, see Appendix below (p. 186).

When, as in the rest of this chapter, and in the two chapters following, just two techniques are being considered, I shall as usual use stars to mark the parameters of the *old* technique.

4. The efficiency curve of the techinque (a_0, a_1) then has the equation

$$k_0 = q_0 + q_1(R^{-1} + R^{-2} + \cdots + R^{-n}) = 0.$$

Now

$$R^{-1} + \cdots R^{-n} = R^{-1}(1 - R^{-n})/(1 - R^{-1}) = (1/r)(1 - R^{-n}).$$

So the efficiency equation may be written

$$wa_0 = (1 - wa_1)(1/r)(1 - R^{-n})$$

or

$$(1/w) = a_1 + a_0 r_n, \quad \text{where} \quad r_n = r/(1 - R^{-n}).$$

Now this r_n is readily recognizable as interest + depreciation—the *gross rate of interest*. Since it depends on n (the 'life' of the 'machine') as well as on r, I write it r_n. Since

$$(1/r_n) = R^{-1} + \cdots + R^{-n}$$

which diminishes as r increases (for given n) it is clear that r_n increases with r. When $r = 0$, $R = 1$, so $r_n = (1/n)$. Thus for given r, r_n is determined, and for given r_n, r is determined (n given). For positive r, $r_n > (1/n)$.

When the efficiency equation is written in this manner, it is in fact being re-stated as a cost equation; for $(1/w)$ is the price of the product in wage-units, a_1 is the running cost, $a_0 r_n$ is interest and depreciation on cost of construction. So if we consider a switch from one technique to another, the Index of Improvement, being the relative reduction in cost on the new technique, is

$$I(r) = (w/w^*) = (a_0^* r_n + a_1^*)/(a_0 r_n + a_1),$$

r_n being, as explained, a function of r. r_n is always positive, so $I(r)$ must always lie between the two *sectoral cost-ratios* (a_0^*/a_0) and (a_1^*/a_1). The former, which I shall call h, is the index of saving in constructional cost; the latter, H, is the index of saving in utilizational or running cost. In the relation between h and H we have, in the Standard Case, a firm and unambiguous representation of the bias.

For if $h = H$, $I(r)$, since it is between them must be equal to them. Thus it is the same whatever r_n and so whatever r; the change is unbiased. When h and H are unequal, a fall in r (and so in r_n) takes $I(r)$ nearer to H. So when $h < H$, a fall in the rate of interest raises the index; the switch is forward-biased. It is backward-biased in the contrary case.

Backward-biased improvements are accordingly identified (in this world of Simple Profiles) as those in which the main saving in cost is on the side of construction; that is the sense in which they are 'capital-saving'. But I have always been careful, in this book, not to identify *capital* with plant and machinery; certainly not with plant and machinery alone. The bias is a matter of the contrast between construction and utilization—not between labour and capital.

5. There is a further distinction which is at once suggested. Since I is between h and H, it is not possible, if the switch is to be profitable ($I > 1$) for both h and H to be less than 1; there must be saving somewhere. But it is not ruled out that one of the sectoral ratios may be less than 1, while the other is greater than 1, sufficiently greater to compensate. It would seem natural to describe a switch of the latter sort as being strongly biased; while if the sectoral ratios, though unequal, are both greater than 1, we should say that the switch is weakly biased.

Let us, however, look at the matter diagrammatically (Fig. 9). In this diagram the efficiency curves are drawn in their cost form, $(1/w)$ being expressed as a function of r_n; so they appear as upward-sloping straight lines. The slope of the line is a_0, while a_1 is the intercept on the vertical axis. C is the representation of the new, C^* of the old technique; we consider various C in relation to a given C^*.

If $h = 1$, $a_0 = a_0^*$, so that C and C^* are parallel. C must lie below C^* if the switch is to be profitable. If $h < 1$, C (drawn as C_1) slopes more steeply than C^*; thus if it lies below C^* anywhere, it must lie below it on the left. There must then be an intersection; at a high rate of interest (low rate of wages) the switch would not be profitable, but at a higher rate of wages it would be profitable. So a switch that is made *because* wages are high is bound to be strongly forward-biased. It is nevertheless quite possible that such a switch may be made because of technical invention, not being induced by a rise in wages. It must be profitable to make it at the current rate of wages; all that is signified by the strong forward bias is that there is some rate of wages (perhaps much lower than the actual) at which it would not be profitable.

The strong forward bias (defined by $h < 1$) has this useful property; what of the backward bias? The position here is not quite symmetrical. If $H < 1$, C (shown as C_2) is above C^* on the vertical axis. So again, if the switch is (ever) to be profitable,

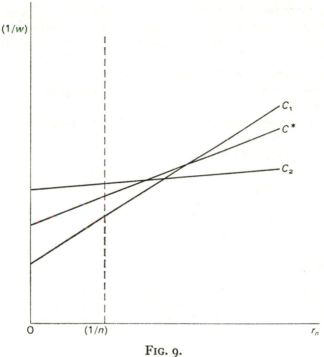

FIG. 9.

there must be an intersection. But here it is necessary to remember that with a positive rate of interest, the gross rate $r_n > (1/n)$. Thus if the intersection is to the left of the dotted line—drawn at $r_n = (1/n)$, C will still be lower than C^* at any positive rate of interest. It is only when the intersection is to the right of the dotted line (as with C_2 as drawn) that the profitability of the switch depends upon the rate of interest. So $H < 1$ is too weak a condition to demarcate strong backward biases in this probably more interesting sense. There will be some switches with $H < 1$ that are still, in this other sense, weakly biased.[1]

I shall not write down the test for strong backward bias, in this other sense, for we shall not need it. We shall find, in subsequent chapters, that the distinction between strong and weak forward biases is very important; but that the corresponding distinction on the backward side, however defined, does not much matter. One of the reasons for this is rather evident.

Whenever C is substituted for $C*$ as a consequence of a rise in wages, there must be a strong forward bias. We shall certainly expect that in a progressive economy such substitutions will be occurring; so strong forward biases must certainly be taken into account.[2] The opposite case, of a change in technique that occurs as a consequence of a fall in wages, looks relatively exceptional. In the course of transition to a more productive technology, it should not normally occur.

It must however again be emphasized that the switches we are to examine, though they may sometimes be in response to a change in wages, are not necessarily so. We shall in fact begin with the study of the effects of technical changes which are not in response to changes in wages, but are solely the result of changes in technology. There is no reason at all why such changes should be unbiased; they may be biased, strongly or weakly, in either direction. Even so, we shall find that the place where we draw the line between strong and weak *backward* biases is of little importance.

[1] It will be observed that there is no corresponding difficulty in the case of the strong forward bias. If C_1 had intersected $C*$ to the left of the dotted line, there would have been *no* rate of interest at which the switch would have been profitable. So it is only intersections lying to the right of the dotted line which come into question.

[2] As they will be, in this sense, in Chapter X.

THE FIXWAGE PATH

1. I PROCEED in this chapter to work out the Fixwage path in the Standard Case. I begin with this, rather than the Full Employment path, as it is somewhat easier. Even so, many readers will prefer to read this chapter in conjunction with sects. 9–11 of the Appendix, where the argument is formally set out in mathematical terms.

We begin (since we are to analyse a Traverse) with a steady state under an *old* technique. Then at time o (which is the start of year o) there is a change in technology, by which new processes become available that were not available before. At the given wage (carried over from the old steady state and remaining inflexible) there will be some particular process which is now the most profitable; we may suppose that it is one of the new techniques, since otherwise the change would be ineffective. Since the wage is fixed and remains fixed, that same new technique will continue to be dominant, throughout the Traverse which is to be discussed. Thus there is no more than a single switch, from the old technique (C^*) to the new technique (C).

Since it is profitable to switch from C^* to C, the rate of return on C must be higher. The rate of interest will thus rise, from r^* to r. Since the wage is fixed, the rate of interest will remain at r, so long as there is no further change in technology.

What remains to be established is the growth of the system, in particular the path that will be followed by employment (A_T). We are assuming Full Performance, so this depends on saving. What assumption we make about saving is crucial for the determination of the path.

There are various possible assumptions. To work out the path for each separately would be laborious, and unnecessary. It will suffice to work it out for some particular assumption, indicating subsequently what changes would have to be made if that assumption were varied.

What assumption we choose for this purpose can be decided by convenience. For the analysis of steady states, the most convenient assumption about saving is to make it a constant proportion of profits. Here, however, that is not convenient. For though (as we have just seen) the rate of profit (or interest) is in our case already determined, the growth rate which is determined by the familiar $g = sr$, with s given and r given, is the growth rate of the value of capital (K_T); out of the steady state, this is not the same as the growth rate of other variables. To proceed from the growth rate of K_T to that of other variables, in the course of a Traverse, is by no means easy.

What is fairly easy, in the present case, is to make the other assumption that was mentioned in Chapter V—that the Take-out (Q_T), considered as 'consumption out of profits', is unaffected by the change in technique. It is the same as it would have been if the change had not occurred. In order to get the *effect* of the change, we must compare what actually happens with what would have happened otherwise; that is to say, we compare the actual path with a continuation of the old path, the *reference path* we may call it. We shall thus assume that $Q_T = Q_T^*$, where Q_T^* is the take-out at time T on the reference path.

This Q-assumption would not be a reasonable assumption for the study of steady states; but for the study of Traverse it seems quite a reasonable assumption. That consumption out of profits should for a while be unaffected by the change in profits is surely a fair approximation to what is likely to happen.

2. It has already been remarked[1] that in a Traverse two phases may be distinguished: (1) an Early Phase, in which old processes started before time 0 remain uncompleted, and (2) a Late Phase in which all such processes have been completed, but in which the path of the economy remains substantially affected by the consequences of what happened during the Early Phase. To this classification we may however add a Preparatory Phase, during which the first new-style machines are being constructed— though they are not, so far, producing any final output. The length of the construction period being one year, the Preparatory Phase is year 0. Since the machines last for n years, the Early Phase extends from the beginning of year 1 to the end of year n.

Up to the end of the Early Phase, old processes (begun before time 0) are continuing on the actual, just as they would do on the

---

[1] Above, p. 83.

reference path. (For as we have seen[1] with Simple Profiles there will be no truncation of old processes.) Thus we need only compare the processes started after time o (the beginning of year o). I shall call such processes, whether on the actual or on the reference path, *fresh* processes, the others being *stale* processes.

During the Preparatory Phase (year o) no fresh processes, whether on actual or on reference path, are producing any final output. All final output comes from stale processes. So if the part of that output which is taken out is unchanged ($Q_0 = Q_0^*$) the part that is available for wages is also unchanged. $wA_0 = wA_0^*$; and so, since w is fixed, $A_0 = A_0^*$. Total employment is unchanged; employment on stale processes is unchanged, so employment on fresh processes is also unchanged. All that can happen in the Preparatory Phase is that the labour which would have been employed in making old-style machines is transferred to the making of new ones.

I pass to year 1 (the beginning of the Early Phase). Total employment, it must be remembered, is now a variable; we shall see in due course how it is determined. The key to what happens is the course of *constructional employment*—the size of the labour force engaged on making machines. In view of the Fixwage assumption, this varies exactly with constructional expenditure— or, as it is here not inappropriate to call it, *gross investment*.[2] We have seen that in year o gross investment is unaffected by the change in technique; but in year 1, it must be raised.

For if the change in technique is to be profitable, the rate of return on the new process must be higher than on the old. Since old and new machines have the same life, a higher net return means a higher gross return; so the difference between value of output and value of current input, on a set of machines of given construction cost, must be raised. The gross profit (in this sense) that is earned on fresh processes must be greater, already in year 1, on the actual path than on the reference path; while the gross profit earned on stale processes is the same on both paths. Total gross profit is accordingly raised. No more is devoted to any other purpose than payment of wages (by the Q-assumption);

---

[1] Above, p. 83.
[2] It will be noticed that when we are working with Simple Profiles we can make free use of 'gross' concepts, such as are popular among applied economists. In more general theory they have little meaning.

the additional profit must therefore be saved and (in Full Performance) invested. It can only be invested in starting new processes. Thus already in year 1, gross investment will be higher on the actual than on the reference path. It is higher by the reinvestment of the higher profits made on the fresh processes started in year 0.

When we pass to year 2, the same repeats, on a larger scale. The higher gross profits made on the new-style processes started in year 0 persist; but to these are added higher gross profits on processes started in year 1 (the number of these processes having

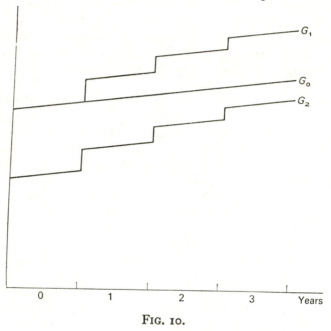

FIG. 10.

been already expanded by what has happened in year 1). So gross investment in year 2 is expanded, relatively to what it would have been on the reference path, in a greater proportion than gross investment in year 1. Throughout the Early Phase, this increase will continue.

The course is as shown on Fig. 10. This is a time-chart, drawn on log scale, so that constant growth paths appear as straight lines. G_0 is the reference path, the path of gross investment as it would have been if there had been no change in technique (the old steady state continuing). G_1 is the path that has just been described. It rises by steps, year by year, always rising relatively to the reference path, though at a diminishing rate.[1] That is the course in the Early Phase, of Gross Investment or constructional employment.

3. But what, now, of total employment? Employment on stale processes is the same as on the reference path; employment on construction moves as just indicated; what remains to be considered is the rest of the employment on fresh processes—employment on running the fresh machines. This can be most easily allowed for if we go back to the Social Accounting Equation $Q_T = B_T - wA_T$, which must hold, on actual and reference path alike. So if $Q_T = Q_T^*$, $B_T - B_T^* = w(A_T - A_T^*)$; the course of total employment, relatively to the reference path, is the same as the course of final output. This also may be represented on our diagram (Fig. 10).

G_1, as drawn, shows gross investment in terms of cost. *This is not the same as gross investment in terms of output capacity.* Since it has been our practice to define a unit process as having unit output capacity ($b_1 = 1$), the condition for the change in technique to leave the relation between cost and output capacity unchanged is $a_0 = a_0^*$, or $h = 1$. So if $h = 1$, G_1 is also the path of gross investment in terms of output capacity. But it takes a year for projected output capacity to generate effective output (since it takes a year to make the machine) so actual increases in output are shown by G_1, lagged one year.

Keep $h = 1$, and consider year 1. Constructional employment, in year 0, was the same on the actual as on the reference path, so output, in year 1, will be the same on both paths. The new machines give more profit, entirely because they have lower running costs. Less labour will thus be employed in running the new machines, but total employment will be the same, the labour not required for the running of the machines being transferred to construction. (We abstract, of course, from difficulties of transfer; labour is assumed 'homogeneous'.) That is what happens in year 1.

It is in year 2 that expansion, in output and in employment, first begins. It is due to the additional machines produced, as we

[1] As follows at once from the formula for x_T, (9.2) in the Appendix.

saw they would be, in year 1. So the rise in gross investment, which on the diagram is associated with year 1, is reflected in a rise in output and total employment, one year later. We have only to displace the path G_1 one year to the right, and it can be used to show *increases* in output and employment.

That is what happens when $h = 1$. If $h > 1$, G_1 must be lifted, as well as displaced to the right, if it is to show increases in output. It must be raised throughout, even in year 1; and raised thereafter by a constant amount, on our log scale. The effects on output and employment will be by so much the more favourable.

If, on the other hand, $h < 1$ (the *strong forward bias*) the path must be lowered, again by a constant amount, into a position such as is shown by G_2. G_2 is still rising, relatively to the reference path, and its growth is always greater than that of the reference path; so it must intersect the reference path (G_0) sooner or later. But there is first a *reduction* in output-capacity; so output and employment are reduced in year 1 below what they would have been. And for several 'years', it may be, the fall persists. All the time that G_2 is below G_0 output capacity goes on falling; only at the intersection does the fall stop. It will even then be several 'years' before output recovers to the reference level; and then goes on ahead.

We can see how this happens. It is still the case that in year 0 the same labour is employed in making machines as on the reference path. But when $h < 1$, the new machines have less output capacity than those which they substitute. It is nevertheless profitable to introduce them; it can only be profitable if they offer a *great* saving in running cost. Thus in year 1 there is a sharp fall in employment in running fresh machines. There was such a fall with $h = 1$; but the additional demand for labour in construction then exactly matched the fall in question, so that total employment, in year 1, could remain unchanged. With $h < 1$, it fails to match; so there is net unemployment, on actual path as compared with reference path. Even so, there is the additional construction; so in year 2 there is something to offset the 'technological unemployment' which continues. At the point of intersection, the additional output capacity, due to constantly increasing investment, at last begins to offset the 'technological unemployment'.

4. These are the possible cases, in the Early Phase[1]; when we go on to the Late Phase, what difference is made?

It is characteristic of the Early Phase that the difference in Net Investment, between actual path and reference path, is the same as the difference in Gross Investment. For the difference in Gross Investment (whether measured at cost or in output capacity) is entirely a matter of the difference in fresh machines (those started since the beginning of year o). There is in each case a discarding of machines, from the termination of processes; but these are all stale machines, the same on each path. That is why we have been able to work in Gross Investment terms.

In the Late Phase, we lose this convenience. We still maintain the old reference path, on which the deduction from gross to net is a matter of the discarding of old machines; but on the actual path it is now a matter of the discarding of new machines, the new machines which already have the higher return. There is still a gain in productivity, on actual path as compared with reference path, but it is not so large as it would have been if the Early Phase had continued. What in consequence happens is that r, the net rate of return, comes to take the place which was occupied by r_n, the gross rate, in the Early Phase.

In the Early Phase, it will be noticed, everything is exactly the same as it would have been if the new machines were going to last for ever. That is why we could work in terms of gross rates. It is when the new machines begin to require replacement that the net rate becomes dominant.

There will have to be a shift to dominance of the net rate if the system is—even in the very long run—to approximate to a steady state. For in a Fixwage steady state the rate of growth is governed by the net rate of return; the gross rate has nothing to do with it.

If, even in that limit, we stick to our Q-assumption—though to stick to it in that limit is rather ridiculous—we have a growth rate of consumption out of profits which is less than the net rate of return; so a larger and larger proportion of profits must be saved. So the steady state, to which the system tends, is that 'Golden Age' in which consumption out of profits is negligible and the system expands at the net rate of return. But it will, of course, be approached asymptotically.

---

[1] It will be noticed that it is only the strong *forward* bias which constitutes a special case. Here, in Fixwage theory, backward bias creates no special problem.

The general nature of the path (of output or of employment), which emerges is such as is shown in Fig. 11. I show the case where $h = 1$; and I round off the 'years' so as to show a continuous curve. As before the diagram is drawn on log scale. The reference path OR is thus a straight line. The actual path begins, in its Early Phase, by 'aiming' at a constant growth at the gross rate of return (shown by the line E–EP); but at the end of the Early Phase it changes direction gradually, so that it ultimately aims at

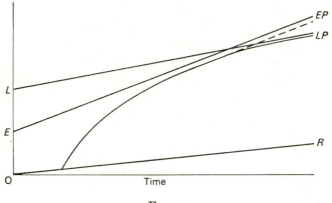

FIG. 11.

constant growth at the net rate (shown by L–LP). If $h < 1$, there will be an initial setback, followed by the same kind of growth.[1]

5. That completes the determination of the Fixwage path, under our Q-assumption. We have still to ask how much difference would be made, if that assumption were relaxed.

It is directly evident, from steady state theory, that if we had made the conventional assumption that consumption out of profits is a fixed proportion of profits, the take-out would (ultimately) expand more rapidly than on the reference path, because of the rise in the rate of profit; so the ultimate expansion, instead of being at rate r, would have been at a rate less than r. We may evidently generalize from this; concluding that any rise in consumption, in response to the rise in profitability, will damp down the ultimate expansion. The ultimate growth rate will still be

[1] A mathematical justification of the path that is shown in Fig. 11 (it needs justification) will be found in Appendix, sect. 11.

higher than on the reference path, but not so fabulously higher as we have made it.

What however of the Early Phase? There is a case for saying that in the Early Phase, or at least in the Preparatory Phase, the take-out should be reduced. This may be argued on the ground of a higher incentive to save, from the higher rate of interest (or expected rate of profit); it is not inconceivable that those who are starting the new processes should save more, to take advantage of their new opportunities. But the same may also be argued on another ground. There is an improvement in the position of those who have free funds with which to start new processes; but there is also a corresponding deterioration in the position of those whose capital is sunk in old processes, now become obsolescent. We have assumed that there is no effect on the take-out by either class, or that such effects as there are offset one another. It could nevertheless happen that the gainers do not immediately expand their consumption, since their gains are for the moment prospective rather than actual; while the losers contract theirs, as soon as they realize their diminished profits.[1] If this should happen, there would be a fall in the take-out at the beginning of the Traverse, which might do something to offset the setback which we have found in the case of a strong forward bias. But such alleviation as could be expected in these ways would surely be very transitory; and the setback which we have calculated does not look as if it would be as transitory as that.

6. One of the things which we have done in this chapter is to clear up an ancient controversy. For the setback which we have

---

[1] That profit on the stale processes will be diminished can be proved, if we are prepared to accept that the profit in question is interest on value of capital, measured forward.

The initial capital, at time zero, consists entirely of old machines, and the future net outputs of those machines are unaffected by the change in technology —since the wage is fixed and there is no truncation. When the rate of interest rises, as we have seen it will rise, these net outputs must be discounted at the higher rate. The initial capital value will then fall, but to this lower value a higher rate of interest is applied. It can be shown that the rise in interest will not offset the fall in capital value.

For, applying the Social Accounting equation to the reference path, $Q_0^* = r^* K_0^* - (K_1^* - K_0^*) = (r^* - g)K_0^*$, so that $K_0^* = Q_0^*/(r^* - g)$. The net outputs of the old processes and the old (pre-time o) rates of start are all hidden in Q_0^* and g. Capital value changes from $Q_0^*/(r^* - g)$ to $Q_0^*/(r - g)$, being accordingly reduced. Profit changes from $r^* Q_0^*/(r^* - g)$ to $r Q_0^*/(r - g)$ and is therefore also reduced, since $r^*(r - g) > r(r^* - g)$ when $r > r^*$.

identified is precisely that which was distinguished by Ricardo, in the famous chapter 'On Machinery', which he added to his last edition of his *Principles* (1821). Our assumptions—the perfectly elastic supply of labour, and the Full Performance path, which makes employment vary positively with saving—are the same as Ricardo's. He evidently believed that he had taken them from Adam Smith, though whether they are exactly Smith's assumptions is a matter for argument. Smith had been confident that there would always be sufficient employment if there were sufficient saving. Ricardo, of course, even in his first edition (1817), had another bugbear; but, apart from the question of land scarcity, then his principal preoccupation, he followed Smith, or thought of himself as following Smith. Then, in the third edition, comes the qualification. The introduction of 'machinery' has an adverse effect on employment *in the short run.*

He had in fact learned to distinguish between investment at cost and investment of output capacity. He saw that when there was a discrepancy, the short-run effect would be a fall in production ('gross revenue' he calls it) and hence in employment of labour. And he saw that the harmful effect might persist, for quite a time. But not indefinitely.

The increase in net incomes (*as we should say, profits*), estimated in commodities (*as we are reckoning them*), which is always the consequence of improved machinery, will lead to new savings and accumulations. These savings, it must be remembered, are annual, and must soon create a fund much larger than the gross revenue originally lost by the discovery of the machine, when the demand for labour will be as great as before.[1]

This is in substance what we have been saying.

It may nevertheless be asked: in associating his exception with 'machinery' was not Ricardo overstating his case? On our analysis, the exception does not arise from any 'improved machinery'; only from such improvements as have a strong forward bias. It may appear that Ricardo was going further; and if so going too far.

I think we must remember how the problem presented itself to him. He was becoming conscious of the Industrial Revolution; rather late, some would say, but no one, at that depth, had

---

[1] Ricardo, *Principles*, Sraffa edition, p. 396.

thought it out earlier. What, in that context, he will surely have had in mind is not 'improved machinery' (though he says 'improved machinery') but the introduction of machinery: the introduction of a strongly fixed-capital-using technique in place of one which, as an approximation, could be regarded as circulating-capital-using only. The latter, in terms of our model, would be represented by a profile in which a_0^* and a_1^* were much the same. To pass from that to a technique in which fixed capital was substituted for circulating must involve a *rise* in the 'constructional' or preparatory coefficient ($a_0 > a_0^*$, so that $h < 1$). The *introduction* of machinery must, almost inevitably, be a switch with a strong forward bias. May it not be that this is what Ricardo (mainly) meant?

If so, he still has a message. It can be put in terms of our model, or in what (nowadays) are more conventional terms. To industrialize, without the savings to support your industrialization, is to ask for trouble. That is a principle which practical economists have learned from experience. It deserves a place, a regular place, in academic economics also.

THE FULL EMPLOYMENT PATH

1. I PROCEED to make a corresponding analysis of the Full Employment path. As before, we start from a steady state under an old technique, and suppose that at time o a new and more profitable technique is introduced. We keep all the Standard assumptions. Each technique has a Simple Profile; the durations of the constructional period and of the utilizational period are the same in the two techniques. But whereas in the last chapter the wage was fixed and employment variable, here the wage may be variable but employment is constrained to move as it did in the old steady state. There is full employment of a labour supply which increases at this given growth rate.

Since the wage is variable, it would be fair to assume that the technique which is chosen for new processes will vary, in response to such changes in wages as occur. This complicates the problem considerably, for we can no longer confine ourselves to the effect of a single technical switch. Yet the single switches, which are here in question, are different from those which we have analysed previously; we need to understand them before we can go on. There is nothing for it but to break up the enquiry into two parts. I shall therefore, in this chapter, confine attention to the switch from one *given* technique to another. There will, in consequence of that switch, be effects on wages; but the effects on choice of technique of those changes in wages, and the effects on wages of those *induced* technical changes, will be held over to the next chapter. In the present chapter those effects will be neglected.

There is of course no question that this is an important decision. Current (and traditional) theories of wages, under Full Employment, are divisible into those which rely upon technical substitution—marginal productivity theories in the widest sense—and those for which it is no more than a secondary complication. By deciding to postpone the question of substitution, we are committing ourselves, for the time being, to the latter group. When we analyse the Traverse as proceeding from one given technique to another, we find that the course of output is fully determined by the techniques and by the Full Employment condition; we can work it out without saying anything about wages. We must determine wages, as a separate step, by introducing some assumption about saving—in the manner of Mill or of Professor Kaldor. In the present chapter, but only in the present chapter, our theory of wages is a wage-fund theory.

2. So we must begin with the determination of output. Or rather (as usual) we must begin with the rate of starts; or what comes to the same thing with Simple Profiles, constructional employment. I now say constructional employment, rather than gross investment; for labour is now the scarce factor, and the distribution of the labour force is what matters.

Since total employment is to be the same as it *would have been*, any change in constructional employment (relatively to the reference path) must be matched by an equal and opposite change in utilizational employment. In year 0, all the utilizational employment is on old processes; if the old processes are not to be truncated, it must be the same as on the reference path. Thus in year 0, there can be no change in constructional employment, relatively to the reference path; all that can happen is that the labour that would have made the old machines is transferred to making the new.

What happens later—in year 1 and in subsequent years—depends on the *bias*. But in quite a different way from that which we found on the Fixwage hypothesis. For here it is impossible for constructional employment to increase without limit; it is constrained at every date by the limit that is set by the total supply of labour. It is the distribution of labour between the sectors which matches the bias. With a forward bias, there is a relative increase in constructional employment; with a backward bias, a relative decline.

Let us begin by working through the *neutral* case, in which there is no bias. $h = H$; there is the same proportional cost-saving in each sector. The new machines, that are produced in period 0 with the same labour as would have produced the old machines, have a larger output-capacity; but when they come into use, there is just the same cost-saving at the utilizational end, so they need just the same labour to work them as the old machines would have required. So there can be full employment in period 1 without any transfer of labour. All that happens in period 1 is an increase in final output, due to the increase in output capacity of the period o machines.

If that happens in period 1, there is no reason why period 2 should not repeat the same story. But in period 2 both the first and second batches of new machines are producing, so there is a further increase in final output. And so on. The same will in principle hold up to the end of the Early Phase, when all of the old machines have been replaced. There will then be no further increase in output, relatively to the reference path; the system will in fact have settled into a new equilibrium.

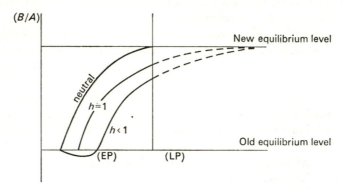

FIG. 12.

One can verify that it is in fact a new steady state from the following consideration. Since the proportion of the labour force engaged in construction has remained unchanged throughout the Early Phase, the stock of new machines will have been growing regularly, at the growth rate of the labour force, which is the growth rate it will have to have in the new equilibrium. So, at the end of the Early Phase, the stock of new machines has the *right* age-distribution. No further adjustment is required before it can fit a steady state.

The path of 'productivity' (B/A) is thus as shown in the curve marked 'neutral' in Fig. 12. As one would expect[1] the rate of increase falls off gradually, so that there is a smooth transition to the new steady state.

[1] And, as is proved in Appendix, sect. 13.

3. Let us now consider what happens when there is a forward bias. The mark of the forward bias, in the present application, is that the new machines, produced by a given amount of constructional labour, require less labour to work them than old machines, produced by the same labour, would have done. From the point of view of the machine-using industry, there is 'technological unemployment'. But in our model there is no resulting unemployment, since the displaced labour is immediately transferred.

In year 0, of course, there is no displacement; for in year 0, only old machines are in use. But the machines that are produced in year 0 are new machines; so when they come into use, in year 1, there is a fall in the demand for utilizational labour. If full employment is to be maintained, the displaced labour must be transferred to construction. So, already in year 1, there is an increase in the labour force engaged in construction (relatively to the reference path); or what comes to the same thing, the proportion of the labour force that is engaged in construction must be raised.

Now, without concerning ourselves (for the moment) with the effect on output, let us go on to year 2. The new machines, produced in year 1, will again be diminishing the demand for utilizational labour; but now there is something to set on the other side. For because of the transfer to construction in year 1, there are more new machines in year 2 than there would have been in the absence of this transfer. There was no such secondary effect in year 1, but there is in year 2. It will, at the least, damp down the primary effect.

Is it possible that the secondary effect may offset, or more than offset, the primary? We shall have to work it out. Total employment is to be the same on the actual as on the reference path. Employment on stale processes is the same, so employment on fresh processes (those started after the beginning of year 0) must be the same. Now on the actual path employment on fresh processes in year 0 is a_0x_0; in year 1 it is $a_0x_1 + a_1x_0$; in year 2 $a_0x_2 + a_1(x_1 + x_0)$; and so on. The increase in fresh employment from year 0 to year 1 is $a_0x_1 + a_1x_0 - a_0x_0$; from year 1 to year 2 it is $a_0x_2 + a_1x_1 - a_0x_1$; and so on. The increase from year T to year $T + 1$ will thus be

$$a_0x_{T+1} + a_1x_T - a_0x_T$$

and this must be the same as on the reference path. But on the reference path all starts (x^*) have growth rate g; so the increase in fresh employment on the reference path, which is

$$a_0^* x_{T+1}^* + a_1^* x_T^* - a_0^* x_T^*$$

must have growth rate g. So the increase in fresh employment on the actual path also must have growth rate g, which is the growth rate of the labour force.

Thus if we divide the increase in fresh employment from T to $T+1$ by the total labour force at year T(which is A_T), the result must be a constant, the same from year to year.

Now $a_0 x_T / A_T$ is the share of constructional employment in total employment in year T; call it c_T. Thus what we have found is that

$$a_0(A_{T+1}/A_T)c_{T+1} + (a_1 - a_0)c_T$$

is the same from year to year. $(A_{T+1}/A_T) = (1 + g) = G$, the growth multiplier. Put U for $1 - (a_1/a_0)$. Then

$$c_{T+1} - (U/G)c_T = c_T - (U/G)c_{T-1}$$

or $$c_{T+1} - c_T = (U/G)(c_T - c_{T-1})$$

This is what we have been seeking. The increase in the fraction of the labour force employed in construction, from year 1 to year 2, is (U/G) of its increase from year 0 to year 1. It is at once apparent that it is the (a_1/a_0) in U which produces the secondary effect. The primary effect will be larger than the secondary, so long as U is positive; that is to say, so long as $a_0 > a_1$.

Now this is curious. It is not immediately obvious that we should have to assume $a_0 > a_1$; that the construction coefficient, per unit of output and unit of time, should be greater than the utilization coefficient, similarly reckoned. But if this is not the case, so that U is negative, there will be a positive swing, from employment in utilization to employment in construction, in year 1; then a swing back to utilization in year 2; back again to construction in year 3; and so on. If U is negative, there must be this oscillation from 'year' to 'year'.

Nothing like this appeared when we were studying the Fixwage path. It is, perhaps, just a preliminary warning that Full Employment, under the rather fixed technical coefficients we are assuming, may be by no means easy to achieve.

There is however a reason why it may, after all, be justifiable to assume U positive. We should think of the initial period of our process as requiring investment in fixed capital, and also investment in circulating capital, such as will be required for the production of final output in year 1. If both sorts of investment are present in a_0 and only one of them in a_1, the condition which makes U positive should be realized. What is made rather suspect, in the light of this discovery, is the purely circulating capital model, in which there is no investment in fixed capital. But for that model the Simple Profile is not a good fit.

4. Let us therefore assume that $a_0 > a_1$. Then U is positive and < 1. So (U/G) is positive and < 1. Then, with a forward bias, the proportion of the labour force engaged in construction is unchanged in year 0; increases by a fraction, which depends on the bias, in year 1; increases by (U/G) of that fraction in year 2; by $(U/G)^2$ of that fraction in year 3; and so on. It appears to be converging on a new equilibrium.

But this (as we found in the parallel Fixwage case) is not correct. The 'equilibrium' thus approached is only a pseudo-equilibrium; it is the goal at which the path appears to be aiming in the Early Phase. The path we have just described is no more than an Early Phase path. At the end of the Early Phase, its 'equilibrium' will not have been reached.

In the Late Phase the old machines have disappeared; so the primary effect disappears; there is no more displacement of labour by the substitution of new machines for old. But because of the expansion in constructional employment that has occurred during the Early Phase more new machines are being produced than are needed to replace those being discarded (together with what are required to match the growth rate of the labour force). These need labour to work them; it can only be provided by *diminishing* constructional employment. Thus (even though U is positive) there must in the Late Phase be some reflux of labour from construction to utilization.[1]

5. What, in the meantime, has been happening to final output? There is where we have to distinguish between the weak and the strong bias. Let us begin by taking the border-line case ($h = 1$). Here there is neither gain nor loss in output-capacity from

---

[1] As is proved in Appendix, sect. 14.

transferring labour from the production of old to the production of new machines; the only gain in output comes from the additional constructional employment (lagged one year). Since in year o there was no additional constructional employment, there can be no gain in output in year 1 (as there was, it will be remembered, in the *neutral* case). But in year 2 there is a gain in output, due to the additional constructional employment in year 1; and this rise will continue throughout the Early Phase. Now we saw that in the *neutral* case, productivity (B/A) would at the end of the Early Phase have reached its final equilibrium level; but in this forward-biased case it will not have reached it. For we have seen that constructional employment will be running at more than its equilibrium level; so there is still some gain in output which is to come. Thus there is a further rise in productivity in the Late Phase, though the rate of rise, in the Late Phase, will be diminishing.[1]

The path of productivity, when $h = 1$, thus appears to be as drawn in the curve so marked in Fig. 12. The beginning of the rise is delayed, and all the way the curve lags behind the *neutral* curve.

It is easy to see that when $h < 1$ the path must be such as is drawn in the curve so marked on the same diagram. There is a further retardation, which must exhibit itself in an actual *fall* in productivity during some early periods. It is directly evident that in year 1 there must, when $h < 1$, be a fall in productivity. For there has then been no time for a secondary effect, and the primary effect is the substitution of machines with lower output-capacity.

This, of course, corresponds to the set-back which we found in the Fixwage case. It is inevitable that in the first periods, the Fixwage path and the Full Employment path should behave rather similarly.

As drawn in Fig. 12, the paths are shown as 'aiming' at the same final equilibrium. This is useful as a means of indicating their structure, but there is a most important way in which it gives a wrong impression. We should remember what was learned in Chapter VI about the efficiency curves of the techniques. The equilibrium rise in productivity is measured by $I(g)$, but the initial cost-reduction is measured by $I(r^*)$; the relation between

---

[1] As is also proved in Appendix, sect. 14.

them is affected by the bias. In the *neutral* case $I(r^*) = I(g)$; but with a forward-biased improvement $I(r^*) < I(g)$, if $r^* > g$, as we continue to assume. Thus if we make the more interesting comparison, between techniques that are such that the initial cost-reduction is the same, the forward-biased improvement will have the higher equilibrium, higher the greater the bias. So the forward-biased improvement yields more in the end; but it loses ground—relatively and perhaps absolutely—on the way.

6. Most of what has been said applies, with just a change of sign, to the backward bias.

The general effect of a backward bias is a shift of labour from construction to utilization. All the increases in constructional employment become decreases; but we may still take it that U is positive, so just as the increase slowed up, the decrease will slow up. As before, it appears to be aiming, in the Early Phase, at a new equilibrium. But at the end of the Early Phase it will have gone too far. So there must be some reflux towards the final equilibrium.

These effects on the distribution of employment are quite symmetrical, between backward and forward biases; but when we come to productivity there is a difference. For there is nothing here which corresponds to our border-line case ($h = 1$). It is necessary, if a backward-biased improvement is to be profitable, that $h > 1$. The new machines, produced in year o, have a larger output-capacity; so in year 1 productivity must be raised. But here, in the Early Phase, constructional employment will be (relatively) falling; so the output of new machines will be similarly falling; and it is possible that even before the end of the Early Phase, this may lead to a fall in new output-capacity. There is certainly a brake on the rise in productivity; and it is perfectly possible that even before the end of the Early Phase, there may be an actual fall.

To distinguish a strong backward bias as one in which there will be a fall in productivity, before the end of the Early Phase, does not however signify much. For in the Late Phase there must be a fall; there must be a fall, even with quite a weak backward bias. For, as we have seen, there must in the Late Phase be a reflux to construction; and this cannot occur without a (relative) fall in utilizational labour, which implies a fall in productivity (of final output).

With a backward bias, there must at some stage be a fall in productivity—in the Late Phase, if not earlier; there will always be a peak and then a decline; the stronger the bias, the earlier the peak will come. It may come within the Early Phase, or in the Late Phase; but the shape of the path, wherever the peak comes, is much the same. It is always of the type that is shown in Fig. 13.

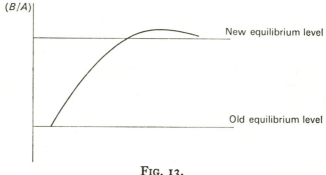

FIG. 13.

When there is a backward bias, $I(g) < I(r^*)$; so the ultimate gain in productivity is less than the initial cost-reduction. Quite generally therefore the forward bias does better in the long run than in the short; while the backward bias does better in the short run than in the long. That is the simplest, and most fundamental, difference between them.

7. I come, at last, to the determination of wages (w). The wage is determined, as by now we shall have come to expect, by saving propensities; but we should be clear just what that means. With given techniques, and given employment of labour, production and distribution are entirely separated. We have seen what determines the amount of final product; it will be just the same, provided full employment is maintained, however it is distributed. On our hypotheses, whatever is produced is consumed; so there must be a sense in which the real saving of the economy, its real accumulation of capital, is independent of what people want to save. But these are peculiarities, not even of our model, but of the questions which in this chapter we have been asking of it. It is only at this stage that they have their place. But at this stage they do have it; and the consequences that follow from them must be given.

It is the distribution of the final product (consumption) which is here in question; so it is with respect to that distribution that savings propensities are most conveniently defined. One such assumption about saving propensities is our regular Q-assumption—that there is no saving out of wages and that consumption out of profits is the same as on the reference path. On this assumption the course of wages will be the same as that of productivity, for the whole of the excess product (the difference between actual output and what it would have been) goes to wages. If we make the obvious alternative assumption, that the proportional division of consumption is unchanged, so that (Q/B) is unchanged, we get a very similar result, for the excess wage is then a constant proportion of the excess product. And little difference would be made if we admitted saving out of wages, so long as the proportion of wages saved did not change. The wage, on both actual and reference path, would then be raised, but in the same proportion, so that the behaviour of the excess wage would still be the same.

The movement of productivity (B/A) will thus reflect, fairly well, the movement of wages. Excepting in the (surely) extreme case where movements in consumption out of profits eat up the whole of changes in productivity, wages will rise when productivity rises, and fall when productivity falls.

X

SUBSTITUTION

1. THERE is still one thing to be done, one very important thing, before we can leave our Standard Case and its Simple Profiles. We have hitherto supposed that the new technique, to which the Traverse is to be made, is given; what is to happen when there is a choice of techniques, so that the dominant technique may change in the course of the Traverse? This was a question, it will be noticed, which did not arise in Fixwage theory, where there must be just one dominant technique in any technology; but in Full Employment theory, where the wage will vary during the Traverse, we ought to allow for the possibility that the technique that is chosen for new processes will change, in response to changing wages.

Since each individual process extends over time, the choice should in general depend on expected wages as well as on current wages; but as I have previously explained,[1] I shall in this book leave that complication out of account. I shall assume *static expectations*—that the wage that is ruling at time T is expected to remain unchanged, at least so long as the processes started at time T are expected to continue. Since these expectations are 'wrong', the path that is chosen will not be an optimum path; it may sometimes behave in curious ways that are to be attributed to its non-optimality. But in positive economics it has its place; there is no simple assumption which throws more light on the kinds of things that are likely to happen.

As before, we start from a situation in which an *old* technique, belonging to an *old* technology, is dominant; and it will be convenient to make our usual assumption that initially the economy is in a steady state under that old technique.[2] There is then introduced, at time o, a new range of practicable techniques. If the invention of these new techniques is to be effective, some of them must be more profitable than the old technique at the initial rate

---

[1] Above, p. 56.

[2] We shall however find, as we proceed in this chapter, that ways of relaxing this assumption will be presenting themselves.

of wages. One must then be the most profitable; so for processes started at time o, and perhaps for some time afterwards, this new technique will be adopted. Nevertheless, in the course of adjustment to that first new technique, the wage will change, in the manner to which we are now accustomed; and it may well be that as a consequence of the change in wages, another technique becomes the most profitable. Thus between time o and time T_1, newly started processes use the first new technique, while there are (of course) old processes that are still unfinished; while after T_1 newly started processes use the second technique, while old processes and first new technique processes are still unfinished. At time T_2 there is (or may be) a second such switch; and so on. This is the sequence we have to work out in detail.

It is a sequence, it will be noticed, which depends on three effects. The first runs from wages to choice of technique; the second from choice of technique to productivity (B/A); the third from productivity to wages. The first and second depend on the techniques (the parameters of the techniques); but the third is quite different, for it depends on saving. With any reasonable assumption about saving, a rise in productivity will lead to a rise in wages. So I shall begin by supposing that there is some rule by which rises in productivity are transmitted into rises in wages; the effects of changes in saving propensities, changing the 'rule', can be considered later.

2. Let us set out the problem in efficiency curve terms. Fig. 14 is the regular efficiency curve diagram (as used, for instance, in Chapter IV above). E_1, E_2, E_3 are efficiency curves of alternative techniques in the *new* technology. (I have drawn them as straight lines; since—as we know—the efficiency curves of Simple Profile techniques, with the same durations, are transformable into straight lines, this does not matter.) It is unnecessary to draw the efficiency curve of the old technique; for all that here concerns us is the initial equilibrium under that technique, marked as P^*. Its co-ordinates, oW^* and or^*, are the initial wage and initial rate of profit (or interest).

When the new technology is introduced, giving a choice between the new techniques that are shown, there will first of all, at time o, be a switch to E_1, for the processes to be started, since at the initial wage oW^* this is the technique that gives the highest

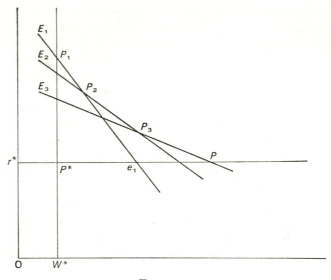

FIG. 14.

return. This switch is shown on the diagram as a movement from
P^* to P_1. Now (excepting in the case when this initial switch is
strongly forward-biased) the effect of the switch will be a rise in
productivity; and we are to take it that the rise in productivity
will be reflected in a rise in wages. The rise in wages will be
represented on the diagram by a movement along E_1 downwards
from P_1. The wage will be rising and the rate of profit falling;
with no change, at that stage, in the technique E_1 that is used for
new processes.

This will continue, until P_2 is reached, when technique E_2
becomes the more profitable. The 'representation' will then begin
to move along the curve E_2, until P_3 is reached when there will
be a similar switch to E_3. And so on. The 'representation' will in
fact continue to move along the efficiency frontier of the new
technology.

It will continue to do so until a new equilibrium is reached.
Where that equilibrium is depends upon the rule about saving. If
we make what (here) seems to be the simplest assumption—that
saving is a fixed proportion of profits, so that $g = sr$, with s constant—there can be no final equilibrium until a rate of profit is
reached which is the same as it was in the initial equilibrium. So

the final equilibrium is at P, where $r*P*$ intersects the frontier. (On other assumptions about saving, it may lie below P or above it.) Thus, so it appears, there will be a sequence of switches until a technique is reached under which this condition can be satisfied, in equilibrium, without further switch.

3. That is one way of setting out the sequence, but it tells no more than a part of the story. Taken by itself, even as an account of what happens with Simple Profiles, it is quite misleading. At each of the switches, it will be noticed, there is a change that is prompted by a rise in wages. So it must be directed, in some sense, towards economizing in labour. Yet it appears from the diagram that it has the effect of making the wage rise *more* than it would have done otherwise! If there had been no *substitution*, technique E_1 being maintained throughout, the final equilibrium would have been at e_1, instead of at P, where we have found it. So the effect of substitution *against* labour is to make wages *higher*!

In spite of its strangeness, there is in fact nothing wrong with this proposition—when it is understood as a property of the final equilibrium. The paradox has arisen because the diagram has concealed what will have happened—what must have happened —on the way. Fig. 14 is no more than a piece of steady state analysis; and for the study of a Traverse that is not good enough. All that is shown on the diagram is a relation between wages and interest; all that is 'represented' is the fact that when the wage is such-and-such, the rate of interest must be at the figure that corresponds. Nothing is said on *when* that position will be reached. There is a missing co-ordinate—Time.

Consider the switch from E_1 to E_2, each of these techniques having a Simple Profile (*durations* being the same, so that the rest of our Standard assumptions apply). It is at once apparent that since the efficiency curves intersect, E_2 being superior to E_1 at a lower rate of interest but inferior at a higher, the switch must be forward-biased; it must indeed be *strongly* forward-biased. For it is always true that as r falls, the index $I(r)$ moves from h towards H; so if, in doing so, it rises from < 1 to > 1, it follows that $h < 1$ (and of course $H > 1$). Thus the switch is strongly forward-biased; so our analysis, in Chapter IX, of what happens when there is a strong forward bias, will apply.

It must not, however, be taken too dramatically. What we were considering, in our previous analysis, was a single switch to a new technique, by an economy which was formerly in a steady state, with constant productivity and constant wage. That is not the problem which here confronts us. At the point of the switch to E_2, the economy is in process of adjustment to E_1; it is in the middle of a Traverse such as we were formerly examining. The technique E_2 is strongly forward-biased with respect to E_1: but this need not imply that it is strongly forward-biased with respect to the old technique (E_0 as we may now call it).

Suppose for instance that the original switch (from E_0 to E_1) was unbiased. Then, as we know, the h of that switch (h_{01} say) must be > 1, since otherwise that original switch would not be profitable. We have just learned that $h_{12} < 1$; but this does not necessarily imply that h_{02} (which $= h_{01}h_{12}$, as is obvious) must be < 1. What is implied by $h_{12} < 1$ is that the path of productivity, after the switch to E_2, will be lower, *for a while*, than it would have been if the switch to E_2 had not occurred. But this does not mean that there must be an actual fall in productivity; and so, by our convention, in the wage.

But it is not sufficient just to look at the constructional co-efficients of the techniques (for it is the ratios of these, it will be remembered, that our h's measure). We are still giving too little attention to Time.

We found, in Chapter IX, that in the case of a single *unbiased* switch the sharpest rise in productivity comes at the beginning (consider the curve marked *neutral* on Fig. 12). The rise is then completed at the end of the Early Phase; as the end of the Early Phase is approached, the rise levels off. Thus if the switch from E_1 to E_2 comes late, the economy will nearly have reached an equilibrium under E_1 before the second switch occurs; then, if $h_{12} < 1$, what happens is much the same as if a switch with a strong forward bias had supervened upon a steady state, with the consequence with which we are familiar—a (temporary) fall in productivity. But if the second switch comes early, it is super-imposed upon a first switch which is still in full vigour. There should then be no more than a retardation of the rise, without actual setback.

We can now see just why it is that Fig. 14 is so misleading. It is like a map which pays no attention to the state of the roads. If the rate of progress along each of the paths that are shown were the same, we could draw the conclusion that wages would always be raised by substitution; so that by the time the non-substitution path (along E_1) had reached its equilibrium, the substitution path (along the frontier) would have reached a wage that was higher. But now we find that the rate of advance along the frontier is *retarded*. At each of its switch-points there is a slowing up. So there is no reason to expect that the frontier path will reach a higher wage *in equal time*. Ultimately, indeed, it is bound to win; but a long-run gain, not a short-run gain, is what it offers.

4. The function of substitution, in an expanding economy, is to slow up the rises in wages that come from technical improvement; but the effect of the retardation is to stretch out the rise, making it a longer rise, so that a larger rise, than would otherwise have occurred, is ultimately achieved. That is the Principal Proposition I am advancing in this chapter. It is surely an important proposition, perhaps the most important in all this book. But it has taken a long series of specializing assumptions for it to be reached. It is only on the basis of those assumptions that we have established it. On more general assumptions, it will probably be subject to exception, or at least to qualification. Something should be said on possible qualifications before going further.

There is one qualification to be made, even within our Standard model (all techniques having Simple Profiles with the same durations). I have shown that it is not necessary for substitution to do more, at the switch-point, than check the rise in wages; it need not go so far as to cause an actual fall. But there seems to be no reason why a fall should be excluded; what, in that case, is to happen? If the switch to E_2 caused an actual (short-run) fall in wages, this would be shown on Fig. 14 as a backward movement along E_2. But the effect of that would be that the E_1 technique again became the more profitable; so that (it appears) there would be a switch back to E_1. Now it is inherent in our argument that the effects on productivity (and hence on real wages) of changes in technique are not instantaneous; they are subject to considerable lags. There should thus be an oscillation; first E_2, then E_1, then again E_2, then again E_1 would be adopted for new processes. (These processes, it will be remembered, will be going on concurrently.) The net effect of this kind of substitution is that the fall in wages, which would have resulted from a simple

switch, is damped; but the time which must elapse before productivity rises decisively, is lengthened out. It would seem that
with this amendment the picture that was drawn by our preceding argument is not substantially changed.

There might well be a similar 'damping' substitution, if the
original switch (from P^* to P_1 on the diagram) was strongly
forward-biased. Then, in the absence of substitution, the 'representation' would begin by moving *backwards* along E_1. That,
however, might again induce a substitution which had a damping
effect.

None of this changes our proposition seriously; the main effect
of substitution, in a growth process, appears as stated. But what
would happen if we went outside the Standard model? That is a
large question, which I am quite unable to discuss at all adequately; it may however be suggested that the specialized
assumptions of that model may not, after all, have been so re-
strictive. The Efficiency curve diagram is not in itself dependent
on the Simple Profile assumption; it is indeed so general that it
makes little use of our general 'Austrian' assumption of the
separable processes. Something very like it must come up in any
(or nearly any) growth theory. But however it is introduced, it
will still be liable to lead to its characteristic paradox—it will still
appear to be showing that substitution against 'labour' tends to
benefit 'labour'. Something of the kind of our theory of the
strong forward bias (or of Ricardo on machinery) is then needed
to complete it—to make it make sense. Variations in the length of
time taken to traverse what look like equal 'distances' on the
diagram must be introduced, in some way or other.

There is however one qualification, which has to be made
when we leave the Standard assumptions, which might be
thought to make a substantial difference. With Simple Profiles,
and equal durations, re-switching (we know) is excluded; it is
impossible that the efficiency curves of different techniques
should intersect more than once. When we leave these Standard
assumptions, re-switching becomes possible. It will however be
noticed that the only multiple intersections which can affect this
analysis are such as occur between the highest and lowest rates of
profit that appear in the sequence; intersections outside that
range make no difference. The critical case is that shown in
Fig. 15, which reproduces Fig. 14 excepting that E_1 and E_3 are

now the same curve. So there is a switch from E_1 to E_2 at P_2, and then back to E_1 at P_3. If E_1 (with this property) and E_2 are the only techniques in the new technology, e_1 (where E_1 intersects $r*P*$) is the final equilibrium point, *whether or not the switch to E_2 occurs.* The switch to E_2 is *abortive.*

The final equilibrium is the same; but that does not mean that from our point of view the paths are indifferent. There is still a question whether the equilibrium will be reached in the same

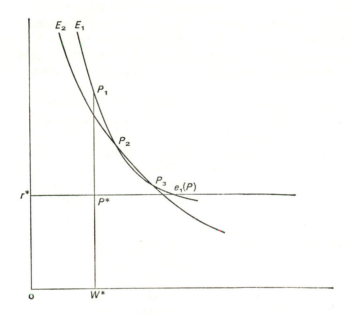

FIG. 15.

time, on the one path or on the other. On this, however, while recognizing the problem, I have little to say. It is clear that at each switch the change is forward-biased; the fact that a switch from E_1 to E_2 is forward-biased at one rate of profit and backward-biased at another is what is responsible for the re-switching phenomenon. There may thus be some presumption that there is slowing-up at each switch-point; so that e_1 will be reached more rapidly on the non-substitution path. But the effect of the bias on productivity has only been demonstrated for the Standard model;

it is not very safe to carry it over to a non-Standard (and inherently tricky) case like this.

It is however apparent, from Fig. 15, that more is required than mere multiple intersection of particular efficiency curves if our Proposition is to be disturbed by re-switching. It is not sufficient that some of the relevant techniques should have multiple intersections. If the substitution process, as a whole, is to be abortive, the same technique must be dominant, both at the initial wage (at P_1) and at the equilibrium wage (at P). Only if this condition holds will the final equilibrium be the same, with or without substitution. Otherwise there may be abortive substitutions on the way; nevertheless, as a whole, the substitution will work in what we have found to be a normal manner. It seems safe to regard the exception, thus defined, as so extreme that it can be disregarded.

5. By whatever route we have come, we find ourselves impelled to distinguish between *autonomous* technical changes, which shift the frontier, and *induced* changes, which proceed along the frontier. It may be granted that in an economy with active innovation, autonomous changes will be incessant. Each will set up its own train of effects, effects that are (of course) superimposed upon one another. Nevertheless, for the sake of understanding, each autonomous change must be taken separately.

Induced changes follow on the autonomous change, but not immediately. The new technology is first introduced in the form (our E_1) which is the most profitable at the initial wage (or, more generally, at initial prices). The effect of this first switch is to raise the rate of profit; it must raise the rate of profit, since otherwise it would not be made. That is the first effect; but as the new technique works through to the flow of final product, there are further effects. It is here that one must distinguish between the abnormal case, where the autonomous improvement has a strong forward bias, and the normal case, in which there is no bias, or only a weak bias—in either direction. In the normal case, the flow of product will expand (as soon as it is affected); so wages will rise, and the rate of profit will begin to fall. The induced changes then come in as attempts to arrest the fall in profit. They do arrest it; they do check the rise in wages; but in so doing they open new opportunities for the exploitation of the new technology. The initial autonomous improvement will have a larger

ultimate effect on production (and hence on wages) if it has a long
series of possible induced changes following from it, than if it has
only a short series; or than it would have, if the induced changes
were prevented from occurring.

It is of course assumed, in the generation of this sequence, that
saving propensities are such that higher productivity leads to
higher wages—on the Full Employment path, with which (as
always in this chapter) we are alone concerned. It will however
be noticed that the course of the sequence is affected, in what (in
terms of our analysis) is a new way, by the rate of saving. While
we were taking the new technique, to which the Traverse was to
be made, as being *given* (as we did in the preceding chapter),
there was just an effect of saving on wages; there was no effect on
productivity. There was just one course of productivity by which
the economy could adjust itself to the new technique; the way in
which the new technique was reflected in wages was a matter of
saving, the productivity of the technique was not. When technique is variable, that is all changed. The more rapid rise in
wages, which would occur if the saving propensity were greater,
would bring forward the date at which each switch-point would
be reached. So the induced changes would come faster; the substitution process, all along, would be speeded up. If we stick to
the formula for saving which gives $g = sr$ in the final equilibrium,
a rise in s will lower the equilibrium rate of profit; so it will push
the equilibrium point to the right along the frontier. Thus it will
cause a technique which lies further along the frontier (if we like,
a more capital-intensive technique) to be adopted. But this is not
an effect on the final equilibrium only; it is an effect which is felt
all along the sequence. And since, with a flow of autonomous improvement, the final equilibrium under given technology will
never be reached, this *general* effect of saving is very important.[1]

All this assumes that the autonomous improvement, which
leads the sequence, is not strongly forward-biased. In most
applications, one would suppose, that would be reasonable. For
the strong forward bias is itself an extreme case; there is plenty of
room within the spectrum for weak biases (forward or backward)

---

[1] This is of course the effect which is represented by production function
theorists as an effect of 'capital' on 'product'—the marginal productivity of
capital. The effect, so it seems to me, must be recognized, however we represent
it.

which have a 'normal' effect. When we are considering a sequence of autonomous improvements, it should usually be fair to suppose that the representative improvement is not strongly forward biased. I have nevertheless suggested elsewhere[1] that there may be cases in which a predominance of strong forward biases, over a considerable period, may not be an unreasonable hypothesis. Such is perhaps the case of the beginning of industrialism, the first introduction of strongly fixed-capital-using techniques—the case which, as was suggested above,[2] may well have been mainly in the mind of Ricardo, when he wrote his *machinery* chapter. What, on our analysis, should be said on that case, is that the stage when the new technique leads to a rise in wages—with or without substitution—may be long deferred.

6. When, however, we come to history—or to applied economics —should we not go further? I have so far been telling the story in the conventional terms, of shifts in technology and switches within the technology; but, at the point we have reached, do not the 'technology' and the 'technological frontier' themselves become suspect? They are essential tools of static analysis; but in dynamic analysis, such as this, do we need them? We should be much happier without them. The notion of a 'technology', as a collection of techniques, laid up in a library (or museum) to be taken down from their shelves as required, has been deservedly criticized; in itself it is a caricature of the inventive process. Let us try to get rid of it.

Why should we not say that every change in technique is an *invention*, which may be large or small? It certainly partakes, to some degree, of the character of an invention; for it requires, for its application, some new knowledge, or some new expertise. There is no firm line, on the score of novelty, between shifts that change the technology and shifts that do not.[3]

The distinction which we have been making, between autonomous and induced improvements—now to be describable, in the familiar manner, as autonomous and induced *inventions*—is,

---

[1] In my *Theory of Economic History* (1969), Ch. 9. See also my discussion with Professor Beach, *Econ. Jour.* December 1971.

[2] Above, pp. 98–9.

[3] It will therefore be noticed that on this plane of discourse there can *by definition* be no re-switching. Every technique to which a switch is made is a new technique. In practice, isn't it?

nevertheless, still with us. Every invention marks a change in technique. Each technique (still) will have an efficiency curve, indicating rates of return on that technique at various levels of wages. If the invention is to be *effective*, the new curve must lie outside the old at the current level of wages. There remains a distinction between the case where the new curve lies wholly outside the old, and that where the new curve lies outside the old at the existing level of wages, but not at other levels. That is nearly what we need, but not quite. For it draws its class of autonomous inventions much too narrowly. It will clearly be irrelevant if the new curve intersects the old at some level of wages which is far from the actual—so that if the level of wages were quite different from the actual, the invention would cease to be effective. What we need is to define induced inventions as those which are such that *as a result of the current movement of wages*, but only so, they become effective. These are the inventions which we have formerly exhibited as movements along the technological frontier; but they need no technological frontier to be definable.

It seems to me that by making this amendment, one takes a long step nearer reality. One is almost in sight of something which would be recognizable by the economic historian. He would probably find it easier to begin with another classification, into primary and secondary—primary inventions being those in which some technological 'revolution' is first expressed, secondary inventions its further adaptations. Such a classification is technological, not economic; but our classification, in the form we have just given it, fits in. Our induced inventions are just one class of secondary invention. There are other types—particularly such as result from the purely technical working-out of the 'revolution'. We should regard that sort of secondary invention as autonomous. Our induced inventions are responses to the economic effects of the working out; but they are just as much a part of the 'tail' of consequences that follow from the 'revolution' as the secondary effects of more technical character.

It is natural to think of induced inventions as being directed to overcoming economic scarcities; but we should be clear that it is to the effectiveness of the invention that the classification refers, not to the motive for making it. We are not concerned, in this analysis, with the way the inventions come into being; but we are deeply concerned with the fact that they cannot be applied—they cannot be successfully applied—until they have been 'costed'; that is to say, until prices have acted as a sieve.

7. In the 'practical' application just suggested, the scarcities to be overcome by induced invention may be of many kinds; scarcity of labour (undifferentiated labour) is just one example. It appears in our model as the only example because we have been taking 'labour' to be the only input. It will however be remembered that 'labour' was just the name which we gave to our one original input[1]; it becomes of great importance, in this place, to remember that 'labour' is to be understood in this wider sense. The application to actual labour is only one of many applications; we can substitute other factors, or other classifications of factors, and most of the formal theory can be preserved.

The Fixwage theory of Chapter VIII, when so regarded, appears as nothing else but an analysis of a growth process which is unimpeded by natural scarcities. There is no scarcity, which cannot in time be overcome, not even of labour. There can then be no falling rate of profit, no substitution, no induced invention. When it is taken in that way, we see why we need it. We cannot appreciate the effect of scarcities of original factors, until we see what would happen in their absence. The Full Employment theory of Chapter IX is a theory of growth with one original factor, not absolutely restricted in supply, but increasing autonomously. It needed to be completed by an analysis of induced invention (just given), as the other theory did not.

If the original factor was strictly fixed in supply, the whole of the Full Employment theory would still be valid; we must just set $g = 0$. There is no difficulty in doing that, as a matter of algebra; it is indeed a great simplification. I shall not trouble to write it out, in our 'language'; I shall merely observe that in another 'language' it is quite familiar. It is nothing else but the formal model of the English classical economists—Ricardo and Mill.

In Ricardo and Mill there is just one original factor—land. Labour appears to come in, but the perfectly elastic supply of labour, at a fixed real wage, implies that labour is, formally, an intermediate product.[2] The subsistence of labour is produced, as

---

[1] Above, p. 37.

[2] As has been observed by Samuelson, in his paper on Ricardo (*Collected Papers*, i. 273).

part of the process of production; and this is transmuted, as what is still in formal terms part of the process of production, into labour services.[1] The single original factor, land, is fixed in supply.

Because the original factor is fixed in supply, the final equilibrium, under given technology, is the Stationary State. That is what they say; and it is perfectly consistent with what we have been saying. One has simply to grant them their *empirical* assumption, that the scope for induced invention, directed toward economizing in land, is rather narrow; and all else follows. As Mill put it (in 1848):

> When a country has long possessed a large production, and a large net income to make savings from, and when, therefore, the means have long existed of making a great annual addition to capital; (the country not having, like America, a large reserve of fertile land still unused) it is one of the characteristics of such a country, that the rate of profit is habitually within, as it were, a hand's breadth of the minimum, and the country therefore on the very verge of the stationary state. By this I do not mean that this state is likely, in any of the great countries of Europe, to be soon actually reached, or that capital does not still yield a profit considerably greater than what is barely sufficient to induce the people of those countries to save and accumulate. My meaning is, that it would require but a short time to reduce profits to the minimum, if capital continued to increase at its present rate, and no circumstances having a tendency to raise the rate of profit occurred in the meantime. The expansion of capital would soon reach its ultimate boundary, if the boundary itself did not continually open and leave more space.[2]

Autonomous invention might still come to the rescue.

8. One can perhaps go a little further. When the theory of this chapter is re-thought in Ricardo–Mill terms, it suggests an interesting conclusion. For wages we are now to read rents. What we shall then learn from our Principal Proposition is that induced invention, though it may very probably cause a fall in rents in the short run, must in the longer run raise them. The same will apply to any autonomous invention which raises the rate of profit. It will thus apply to any 'economically desirable' improvement,

[1] We could have expressed our Fixwage model in that way; but it seemed more interesting to introduce labour explicitly.

[2] Principles, Book IV, ch. 4, sect. 4.

even (for instance) to Free Trade in Corn. All the gains from the efforts of business men and inventors—and even of economists— must ultimately go nowhere else but into the landlord's pocket.[1]

I believe that Ricardo and Mill did draw this conclusion; but they had no love for the landlord, and it horrified them. Their reactions to it, however, were different. The moral, as Ricardo saw it, was that all effort must be made to postpone the stationary state as long as possible. It should be possible, by continual *improvement*, to keep up the rate of profit; and by the consequential steady increase in the demand for labour, keep wages running just a little ahead of subsistence. (For though in the long run the supply of labour is elastic—only too elastic—it needs a little time in which to catch up.[2]) Mill, on the other hand, believed that the elastic supply of labour should, and could, be combated directly. The major difference between them is not at all a matter of formal analysis; it simply consists in Ricardo's pessimism, and Mill's optimism, in the matter of population control. So it is that in Mill labour is beginning (perhaps only beginning) to become the scarce factor; some of the gains from progress, even the long-run gains, can therefore pass from land to labour. So it is that he can say 'I cannot regard the stationary state of capital and wealth with the unaffected aversion so generally manifested towards it by political economists of the old school'; and he can allow his civilized sentiments to build it up into a Utopia.[3]

I must not go into that. All that, in this place, is relevant, is that we are all of us—Ricardo, Mill, and I—saying what in terms of economic principle is the same thing.

[1] As an owner of building land, if not of agricultural!
[2] This is very well stated by Adam Smith (Wealth of Nations, Book I, ch. 8). There is no reason to suppose that it would not have been taken for granted by Ricardo.
[3] Principles, Book IV, ch. 6, sect. 2.

SHORTENING AND LENGTHENING

1. I HAVE completed, in the preceding chapter, all I have to say on the Standard Case. It claimed no more than to be an instrument of exploration; as such, I think it has proved its worth. Though its assumptions are so narrow, it has enabled us to get a glimpse of things which certainly look as if they should have a wider application. One is nevertheless conscious, while one is using it, of the thinness of the plank on which one is walking. We have been piling simplification upon simplification, specialization upon specialization; cannot some of them, at least, be removed?

In the present chapter and in that which follows it, I shall report on what I have been able to do in the way of extension; it is not, I fear, very much. There is no second Standard Case which seems to be analysable in comparable detail. All I can do is to test out some of the Standard Case assumptions, in order to get a general idea of the kinds of complication which arise in their absence. There are several directions in which this can be done; so what follows will divide up into rather separate enquiries.

There is one of these enquiries for which we do not need to leave the Simple Profile. In the Standard Case we did not just assume Simple Profiles; we also assumed that the Simple Profiles, of the old technique and of the new, had the same *durations*, the same length of construction period and the same length of utilization period. We can see what happens when this particular Standard assumption is dropped.

Most of what I can say relates to the construction period. This, it may well be felt, is the less interesting question. It would be nice to make an analysis of changes in the utilization period— that is to say, of changes in the *life* of the machine. Unfortunately (as we have already found in our study of the Standard Case) we can say much more about the Early Phase of a Traverse than about the Late Phase; and it is clear that changes in the life of the machine are entirely a Late Phase problem. That is why it is hard to do much about them.

Changes in the construction period are less interesting, but they do have some interest—particularly, perhaps, a historical interest. For changes in the construction period are changes in the waiting period—in the period which must elapse before *any* final output is forthcoming. Any economic theory which begins from circulating capital must lay great stress on this waiting period; it is at the centre of attention in an 'Austrian' theory, such as that of Böhm–Bawerk. In spite of the considerable stress that was laid on circulating capital in the classical theories of Mill and Ricardo, the most important properties of their model do survive (as we have found) in the Standard Case. It was indeed quite tempting to describe the Standard Case model as a classical model. I have however claimed that our general approach is in the Austrian tradition. As such, it clearly calls out to be extended so as to take account of this characteristically Austrian problem.

We shall find, in the course of our enquiry, that shortening and lengthening (of the construction period) do not change the general picture very drastically, so long as we confine our attention to the Full Employment path. With that, accordingly, I shall begin. We shall however see, when we come to them, that the effects on the Fixwage path are much more dramatic. We have not so far needed to use the Fixwage path as anything more than a basis for comparison. The properties which here emerge do however have some independent interest. They give us new reasons for giving the Fixwage path some attention.

2. Since Time is irreversible, the effects of shortening and of lengthening are not quite symmetrical; so we shall have to take them separately. I begin with shortening—the effects of a shortening of the construction period on the Full Employment path.

It will simplify the exposition (without, in fact, diminishing its generality) if we adopt the following conventions. We have previously taken the length of the construction period to be one year; let us now take the length of the construction period of the *new* technique to be one year, while the (longer) length of the construction period of the old technique is one year plus one month. (That the number of calendar months in the calendar year is twelve does not here signify; it will however help if we give to the early and late months in the year their familiar names.) As usual, we suppose that the new technique is introduced at the beginning of year o—in January year o, we may now allow ourselves to say.

We have first, as usual, to determine rates of start—from the Full Employment condition.

We keep to our usual assumption that 'stale' processes—those started before year o—are to be kept fully manned. Thus the Full Employment condition reduces, as usual, to the condition that employment on 'fresh' processes (those started in year o and later) should be the same on the actual and on the reference path. Now in the whole of year o all labour employed on fresh processes (on both paths) is constructional labour; so the rate of starts in year o is determined by the condition that the labour employed in construction should be the same as on the reference path—our usual condition. It is only at the end of year o that a difference occurs. There is a critical month, January year 1, when the difference in the construction periods first shows up. In that month, on the reference path, all is as before; the only labour employed on fresh processes is constructional labour. But on the actual path the machines begun in January year o are completed; so they cease to employ constructional labour but they do employ utilizational labour. On our usual assumption[1] that less labour is required (per unit of time, say month) to work the machine than to make it ($a_1 > a_0$), there is, by completion of these machines, a net release of labour. It follows that, in order to maintain full employment on the actual path, constructional employment must be increased; so the rate of starts must be increased. This is so, it must be emphasized, whatever the relation between the input coefficients—whatever the bias. There is always in January year 1, a *special increase* in the rate of starts, which is directly due to the shortening of the construction period.

Now the only month, in year 1, which gets this special increase is January. For when we pass to February, the first of the 'fresh' machines on the reference path will be completed, so that there is a net release of labour, from the completion of machines, on the reference path also. In fact, in the rest of year 1, the relation between actual and reference paths is substantially the same as that to which we are accustomed.

It is substantially the same, but not quite. For if, as we have generally supposed, the supply of labour has a positive growth rate—and the rate of starts on the reference path has therefore the same positive growth rate—the machines that each month

[1] Above, pp. 104–5.

come to completion are one month younger on the actual than on the reference path. So they were started one month later than the corresponding machines on the reference path, and should in consequence embody one month's growth of the general system, which the just completed machines on the reference path do not embody. If we had started from a stationary state, in which the supply of labour was constant over time, this particular qualification (obviously) would not arise. It is a 'growth gain', a phenomenon of shortening *in an expanding economy*.

In later years the same pattern will repeat. In January year 2 there will be an *echo* of the *special increase* in January year 1. For the extra machines which were started in January year 1 will now be completed and will (on balance) be releasing labour; so they will again permit a special increase, though naturally one that is smaller than the first. There will be a smaller special increase in each successive January; gradually, as time goes on, they will die away.

I pass, again as usual, to the effect on final output. Here again we may proceed by comparing the output from 'fresh' processes. In the whole of year 0 there is no fresh output—from either path. In January year 1 there is no fresh output on the reference path but there is on the actual path; so there is a *special* gain here too. In the rest of year 1 the course of output is determined by the difference in output-capacity, between the machines produced one year ago on the actual and those produced one year and one month ago on the reference path. So here there is a second growth gain, due to the machines which come into use on the actual being one month younger than those which come into use on the reference path. It is not the same as the first growth gain, as may be seen by observing that changes in the rate of starts due to the shortening have not had time, in year 1, to affect output. There are of course the usual effects, on output, of the bias. Thus if it should happen that there is a strong forward bias, while output in January year 1 is above the reference path, in the later months of year 1 there will be a fall below the reference path (as in the Standard Case). But, because of the second growth gain, the condition for this to happen is a little stronger than in the Standard Case.

When we pass to year 2, the first growth gain will have had time to affect output, and so will the special gain (in January of year 1) in the rate of starts. All effects together will be raising output, above what it would have been if there had been no shortening. The growth gains produce a steady rise; but to this there is added, in each January, a special bonus. Since every bonus is an increase in output-capacity, they have a cumulative effect. But every bonus is less than its predecessor; gradually, they die away.

All this, it must be emphasized, is what happens in the Early Phase. There will doubtless be echoes in the Late Phase, but these I have been unable to work out.

3. The effects of lengthening the construction period can be brought under similar heads; but what happens under some of them needs a little reconsideration.

It should first be observed that while shortening is a gain in itself—so that a new technique, with the same input- and output-coefficients as the old, but a shorter construction period, would be directly more profitable—lengthening is in itself disadvantageous. It can only be profitable to lengthen the construction period if the lengthening is offset by some other gain. Thus we should not be surprised to find that a lengthened construction period has effects that are somewhat similar to those of a Standard improvement with a strong forward bias—a loss of output, in early stages, being offset by gains later on.

Keeping the year as the new technique's construction period, that of the old will be one year minus one month. So the critical month, when special effects occur, is December. There is no change, in starts or in final output, from what there would have been without lengthening, until December of year o is reached.

In that December there is fresh output on the reference path, but no fresh output on the actual path—so, from one to the other, there is a fall in total output. And while there is release of labour on the reference path, there is no release of labour on the actual path; so the starts on the actual path are no more than can be managed without release of labour; so there is also a setback in starts. This is quite symmetrical with what happens with shortening, except that while the special increase in starts was there dependent on the coefficients of the new process, here it depends on the coefficients of the old process. This has the interesting consequence that even when there is a backward bias, so that we should expect to find a tendency for the ratio of constructional employment to total employment to diminish in the course of the Early Phase, we get this regular effect for non-Decembers, but the December ratios go the other way. Taking both together, the ratio is at its lowest in the first December; as time goes on, the December ratio rises, while the non-December ratio falls—so they tend to come together.[1]

4. I have kept quite strictly, in the preceding, to the Full Employment assumption; it will however be obvious that in this chapter I have been driving it very hard. The redistribution of labour which we found to be needed in the Standard Case, whenever the improvement was biased, was for the most part smooth and gradual. Such changes as these do in fact occur in reality; not indeed without difficulty, but the difficulties are more or less overcome. The quite violent short-run shifts, from one 'month' to another, which have here been turned up by our model, are quite a different matter. One does not have to go far in the direction of realism to judge that such shifts as these must be quite impracticable. But even so, one learns something from the model. It is bound to be impossible, in the face of considerable changes in the construction period of fixed capital, continuously to maintain Full Employment.

And that is not all. For it is not only the rate of starts (hence constructional employment) which when the construction period is variable is subject to violent jerks; the same holds for final output. And unless the part of final output absorbed otherwise than for wages will act as a buffer (and it is not easy to see that there is any automatic reason why it should be) the jerks will be transmitted to the *wage-fund* itself. If Q is unchanged (from what it *would have been*) fluctuations in B mean fluctuations in wA. It may however be supposed that if fluctuations in the wage-fund are matched by fluctuations in employment, the wage (of those still in employment) may be unaltered. But can this happen—in the face of changes in the construction period? That is one of the things we should like to know.

5. For the solution of this problem we must look to the Fixwage path—employment variable, (real) wage not variable. What happens, in the event of lengthening or shortening, on the Fixwage assumption?

---

[1] As is shown in Appendix, sect. 18.

Let us begin with lengthening, where the critical month is December of year o. (Up to then the Fixwage assumption makes no difference.) Full Performance starts in that December are determined by what is left over, from the output of December, after take-out, and after wages have been paid to all labour employed on processes previously started. As usual, we need only look at fresh processes, since all processes started before the beginning of year o will be the same on actual as on reference path. The question is one of availability of *funds* to start new processes. All processes started from February to November of year o will be absorbing funds, on both paths; but the absorption will be the same on each path, so they also may be disregarded. We are left with the processes started in January of year o, and the processes to be started in December.

Consider the position, in this December, on the reference path. The construction period, of the processes started in January, is terminated; by that termination there is a release of funds. There is an absorption of funds in the payment of utilizational labour on the same processes, but there is also an output from those processes. If the process is profitable, the value of the output must be greater than the running cost, so there is a *net* release of funds here also. There are thus two sources of funds, available for the starting of new processes, if not taken out. But in a steady state, with positive total take-out, some part of the funds released must be taken out. That this is so may be most easily seen if we begin by looking at the particular case where the reference state is not merely steady but stationary. Reinvestment is then the same as original investment. The processes started in December must absorb the same funds as those which were started in January (the construction period of which is terminated in December); the funds that are released by the excess of output over running cost must go to the take-out. If the reference path has a positive growth rate, rather more than this of the funds that are released must be reinvested; but if there is to be in total a positive take-out, some part of the gross return that accrues in December from the processes started in January must go to the take-out.

On the actual path there must be the same total take-out, so there should be the same contribution. But where is it to come from? On the actual path there is no release of funds from the termination of January processes; and no excess of output over running cost from those same processes. The contribution cannot be made, even if no new processes are started. Or if we insist that it must be made, the funds to complete other processes, previously started, will not be available.

The *impasse* arises because we have insisted on Full Performance, at constant real wages. As we have seen, it would not arise (or not so acutely) if the wage were variable; and it could of course be avoided by drawing on some external source. The latter, in the form of drawing on stocks, is indeed the practical way of dealing with the difficulty. The shortage is a temporary shortage; the mitigation of temporary shortages is one of the purposes for which stocks are held. A change in technique, such as we are considering, would not normally be adopted unless it offered some advantage; the lengthening is a disadvantage; so it should usually be compensated by some advantage, accruing later on. When that advantage was gained, the time would have come for the stocks to be restored.

There is, in practice, this mitigation; but the importance of the proposition just established remains. Even when the wage is variable, lengthening of the construction period causes jerks. It now appears that when the wage is stabilized, the disturbances to the productive process (as a whole) are intensified. Here again we have a proposition which has only been proved, in this book, under special assumptions; but it certainly looks as if it should have a much wider application.

6. I will not weary the reader with a parallel analysis of shortening, under the Fixwage hypothesis; for the principal things to be said, under that heading, are by now rather obvious.

In the critical month (here January of year 1) there will here be no *impasse*; for there is no shortage of funds—there is overabundance. If it is insisted that there must be Full Performance, there will have to be a violent upward fluctuation in the rate of starts in that January; the jerk will be repeated in successive Januaries, without dying away (as it did on the Full Employment path). But so awkward a path is no more than a mathematical exercise. It is much more important that these fluctuations can be avoided by accumulating stocks; yet such accumulation, in itself, is dangerous. The shortening of the construction period is itself a profitable 'improvement'; there is nothing in the further working out of the improvement which makes it inevitable, or even easy, for the stocks to be re-absorbed. So here we do have a case in which a profitable improvement leads to *over-production*; that could not easily happen in the Standard Case, but here it does seem to happen. The economy will be under-functioning—not from any lack of 'animal Spirits' but for the reason that technical progress has taken a form which is hard to accommodate. This does not have to happen; but it can happen. On our analysis it is not ruled out.

The relevance, to economic fluctuations, of the time-structure of production was the discovery of Professor Hayek[1]; that there is such a relevance our present analysis confirms. The route by which Hayek came to it was from the old Austrian capital theory, a theory which (we can now see) was more competent to deal with circulating capital than with fixed. It was natural, on this approach, to think of accumulation in terms of 'vertical' time-displacements, such as we have been considering in this chapter, as against the 'horizontal' displacements which we studied in our Standard Case, and with which classical theory is more fitted to deal. It should now at last be clear that both sorts of displacement are possible, and that they need to be distinguished. Both raise problems of adjustment; but the adjustments required by vertical displacements are more violent and therefore more difficult. To have drawn attention to vertical displacements was a major contribution; it is due to Professor Hayek.

Where (I may as well emphasize here) I do not go along with him (or with what he said in 1931) is in the view that the disturbances in question have a monetary origin. He had not emancipated himself from the delusion (common to many economists, even the greatest economists) that with money removed 'in a state of barter' everything would somehow fit. One of my objects in writing this book has been to kill that delusion. It could only arise because the theory of the barter economy had been insufficiently worked out. There has been no money in my model; yet it has plenty of adjustment difficulties. It is not true that by getting rid of money, one is automatically in 'equilibrium'—whether that equilibrium is conceived of as a stationary state (Wicksell),

---

[1] *Prices and Production* (1931).

a perfect foresight economy (Hayek[1]) or any kind of steady state. Monetary disorders may indeed be superimposed upon other disorders; but the other disorders are more fundamental.

[1] There is an early work of Professor Hayek's dealing with the perfect foresight equilibrium: 'Das intertemporale Gleichgewicht system' (*Weltwirtschaftliches Archiv*, 1928).

XII

WAYS AHEAD

FROM the point now reached, several roads open out, several which look like being worth exploring. I shall do no more than take a few steps on some of them.

(a) MORE GENERAL PROFILES

I began, in Chapter II, by suggesting that a typical economic process would have a rising and then (probably) a falling phase. The profile of labour inputs (in particular) would be of this shape, though there might well be a kick-up at the end, when the 'machine' was requiring additional maintenance. The Simple Profile, with which we have so long been working, is a rather poor approximation to this economic shape. One of the things which we should like to know is the extent to which our results would be affected if we had used a more realistic profile. The working-out, obviously, would have been more complex; but is there anything essential which would have been changed?

I have made no attempt to calculate a Traverse, from one non-Simple Profile to another. It would be a formidable task; but I expect that in some cases it could be done. All I can offer are some rather suggestive results in the matter of convergence.

With a Simple Profile, as indicated in Chapter VII (and proved in sects. 7–8 of the Appendix), there is assured convergence of a Full Employment path, so long as the constructional input coefficient is greater than the utilizational ($a_0 > a_1$). This does not mean that a Traverse, from *any* initial position, can then be carried through smoothly, with every process that has once been started being carried to completion as planned. We have already seen, in our discussion of Lengthening, that that is not so.[1] All it means is that when a Late Phase has been reached, so that all live processes are of the same Simple type with the same coefficients, a smooth convergence to equilibrium (in the absence of

[1] Above, p. 130.

exogenous disturbances, such as further 'inventions') must occur.[1] How far can we say even this, in the case of a more general input profile $(a_0, a_1, a_2, \ldots, a_n)$?

There are two propositions, which follow from well-known theorems in difference equations, which give us a start.[2]

I. It is a sufficient condition for convergence that the a's should be steadily decreasing:

$$a_0 > a_1 > a_2 > \cdots > a_n.$$

II. It is a necessary condition that $a_0 > a_n$.

Let us say that when $a_m < a_{m-1}$ there is a Down; when $a_m > a_{m-1}$, there is an Up; when $a_m = a_{m-1}$ there is a Pause. The sufficient condition may then be read as All Downs; and the necessary condition as Down on Balance.

All Downs is a very strict condition, not in itself of much direct use. A profile of this type is far away from any in which we may be interested in economics. It is therefore important that All Downs is not a necessary condition. We have indeed already found an example—the Simple Profile itself—where All Downs is not satisfied, though Down on Balance is satisfied. And we know that with a Simple Profile there is convergence.

In the Simple Profile there are no Ups. But it is not the case that it is a sufficient condition for there to be no Ups. There would be no Ups if all a's were equal, but if that were so the necessary condition would not be satisfied. Some Downs are necessary, in order that there should be Down on Balance.[3]

The interesting economic question, which is not settled by these considerations, is whether any Ups can be accommodated. In particular, can Ups be accommodated at the beginning of the process—labour employed on preparatory work, before the peak in constructional activity? It appears, from the mathematics, that

---

[1] Since the Late Phase starts are determined by Repeated Weighted Averaging, no Late Phase start can diverge from its equilibrium value by more than the maximum divergence in the Early Phase. This maximum divergence being consistent with the Early Starts being non-negative, the (lesser) divergence in the Late Phase must still leave the Late Phase starts non-negative. There must therefore be a smooth convergence.

[2] For proofs see Appendix, sects. 20, 21.

[3] Nor is it sufficient that there should be some Downs and no Ups. There is still a requirement that the Downs should be suitably placed. They need to be suitably placed in order that they should be able to 'iron out' differences in the initial x's (determined, it will be remembered, in the Early Phase).

it is in principle *possible* for some such Ups to be accommodated; but it is necessary, if there is to be convergence, that a series of Ups at the beginning should be matched by a series of Downs at the end. Preparatory work at the beginning and a kick-up of maintenance at the end do not fit.

This, I think, makes economic sense. The reason why All Downs works so smoothly is that every process, at every stage after its beginning, is releasing labour. So old processes will always be releasing labour; ample supplies of labour for starting new processes will always be available. The new processes absorb their maximum of labour at their commencement; so the number of new processes which can be started at any date is kept down by the high initial requirement. There is never any danger that this limited number of new processes cannot be carried through.

The reason why Ups are a source of disturbance is that they mark an absorption of labour into *old* processes. It is easy to see that if initial employment is less than peak employment there is a sense in which it is too easy to start new processes. The number of new processes that must be started, in order to re-employ the labour becoming available, is rather large; but as they build up to their peaks, their labour requirement increases, and the point will come when the labour they need is not there. So there is a 'jam'; the processes that have been started cannot be carried through.

Something of this kind is surely recognizable (sometimes) in practice. There are many things that happen in trade booms which cannot be reduced to this phenomenon; but that it is one of the things which have not infrequently happened in trade booms can hardly be denied. 'Speculative' booms, in particular, though their main effect may be distributional, do real productive damage by wasting resources on the beginnings of new developments, which are abortive because the resources that are needed to complete them do not exist. It may be granted that the waste in question would be avoided with better foresight; but if the only available processes have humped profiles of this character (and it may well be that the most productive processes available do have such profiles) it will be hard to avoid crises, while maintaining full employment.[1]

---

[1] I have confined this discussion of non-Simple Profiles to the case of the Full Employment path. There is, of course, a corresponding theory of the Fixwage path; what I have to say about it is given, in mathematical form, in sect. 22 of the

It may be claimed to be a merit of our analysis that it shows up the possibility of such crises; they fit in. But what is to happen when the crisis occurs? That is hardly a matter which can be fruitfully examined within the framework we have so long been using. We have assumed, throughout our discussion of Traverse, that changes in process could only be made at the start of a process—that, in the terminology of Chapter V above, there are no Minor Switches. It is hardly surprising that a model which is so bound down by intertemporal complementarities should be subject to crises. In the real world such rigidities exist; but they are not quite so dominating as we have made them. Cannot we find a way—without going to the other extreme, of turning all 'capital' into 'meccano sets' or 'jelly'—of loosening them just a bit?

(b) MINOR SWITCHES

As explained in Chapter V, what I mean by *minor switches* is much the same as what Marshall meant by short-period adjustments. I cannot use Marshall's term, in spite of its having become such a household word among economists; for (as the reader will by now be well aware) I have to make room for short-period adjustments of other kinds. Minor switches are changes made, in mid-course, to *old* processes. Even when (as we have hitherto been doing, in the whole of Part II) we admit no minor switches, so that old processes have programmes that are completely rigid, some flexibility can still be introduced, in the shortest of short periods, by changing the technique that is adopted for new processes. It is perfectly true that such *major* switches will affect final output only after a lag; that indeed is why Marshall reckoned them to be long-period effects. Nevertheless, as soon as we concern ourselves with the economy as a whole, paying attention to the course of inputs as well as to the course of outputs, we have to treat the major switch as having short-period effects.

There are three kinds of minor switch which in a general treatment would fall to be considered.

Appendix. Here it is absorption of savings, spread over several periods, which causes the strain. Firms can insulate themselves from this sort of trouble, by borrowing, at the start of an investment programme, all the capital they expect to require; it is well to remind ourselves that it is impossible for a whole economy —certainly not for a whole closed economy—to earmark all the real capital it will need *in advance*.

The first is one which must surely occur in practice, every now and then, even with the most rigid programmes—interruptions by Act of God, of Government or (nowadays) of strikers. Sometimes this simply means that the output of some 'week' is lost—net output which should have been positive becomes negative, for gross output is zero, yet some expenditure on maintenance is still required. Sometimes it means that the output which should have been forthcoming in that week is postponed. We need not hesitate to reckon such interruptions as minor switches. It will however be noticed that we cannot usefully accommodate switches of this type so long as we keep to static expectations. If the interruption is expected to be permanent, the process is simply truncated. The study of temporary interruptions is accordingly a part of the more general study of adjustments to circumstances expected to be temporary. I have no doubt at all of the importance of that study; but I may fairly regard it as falling outside the scope of the present work.[1]

The second arises when there is *planned flexibility*. This becomes of importance as soon as we drop the assumption of certain (one-valued) expectations. One of the ways of adjusting to uncertainty—to knowledge of uncertainty, knowledge that one does not know what will happen—is to choose a plan that is easily capable of being adjusted (to some at least of the eventualities judged not improbable) in preference to a more rigid programme which is less adaptable.[2] The programme may then be judged to be carried through *as planned* if the adjustments that are made in its course are no more than such as were allowed for at its beginning; they are minor switches, but they do not imply a substantial change in direction. Here again we have a phenomenon which is doubtless worthy of study; but I shall not pursue that study here.

We are left with the minor switches which are consistent with static, single-valued, expectations. The process has been chosen as that which appeared most profitable at the time when it was started; but in the course of its execution conditions change. If that change had been foreseen, a different technique would have

---

[1] I have made my own contribution to that study in Parts III and IV of *Value and Capital*.

[2] There is a useful study of this kind of adaptability in G. B. Richardson, *Information and Investment* (1960), Ch. 8.

been adopted *at the start*; but it is too late for that. All that can be done is to adapt the 'tail' of the process to the new conditions. Suppose we admit the possibility of this kind of adaptation (but no other) how much difference is made to the analysis of the preceding chapters?

Take first the case of the Fixwage path. As in Chapter VIII, an improved technique is invented at time o. It is adopted for new processes, since it offers a higher rate of return at the fixed rate of wages. The rate of interest rises, so processes of the old type will not now be started. If there were no possibility of minor switches (as previously assumed) the old processes would nevertheless be carried on as planned (with the sole possibility that they might be truncated). The only change that is made by the admission of minor switches is that the *old* processes may now be adjusted to the higher rate of interest.

Consider a particular old process. The part of it which is in the past may be neglected; we need only concern ourselves with the 'tail', which may nevertheless be written in the usual way

$$(q_0, q_1, \ldots q_n) \quad \text{or} \quad (q_t)$$

where the q's, as usual, are net outputs. Since the process would be continued if the rate of interest maintained its old value, the capital value of the 'tail', at the old rate of interest

$$k_0 = \sum_0^n q_t R^{-t}$$

will now be *positive*. We may suppose that even when the rate of interest rises, the capital value still remains positive. But now we admit an alternative 'tail' (q_t^*) which is rejected in favour of (q_t) at the lower rate of interest, but is preferred to (q_t) at the higher rate.[1] So, by the usual 'Samuelson inequalities'

$$\sum q_t R^{-t} > \sum q_t^* R^{-t}$$
$$\sum q_t (R + \delta)^{-t} < \sum q_t^* (R + \delta)^{-t}.$$

All four of these terms being positive, it follows that

$$\frac{\sum q_t (R + \delta)^{-t}}{\sum q_t R^{-t}} < \frac{\sum q_t^* (R + \delta)^{-t}}{\sum q_t^* R^{-t}}. \tag{12.1}$$

---

[1] We need not assume that the alternative tails continue for the same number of weeks, since we can fill up with zeros.

Now if the change in interest is small—and we can deal with a large change in interest by dividing it into small changes and compounding the results—

$$(R + \delta)^{-t} = R^{-t}(1 + \delta/R)^{-t} = R^{-t}(1 - t\,\delta/R)$$

nearly. So from (12.1)

$$1 - \frac{\delta}{R}\frac{\sum tq_t R^{-t}}{\sum q_t R^{-t}} < 1 - \frac{\delta}{R}\cdot\frac{\sum tq_t^* R^{-t}}{\sum q_t^* R^{-t}}$$

or

$$\frac{\delta}{R}\left[\frac{\sum tq_t R^{-t}}{\sum q_t R^{-t}} - \frac{\sum tq_t^* R^{-t}}{\sum q_t^* R^{-t}}\right] > 0. \qquad (12.2)$$

Thus when δ is positive (the rate of interest rises) the change in technique must be such as to lower the *index* $(\sum tq_t R^{-t})/(\sum q_t R^{-t})$ when q_t^* is substituted for q_t.

This index, it will be noticed, has the dimension of *time*. It is a weighted average of the *delays* (0, 1, 2,..., n). A lowering of the index implies a rise in the weights that refer to early dates in the sequence relatively to those that refer to late dates.[1] But it is necessary, if both of the Samuelson inequalities are to be satisfied, that some q's should be greater than their corresponding q^*, and some should be less. Thus the *ordinary* effect of a rise in the rate of interest is to raise early q's and to lower late q's. But the necessary rule is just that the index should be lowered; and it is clear that there are many combinations of rises and falls at different dates which will have this effect.

It will further be noticed that in the formation of the index the q's are weighted by a *particular* discount factor R^{-1}; this is kept unchanged when making the comparison. If this discount factor were changed, the index would be changed. Thus it is perfectly possible for a switch from (q) to (q^*) to lower the index when one rate of discount is used but to raise the index at another rate of discount. So one must not interpret the index in the old Austrian manner, as a 'Period of Production'—a technical property of the stream of net outputs. Here, as in the case of major switches, re-switching is not in principle excluded.[2]

---

[1] This will still be the case even if some of the weights are negative.

[2] The index that has just been described was first presented (and, I think, its properties correctly given) in Chapter XVII of *Value and Capital*. Since in that book I always began from a given stock of capital goods, inherited from the past, all that I said about changes in production plans referred to minor switches. Some of it, I now see, was clumsily expressed; but of the substance I have nothing to withdraw.

I return to the Fixwage path, with minor switches as a result of the rise in the rate of interest. It will suffice, in this place, to suppose that the rise has its *ordinary* effect. A rise in early q's of old processes may take the form of increased final output at early dates (at the expense of output at later dates); or it may take the form of a reduction of input (also matched by a reduction of output at later dates). Whichever of these forms is taken, there is less absorption of 'capital' into old processes, at the early date; so that if nothing else were to happen, the take-out (Q) would be increased. If it is not to be increased (as in our former analysis in Chapter VIII we supposed) there must be an offsetting change; and the only change that is possible is an increase in starts (x). The rate of starts will thus increase at early dates after time o, above what it would have been, though there will be a countervailing reduction at later dates (in the Early Phase).

What effect this has on employment of labour depends on the form which is taken by the rise in the early q's. If there is just a substitution of early output for late output, there will (for the present) be no change in employment on old processes; the increased rate of starts will increase employment on new processes, so total employment will be increased. There will, it is true, be an offsetting decline in employment later on. But it will be remembered that the awkward case (for the Fixwage path) is that in which the change in technique, to the new process, has a strong forward bias (the Ricardo machinery effect). What then happens, in the absence of minor switches, is a temporary decline in employment, which is succeeded by a rise in employment later on. It now appears that *suitable* minor switches may do something to offset this fluctuation. They must however be suitable. If the rise in early q's took the form of diminished employment on old processes (and there is no reason why it should not), diminished employment on old processes must be set against the increased employment on new processes; the net effect on total employment is uncertain.

It is, I think, unnecessary to work out the effect on the Full Employment path in similar detail. All that needs to be said is that there is an effect through wages, *as well as* the effect through interest, just discussed. It is at once apparent[1] that a rise in wages will diminish employment on old processes, while a fall in wages

---

[1] As may be verified, if necessary, by Samuelson inequalities.

will increase it. The rising wage-rate (w), which we have seen to be the *normal* consequence of a switch to a more profitable technique for new processes, will thus tend to cause the old processes to be modified in the direction of using less labour and producing less output; so the rise in total output (and hence in real wages) during the Early Phase of the Traverse will be somewhat retarded. But it is more important that the fall in wages, which we have seen to be the temporary effect of an improvement with strong forward bias (on a Full Employment path with no minor switches) will also be checked, or moderated, if there can be an increase in employment on old processes. The check is temporary, but the fall to be moderated is also temporary. The minor switch, in this important case, has a stabilising effect.

One final point before leaving this topic. It is interesting to note that if one makes the (surely reasonable) assumption that additional output is more *quickly* obtained by increased application of labour to old processes (minor switches) than by starting new processes, there will be a 'Marshallian' short period in which it will be true (in a one final commodity model like ours) that the Full Employment wage is equal to the Marginal Product of Labour. This is by no means inconsistent with Wage Fund doctrine; both relations are simultaneously true. If there had been more saving (less take-out) the wage would have been higher. Less labour would have been employed on old processes, so its Marginal Product would have been higher. This is consistent with full employment, and full performance, if more labour is employed in starting new processes which, in the Marshallian short period, do not yet produce final output. Surely a reasonable result of a rise in saving!

Neither wage fund nor marginal productivity tell the whole story; neither, properly, should be regarded as primary. We do not understand the determination of wages until we see the way they fit together.

(c) MULTIPLICITY OF GOODS

I turn to consider what can be done towards relaxing those basic assumptions which have been with us for so long—the single homogeneous final product, called Good, and the one original factor, called Labour. These are familiar assumptions, common to many forms of growth theory; but they are very strong assumptions, and should surely at some stage be called in question. The principal issues which arise, at the one end and at the other, are quite different. I begin at the product end, the generalization to many goods.

It is conceivable that one might do the generalization directly, re-working the analysis with many final goods introduced explicitly. Rates of start, of productive processes for the various goods, must then be determined by expectations of demands—demands which would presumably be determined by some kind of demand function (a vector of quantities depending on a price-vector and a vector of incomes). It is possible that something significant can be found by such an enquiry; to pursue it, however, is quite beyond my own competence. It is fortunate that there is an alternative, more elementary, approach.

We are of course by no means obliged to interpret the single Good, with which we have hitherto been working, as a single good in a physical sense. Any bundle of goods can be treated as a single good, so long as the proportions in which the component goods are combined are kept constant. So what we are leaving out, by our assumption of the single Good is no more nor less than variation of these proportions.

Such variation, in terms of our model, may be exogenous, or it may be endogenous. Exogenous variation arises from changes in tastes (changes, that is, in preference functions); endogenous variation from changes that arise in the course of a Traverse, changes in distribution being the chief example. Exogenous variation is (up to a point) not very hard to handle. Though one can see the general way in which endogenous variation will work, a formal analysis is much more difficult.

A change in proportions can always be regarded as a change in the specification of the Good; for an old Good (Good I) a new good (Good II) is substituted. We must have some way of valuing Good II in terms of Good I; it is sufficient, for the study of exogenous shifts, to suppose that there is some unit of Good I which initially is worth more than a unit of Good II, while after the change in tastes it is the unit of Good II that has the greater value. (How much of the valuation problem is avoided in this *simpliste* formulation will be obvious; but for the present purpose no more than this seems necessary.) There is a spectrum of techniques (in the sense that has been used in this book, ever since Chapter IV) for producing each Good. Thus for each Good there will be an efficiency frontier (as in Chapter IV) and with given relative values of the two Goods, the two frontiers can be drawn on the same diagram. In an initial steady state, in which Good I is dominant, the wage may be regarded as being expressed in terms of Good I. At that wage the I frontier lies outside the II frontier, so it is Good I that is produced.

When we come to the change in valuation, we have to decide which Good to take as numeraire, or standard of value. If we keep Good I as standard, as (at least for the study of the Early Phase of the Traverse) will probably be convenient, we must keep the wage unchanged (for it is only Good I which is available initially for payment of wages) but must move the efficiency frontier of Good II *upwards*. If there is to be a shift to the production of Good II, the II frontier must lie above the I frontier at the initial wage. The effect is then just the same as it would have been if a more efficient method of production had been discovered; the whole of the preceding analysis of the Traverse will apply. It is unnecessary to go through the whole story again. There will be the usual possibilities of biases, but in all ordinary cases the final equilibrium wage (as in previous chapters of this Part) will lie above the initial wage. Or so it appears—but we must be careful.

The apparent rise in wages, from the old steady state to the new equilibrium, is a consequence of our having taken Good I as our standard of value. If we had taken Good II as standard, the change in valuation would have lowered the efficiency frontier of Good I while leaving unchanged that of Good II. But when we are measuring in terms of Good II, we must reckon that the initial wage (now to be measured in terms of Good II) is reduced—by the change in preferences itself, before anything else happens. There is the same rise in wages in the course of the Traverse; for during the Traverse production is getting adjusted to the new state of demand, and in the course of that adjustment wages, however measured, should be rising. The equilibrium wage is higher than the initial wage in terms of Good II, just as it was when we measured in terms of Good I, for it is the same rise in wages in each case. But whether this indicates a rise in wages *from the old steady state to the new equilibrium* is a matter of valuation.

It is clear that in the new equilibrium, when production of

Good I has been—entirely—replaced by production of Good II, valuation in terms of Good II will be more appropriate. But we can only compare the final wage with the initial wage if we select some value of the one Good in terms of the other, and maintain it throughout. In this case of a change in demand, it will matter a great deal what value we select. That, after all, is by no means surprising.

It is a well-established proposition in Welfare Economics that real incomes, in two situations, can only be compared if we are prepared to accept some common system of valuation—base prices that are kept fixed, systems of preference that are kept fixed, or Social Welfare Function kept fixed. When, as in the present case, there is a change in preferences, no unambiguous measure of gain is in strictness possible. What does survive (and what is undoubtedly important) is that a movement from an organization of production which is ill-adjusted to given preferences to one which is better adjusted to those preferences, should be registered as a gain. But it will not always be shown as a gain, in our statistics; it will only be shown as a gain if weighting is appropriate, or reasonably appropriate.

These complications will evidently persist, in the case of endogenous variation. We ought then to allow for differences in structure between Wage Good and Take-out Good; and for changes in the structure of each in the course of a Traverse. The problems are formidable, and I shall not pursue them here.

(d) MULTIPLICITY OF FACTORS

I shall confine myself, under this head, to the most important case of factor-multiplicity—the simplest case, but also that which is hardest to handle. We have throughout been working with one original factor, which we called Labour, and could not always resist thinking of as Labour; what happens when there is a second original factor, which we may call Land (and think of as Land)? Labour, we supposed in our Full Employment theory, has a given positive growth rate; land, by tradition, which we will accept, has a growth rate of zero. As already observed,[1] there is no difficulty in fitting land into a Fixwage theory; this was in fact already done by Ricardo. For in a Fixwage theory without land, there is no

---

[1] Above, pp. 123-4.

'scarce' original factor; with land, there is just one scarce original factor. So a Fixwage theory with land is formally equivalent to a Full Employment labour theory (with $g = 0$). It fits into place, raising no new problem.

A Full Employment theory, with two original factors—labour having a positive growth rate, land a zero growth rate—is quite a different matter. For it is immediately apparent that in such a theory there can be no steady state with unchanging technique. For if technique does not vary, while the supply of land is fixed over time, the rate of starts of new processes must be fixed over time; so the demand for labour must be fixed over time, and will therefore fail to absorb the increasing supply of labour. To maintain full employment of labour technique must be varying. We are in fact driven to introduce some sort of production function—in order to match an increasing supply of labour with a fixed supply of land.

The theory advanced in this book has been less dependent on the steady state than some other growth theories; it has nevertheless played an essential part, as standard of reference. If that reference is lost, the form of the theory must surely be changed.

There are doubtless several ways in which it could be changed, several devices by which the disparate behaviour of the factors could be fitted in. We might, for instance, suppose (not wholly unrealistically) that shortage of land makes itself felt, not continuously, but at intervals. Between the intervals the system can expand in the way with which we are familiar, without experiencing land shortage; so that between the intervals there can be a (temporary) steady state. The effect of the 'step', at which technique must be changed in order to accommodate the increasing supply of labour, can then be treated as a separate problem.

A more fundamental alternative is to insist that there is one steady state which still survives. There can still be a steady state if the supply of labour, like that of land, is constant over time; so that (with technique, of course, kept unvaried) the steady state is a stationary state. The stationary state can still be used as a reference path, while Traverse analysis is used to determine actual paths—including that which would be followed if the only change that is superimposed upon the stationary state were an exogenous increase in the supply of labour. Along this path (still to be a Full Employment path) wages will have to change; there is now no reason why they should not change. As a result of the change in wages technique will be varied; and we may accept that (at least usually) appropriate change in technique will require falling wages. So much of the classical 'diminishing returns to land' must surely be preserved.

Other sorts of exogenous change may be similarly analysed, by reference to the stationary state—but we need not stop there.[1] For the path which is followed when labour supply increases (and nothing else changes) can itself be used as a reference path—a subsidiary reference path, other paths being analysed in relation to it. Since this Dismal Path (as it may well be called) is only to be used as a reference path, we need not worry about its end—in a Malthusian Apocalypse! A section of the path is all we need. The effects of invention and other more cheerful changes can then be studied by using Traverse analysis to determine differences between actual path and Dismal Path. This, I believe, is the proper solution. I shall not attempt to work it out in detail; most of the tools that are needed for it have I think already been provided.[2]

---

[1] This, I believe, was the procedure that was generally envisaged by nineteenth-century economists, from Ricardo to Wicksell; so one sees why the stationary state was so important to them. Modern economists, it now appears, have left it too far behind; as indicated above, there is a way between these extremes.

[2] For the use of a subsidiary reference path in mathematical theory, see Appendix, sects. 15–16.

PART III

CONTROVERSY

XIII

THE MEASUREMENT OF CAPITAL—
VALUE AND VOLUME

1. W H A T I hope to do, in this final Part, is to throw some light
on the Controversy about Capital, which has drawn so much
attention from economists in the last twenty years. I shall make
no attempt to go through the literature—neither the modern
literature, which has sprung from the famous articles by Joan
Robinson[1] and Robert Solow,[2] nor the classical and 'neo-
classical' literature which (I am convinced) lies behind it. My
object is just to see what light we can get, on these disputed
matters, from the work we have been doing. But it is necessary to
begin more generally, insisting that the issue is a wide one, wider
than it often appears. It is nothing less than an opposition between alternative concepts of capital—each, I think I can show,
a respectable and useful concept of capital; or rather between
families of such concepts, for within each main type there are
several varieties. Part of the trouble with modern discussions is
that they rarely reveal more than a part of the issue; when it is
filled in it becomes more intelligible.

2. Consider (for a closed economy) the stock of real goods, commodities having value, that exists at a moment of time. Many
economists would be prepared to identify that stock with the
Capital of the economy; all, I think, would admit that the Capital
stands in some relation to it. But even those who accept the identi-
fication will grant that for macro-economic purposes we need
some single measure, by which the stock can be represented. All
that we get from the physical goods is a list—so much of this,
so much of that; for macro-economics there must be aggregation.

The obvious aggregate is an aggregate in value terms. Suppose
that it is possible (though whether it is possible turns out to be
one of the questions) to set a market price on each good in the

---

[1] 'The Production Function and the Theory of Capital' (*R. Econ. Studies*,
1954).
[2] 'Technical Progress and the Production Function' (*R. Econs. and Stats.*,
1957).

stock. The Capital of the economy may then be taken to be equal to the total value ($\sum$ price $\times$ quantity in the usual way). According to one party, that is Capital—*capital value.*

Value must always be reckoned in terms of something—money, a particular good chosen as standard, or a bundle of such goods (money value deflated by a price-index number). If a concept such as the capital–output ratio, which belongs to this approach, is to make sense, capital and output must both be measured in the same terms. They may both be measured in money terms; but if the ratio between the money values is to be taken (as it usually is) to be a real (non-monetary) concept, both must be reduced to real terms in the same way. We are accustomed to measuring *real* output by valuing output at constant prices; or, what is approximately the same thing, deflating the money value of output by an index of output prices. If real output is measured in that manner, and the capital–output ratio (the real capital–real output ratio) is to be kept as a pure number, the money value of capital also must be deflated by an index of *output* prices. So it is this which, by the 'value' party (as we may call it) is called Real Capital—the value of capital in terms of final output. The prices at which the individual capital goods are to be valued, to get this Real Capital, are their prices in terms of final output.

These prices, over time, must be expected to be variable. Thus it must be admitted to be possible, if there is a change in technical potentialities, for Real Capital, in this value sense, to change, even though the quantities of capital goods, of given physical specifications, do not change. If the quantities of real goods *produced* remained unchanged, while their prices varied, we should want to say that real *output* remained constant. And we should show that invariance by valuing them at constant prices, even though actual prices had changed. But for Real Capital, in the value sense, we are not valuing at constant prices. So Real Capital, in this sense, has a different kind of reality from Real Output.

But why should we not value at constant prices? Why, while admitting that Real Capital, in the value sense, is a useful concept, should we not also make use of another concept of Real Capital, a *volume* concept, got by valuing at constant prices of the capital goods themselves? This, I think, is what the other party (or, as we shall see, some of the other party) have been trying to do.

The task, at first sight, looks quite straightforward. We have only to take the money value of capital (which already on the other approach was granted to be measurable) and instead of deflating by an index of prices of final output, deflate by an index of the prices of the capital goods themselves. Such index-numbers purport to be available; it is however very doubtful if they are in fact what we want.

There are several difficulties, to some of which we shall be returning later. It is sufficient, in this place, to point to one which is no more than a strong case (a very strong case) of a regular index-number difficulty. It is a difficulty which arises even in the simplest of all index-number comparisons, the comparison of consumption 'bundles'. Even there, it has to be faced. *What is to be done with new goods?* What is to be done at the point when the television set has to be introduced into the bundle?

This, to the statistician, is a familiar difficulty; he has developed ways, though ways that are no more than moderately satisfactory, for dealing with it. At the worst, he can fall back on the consideration that while the appearance of new consumption goods is undoubtedly important, the disappearance of old (though it occurs) is much less so. The latter, at least, may reasonably be neglected. All the sorts of goods that were present at time o may then be taken to be still present at time 1. Accordingly, though we have no Laspeyre quantity-index ($\sum p_0 q_1 / \sum p_0 q_0$)—since the new goods were not present at time o and thus had no prices at that date—a Paasche quantity-index ($\sum p_1 q_1 / \sum p_1 q_0$) can still be preserved. And the Paasche quantity-index is the ratio of the value index ($\sum p_1 q_1 / \sum p_0 q_0$) to the Laspeyre price-index ($\sum p_1 q_0 / \sum p_0 q_0$), which similarly exists. So, though we cannot make the comparison both ways, as would be theoretically desirable, we can make it one way; and with that we may have to be content.

For consumption comparisons, that may be sufficient; though even for consumption comparisons, there is much to be said for trying to go further. But for capital comparisons, it is wholly insufficient. The stock of goods, at the end of the 'year' does not just contain many sorts of goods which were not in the beginning stock; even the goods which appear to be in both stocks will, in the course of the year, have changed their character. It we insist, as we should insist, that what we are to call the *same* good si a good of unchanged specification, it is not merely the case that there are new goods in the end stock; many of the goods which were in the beginning stock will have disappeared. So, in strictness, we do not just lose one of the Laspeyre–Paasche indexes; we lose both. The index-number comparison breaks down altogether.

This is a weighty objection; it is, I think, a more serious objection than that often raised by the 'value' party—that a volume index, in which goods are identified by their physical characteristics, is economically irrelevant. What matters, we are told, is not the physical quantities of goods (when they are intermediate goods, not final products); it is the part which they are capable of playing in the production of something else. I do not think that this is valid. Both producers' goods and consumers' goods are 'economically relevant' only in so far as they yield utilities, directly or indirectly; the measurement of consumers' goods in physical units does not prevent us from making comparisons of real income; why should the measurement of producers' goods in physical units prevent us from making comparisons of real capital? Those who advance this argument have already made up their minds on the 'value' side; the evidence which they bring in support of their case implies that they have already won it.

3. I do not think they have yet won their case; for the objection (the solid objection) just made against the volume measure suggests a comparable weakness in the value measure also. It is necessary (as we saw) even for the value measure that it should be possible to set a market price on each item in the capital goods stock. But there is no reason why that should be so. In practice, indeed, it is quite largely not so.

The point, in statistical work, is unavoidable; and it is perhaps in that setting that it comes out most clearly. Let us put ourselves in the position of a statistician who is asked for a figure for National Capital; and let us grant that what is asked for is a value (here a money value) of National Capital. (We will abstract from problems of external relations and of the Public Sector, problems which can only be dealt with when the rest has been settled.) He has learned that for the measurement of National Income he needs a set of accounts, the running accounts (or flow accounts) of the national economy. So now, when he is asked for a measure of National Capital, he expects to serve it up in the form of a national balance-sheet. But the task of constructing a national balance-sheet is *practically* quite different.

It is characteristic of a running account, of whatever type, that most (though not all) of the items that enter into it are records of actual transactions. When an article is sold, money passes hands; so the value of the article is expressed in money terms, by buyer and seller, in the same way. When money is lent, currently, the same occurs. Thus, if it were the case that all entities within the economy (all private individuals, as well as all traders) kept proper running accounts, and if those accounts contained nothing but transactions items, it would be possible for a national running account to be compiled from them by a purely arithmetical process. Many of the accounts which he would need for this purpose are of course not available to the national income statistician; he has to estimate them. But in making such estimates, he is estimating an actual figure, a figure which exists, or which did exist, though information about it is not available to him; if the information came to hand, it would of course replace the estimate.

Even in the case of running accounts, things are not always so simple. There are items, of which Depreciation and Stock Appreciation are the most important, which do not reflect actual transactions, but are estimates of changes in the value of assets which have not yet been sold. These are estimates in a different sense from that previously mentioned. They are not statistician's estimates of a true figure, which happens to be unavailable; there is no true figure to which they correspond. They are estimates that are relative to a purpose; for different purposes they may be made in different ways. This is of course the basic reason why it has become customary to express the National Accounts in terms of Gross National Product (before deduction of Depreciation) so as to clear them of contamination with the 'arbitrary' depreciation item; though it should be noticed that even with GNP another arbitrary element remains, in stock accumulation. This also may be valued in different ways for different purposes.

What in the case of running accounts is a complication, that can thus to some extent be avoided, in the case of the capital account (or balance-sheet) is central and unavoidable. The assets, the possession of which is recorded in a balance-sheet, are assets that are held, not goods that are sold. They may be sold, when the time comes, but they are not being sold at the date to which the balance-sheet refers. There are no transactions in them, as there are in the items that appear in the running account. So if the statistician is just told to value them at market prices, he is not in general being given any guidance.

There will indeed be some goods (such as raw materials of standard quality) in which there is an active market; purchases and sales are going on all the time. Though the actual goods that are in the possession of the stockholder are not being sold, exactly similar goods are being sold; it is obviously legitimate to apply the price of the one to the other. It will again often happen, as in the case of the more standard type of dwelling-house, that there is an active market in goods that are fairly similar; not exactly similar, since every house has its own location, but near enough for a market price to be assessible, within narrow limits. But these are by no means the general case. For two, at least, of the main classes of capital goods—the plant and machinery of industry, and its goods in process of production—there is, in the relevant sense, no market at all. They have been the object of trade in the past, and they (or what comes out of them) will in the future be sold; but *now*, at the moment when the valuation is to be made, they have no market. They have no market in their present condition. Values can indeed be put upon them in various ways, but these values are not market prices.

4. It is strongly suggested, by this consideration, that something is wrong with both *value* and *volume* measures of capital, as we have so far been taking them in this chapter; neither, in strictness, has been adequately defined. Each, accordingly, is a little out of focus. It is the volume measure, perhaps, which is the more seriously affected; but the value measure does not escape unscathed. Each, it now appears, needs re-formulation. It may be that when they have been re-formulated, we shall find that they can live more quietly together.

We have now reached a point, in the present discussion, when we can begin to get help from the neo-Austrian model, that was developed in the previous Parts of this book.. The model, of course, is artificial; we cannot conclude without examination that what is true in the model will also be true in reality, nor even that distinctions that hold in the model can have real counterparts. It may nevertheless be claimed that the distinctions of the model are (or should be) sharply in focus; they may therefore suggest what it is for which we should be looking.

There was a distinction which appeared in Chapter III (on the Social Accounting of the model) which appears to be relevant. It is the distinction between forward-looking and backward-looking measures of capital. Can we not associate the value measure of capital with the forward look, and the volume measure with the backward look? They are not the same thing, but they are the same kind of thing. With a little adjustment, conformity should be established.

We shall most easily discover the adjustments needed if we start by re-thinking 'value' and 'volume' in terms of the model; then, having got our re-furbished concepts, turn to see what can be made of them in more practical application. Let us begin with 'value'.

In the model, it will be remembered,[1] all capital goods are intermediate products, and there are no markets in intermediate products. To value capital goods at market prices is therefore impossible; that prescription, which we have found to be a snare, is by assumption closed. We nevertheless associated with every process, at every stage of its 'life', a capital value. These values could not be market values; they must thus be subjective values, steps in the process by which technique is chosen, and no more. Their practical counterpart belongs to the Discounted Cash Flow computation of the individual business. Such values can however be aggregated, at least as a matter of arithmetic; some properties of the resulting aggregate were in our former discussion discovered.

When there is a market in an intermediate product, such as a raw material, the price should in principle be determined by the valuations of marginal buyer and marginal seller; and since any stockholder may be buyer, or seller, if he chooses, this price should be equal to the marginal valuation of the stock as a whole. At a moment of time (the moment that is chosen for the capital computation) supply is given; so the marginal valuation determines the price. Such a valuation must be a forward-looking valuation, a capitalization of the marginal stream of net outputs which disposal over the marginal unit will permit. Market prices, of capital goods, may thus themselves be regarded as

[1] Above, pp. 5–6.

forward-looking valuations; so a measure of capital at market prices is itself a forward-looking measure. Thus what we deduce, from rethinking the *value* measure of capital in terms of our model, is that it is, or should be, substantially equivalent to a capitalization of future net outputs; but such capitalization is not in principle dependent upon the existence of a market for capital goods; when the market does not exist, it must be performed directly. It would have to be performed directly in order to get the *true* value to be set upon such intermediate products; information about that true value is, of course, most unlikely to be available. What the statistician, who seeks for a value measure of the capital aggregate, must presumably do, is to look for some indirect method of estimating it.

I shall return to his problem in a later section. All that is necessary, in this place, is to have established the theoretical identity between a value measure, properly generalized, and a forward-looking measure.[1]

5. To build a bridge between volume and backward-looking is more complicated. Let us assure ourselves, before attempting it, that the backward-looking measure is a volume measure, in some broader sense.

It was a fundamental property of the value measure, even as at first enunciated, that it would change, without any change in the physical stock of capital goods, if there were a change in technology, and hence a change in the stream of future net outputs expected from that stock. In that property the generalized forward-looking measure of course shared. It was in order to escape from this consequence that the volume measure (as at first enunciated) was introduced. Now the backward-looking measure, as presented in the model (we are not yet ready to generalize it) also escapes. No change in technology, in the present, can affect what has already happened, in the past. It is the *capital invested* in the past which is registered by the backward-looking measure.

Now just as we found that forward-looking enables us to generalize the value measure to cover goods that have no market, so we find that backward-looking enables us to circumvent the weakness of the crude volume measure (as it will now be fitting to

---

[1] It is the value measure of *capital* that is forward-looking; an associated measure of *income* may not be. See Note at end of this chapter.

call it). For a backward-looking measure (still defined in terms of the model) calls for no comparison between physical characteristics of the capital goods which appear in new and old processes respectively. The backward measure is derived by accumulating past net inputs; these are differences between values of inputs and outputs, all of them being market values, that may readily be supposed to be comparable. Capital invested may surely be measured at constant prices—constant prices of inputs and outputs, and (presumably) also a constant rate of interest used for accumulation. Such a measure, which we may properly call *capital at cost*, when taken in this way at constant prices, will behave in the way that we should expect from a volume index.

Within the model this is, I think, plain sailing; but in practical application there is a further difficulty, a formidable difficulty. Before we can define *capital at cost* more narrowly, we must face it.

In our model, it will be remembered, all processes are mortal. Thus all the processes that are alive at a given date have had a beginning; the total capital invested in all live processes is clearly finite. But in reality existing processes have no clear beginnings. Something is left, to form part of the inheritance from the past enjoyed by (say) modern England, from the roads left by the Romans, and from the clearing of the primitive forest ever so long ago. If this investment, small though it may have been by modern standards, is left to be accumulated over centuries at compound interest, it must dominate *capital at cost* in a way that is clearly preposterous. To make use of a backward measure in this manner will clearly not do.

The remedy is to insist that capital at cost, being a volume measure, is an index-number measure. It is not measured in physical units, tons or cubic feet, but solely by reference to what it was at a base date. So there is no need to go back before that date; the comparison between capital at that date and capital afterwards is what matters. Now the constant prices, at which we are to value, are the prices of the base date; so it is perfectly consistent to use the *value* of capital at the base date as the initial *volume*, everything that happened before that date being, as the business man would say, 'written off'. There is no need to go back to the Normans, or the Romans, or the Garden of Eden! We have simply to adopt the convention that *at the base date* value and volume are the same. Then, as we go forward from the base date, we shall find that value changes in one way, volume in another. The way in which value changes, if it is reckoned according to the method of assessment outlined above, will allow for the changes in technology which subsequently occur; but volume, which is simply the result of the accumulation of subsequent net inputs, valued at base prices and accumulated at the base rate of interest, will make no such allowance. Each could in principle be drawn out on a time-chart, the same time-chart; the two curves having the same starting-point (at the base date) but different courses subsequently.

It may well be supposed that by this device we get a better measure of increments in capital volume than of capital volume itself; but that is not really so. For the increments themselves will be largely affected by interest on the initial capital; an 'error' in the estimation of the initial capital will greatly affect the increments.

6. So the point has come when we must revert, yet again, to the value measure. The state in which we left it is not yet by any means satisfactory.

We have discussed it in terms of the valuation of capital *goods*; and we have allowed ourselves to think of those capital goods being valued *separately*. But this is surely incorrect. The value of a plant, in working order 'as a going concern', is not the same as the sum of the values of the separate items which it contains. This is different from the question that has formerly been in our minds, that of the valuation of 'old' machines. If the latter were the only question, we could certainly say that the value of the plant must be less than it would have been if all items were *new*, just as it must be greater than it would be if all items were sold off second-hand. But, as is indicated without more ado by the 'running-in' phenomenon,[1] the value of the whole plant in working order may well be greater than the sum of the values *new*. There is a complementarity between equipments of various sorts, planned to work together, and accustomed to work together, of which we have not yet (in this chapter) taken account.[2]

---

[1] Of which, it may be remembered, we have taken account in Chapter II.

[2] It is one of the strengths of our *model* that by working in terms of processes (not goods) it does take account, to some degree, of this complementarity. The

There is another matter, also not yet taken into account, which proves to be associated with it. Whose are the expectations, of future net outputs, from which the forward-looking value is to be derived? It is a major complication, which oppresses the statistician as soon as he tries to construct a national balance-sheet, that the expectations of different individuals are not harmonious, and the statements which they record in their balance-sheets of magnitudes which depend on these expectations are not harmonious. A running account, for the whole economy, can be put together by consolidation of separate accounts, for these are largely records of actual transactions, such as sales where the money received by the seller and that paid by the buyer is the same. But the balance-sheet is not a record of such transactions. In addition to the physical assets, so far considered, there are debts and claims, which are not necessarily valued by debtor and creditor, or by company and shareholder, in the same way. So the separate balance-sheets do not fit together, as the running accounts fit together, at least on the whole.[1]

All the statistician can do, in view of this discrepancy, is to select one valuation, which he will choose to regard as *his* valuation, and adjust the rest to fit. There is no other way in which a consistent consolidated balance-sheet can be prepared. But there may be different balance-sheets, presented from the same material, according as one or other of possible valuations is selected.[2] In the case of the most important discrepancy, that of firm versus shareholder, the ideal valuation may well be thought to be that which the firm itself sets upon its own assets (that which, as stated above, is implied in Discounted Cash Flow computations). But a valuation of that sort is seldom revealed. The values which are set in the accounts of the firm are, as one would expect, backward-looking values. The only forward-looking

complementarity, again, is a chief reason why an 'index of capital good prices' is so unsuitable a deflator for reducing capital value to capital volume. The crude volume index is not an index of capital *at work*; it is an index of the value of the bits and pieces sold off at a junk-shop!

[1] Even running accounts do not quite fit together, because of trade credit. If, as is the correct accounting practice, the account is shown in terms of receivables and payables, there may be some lack of fit, because of bad debts.

[2] There has been plenty of experience of this, in relation to the computation of the British National Capital; and I expect the same is true elsewhere. See Note D in the Appendix to my *Social Framework* (4th edition), a note which in successive editions since 1942 has had to be radically changed.

valuation which is on record is the shareholder's valuation—that which is derivable from the prices of the firm's shares on the stock exchange.

This is an actual market price. Is it not as good a market price as any other? Why not accept it, for the computation of capital value, as *the* value of the firm's assets? To make this decision would not solve the whole problem of valuing capital, since in any country there will be large parts of the capital stock to which there are no corresponding securities; but it may well solve what would otherwise be the hardest part of the problem.

Statisticians, however, are obviously reluctant to take this way out; they will of course point to the volatility of equity prices as a reason for distrusting them. On the surface, perhaps, this is not a very convincing reason; but I think it is better than it looks.

As was remarked at the beginning of this chapter, we are looking for a value of capital that can sensibly be deflated by output prices. This must mean that purely monetary influences are to affect the value of capital in terms of money and the value of output in terms of money in the same way. But equity prices do not move in at all similar ways to output prices; for one to be rising and the other falling is not at all rare. A value of capital, derived from equity prices, does not look like providing a capital–output ratio which with any plausibility could be regarded as a *real* concept.

One can perhaps take the matter a little further. The volatility of equity prices is a reflection of volatility in price-expectations (expectations of the course of output and input prices in the relevant future) and in the degree of confidence with which such expectations are held. A value of capital which is to be a *real* measure (real with its own particular kind of reality) cannot be deduced from equity prices unless it is corrected for the future price-changes, which in the equity prices are implied. But there is in general no means of making this correction. It is possible to correct for past price-changes, since they are fact, and some information at least can be had about them. But on future price-changes there is in general no such information.

The future price-changes for which correction is most necessary are those of purely monetary origin; and these, it is true, to some extent correct themselves. For a general expectation of rising prices tends to be reflected in rates of interest, so that purely inflationary expectations do not pull equity prices as much out of line as might at first be supposed. One can even imagine a monetary system which worked so perfectly, the pattern of interest rates for different maturities adjusting itself to the *course* of inflationary expectations, that monetary influences on the ratio of equity prices to output prices would be completely offset. But actual monetary systems, though they do react in this way to some extent, do so very imperfectly. There is a *residual* volatility in the ratio, due to monetary disturbances, which is surely too great for the equity price solution to be very appealing.

7. One can thus understand why it is that statisticians, asked to measure National Capital, are not much tempted to look for a *value* measure. The information which such a measure could convey would surely be too limited. Much labour would have to be bestowed on compilation; it would then in the end be swallowed up by what is 'anybody's guess'. The place of the value measure is in theoretical analysis; but even there it would be well if its weaknesses were better appreciated.

The volume measure also, as we have seen, does not wholly escape the same weaknesses. It also, in its more sophisticated form, requires a value measure *at a base date*. But since the choice of base date is to some extent at the disposal of the investigator, it is possible for him (or will sometimes be possible for him) to choose a date at which monetary conditions are fairly 'normal', so that the relation between capital value and output value is not particularly disturbed. Error in the base will, as we have seen, affect later figures, but it will affect them in a uniform manner, a manner that is easily summarized. It will not prevent the series as a whole from having some solidity.

It must therefore be expected that measures of capital, turned out by statisticians for the use of applied economists, will predominantly be on the volume side. I think that is so already; and as the problem is better understood, it is likely to be so in future to an increasing extent. But what are the consequences of that for theory? That is the question which I shall be examining in the following chapter.

NOTE TO CHAPTER XIII

EX-POST INCOME

THE greater part of this note is a quotation from an article 'Maintaining Capital Intact', which I published in *Economica* during war-time (in 1942) and which is more legibly reprinted in Parker and Harcourt, *Readings in the Concept and Measurement of Income* (Cambridge, 1969). In this article I described the 'Swedish' (that is to say, Lindahl's) definition of ex-post income in the following terms.

.

"THE changes which may have taken place in the price-level of capital goods are not the only reason why the difference between the money value of an article at the beginning of the year and its money value at the end will not do as a measure of depreciation; the underlying reason why this measure will not do is that the beginning-value and end-value were arrived at on a different basis of knowledge. When a particular article from the capital stock was valued in January, there was implicit in that valuation an estimate of what the value would be in December; but the December value which is used for calculating the year's depreciation is not an estimate in the same sense—December is now past, so we *know*. If C_0 is the value of the capital stock at the beginning of the year, C_1 the value of these same goods at the end, then to measure depreciation by $C_0 - C_1$, and net income by

$$\text{consumption} + \text{gross investment} + C_1 - C_0$$

is internally inconsistent. The figures for consumption and gross investment will be based upon the actual historical events of the year; the figure for C_1 also takes into account the actual events of the year though it is still influenced by uncertainty about what will happen when the year is over; but the figure for C_0 was arrived at when the events of the year were still in the future. As far as the events of the year in question are concerned, consumption, gross investment and C_1 all shine in the light of history; but what is history for them is shrouded for C_0 in the mists of futurity. In order to get a true measure for depreciation, hence for net investment, and hence for net income, C_0 must be brought out into the light too.

Let us then define the depreciation of the original stock of capital as the difference between the total value of the goods comprising that original stock as it is at the end of the year (C_1) and the value (C_0') *which would have been put upon the initial stock at the beginning of the year if the events of the year had been correctly foreseen, including among* *those events the capital value C_1 at the end of the year.*[1] Net income is then

$$\text{consumption} + \text{gross investment} + C_1 - C_0'.$$

This, I think is the Swedish definition of *ex post* income; unlike their definition of *ex ante* income, which presents difficulties of interpretation in a world of uncertainty, the definition of *ex post* income is no harder to apply in a practical case than any other method which has been suggested for dealing with the problem of depreciation.

The corrected value for the initial capital stock is of course not easy to arrive at; but what we need is not this corrected value, but the consequential figure for depreciation ($C_0' - C_1$). We can proceed to estimate this by distinguishing, of the various experiences which the initial capital goods will have had during the year, which sorts will cause a divergence between C_0' and C_1. These are the things which will cause true depreciation. By applying the rule to each case as it comes up we ought to be able to discover them.

"IN nearly all the cases where I have been able to try it out, the Swedish definition gives eminently sensible results. They are not always the results which might have been expected beforehand, but they are always intelligible, and they stand looking at from several points of view. Let us check over a few of them.

Normal wear and tear in the course of production is clearly a reason why the value of a capital instrument should be greater at the beginning of a year than at the end, even if the final value was foreseen accurately. Normal wear and tear is therefore an element in true depreciation. So is exceptional wear and tear, due to exceptionally heavy usage; if the exceptionally heavy usage had been foreseen, the gap between the beginning-value and the end-value would have been larger. On the other hand, any deterioration which the machine undergoes outside its utilization does *not* give rise to true depreciation; if such deterioration had been foreseen, the initial capital value would have been written down in consequence; the deterioration is therefore not depreciation, but a capital loss. If a machine remains idle throughout the year, any deterioration which it undergoes is therefore not depreciation, but capital loss; and the use of productive resources to maintain the idle machine in good condition is net investment. This last result may appear surprising at first sight, but it is only reasonable

---

[1] It should be noticed that this supposed foresight only extends to the events of the year under discussion; later events are still in the dark at the end of the year, so they must be left in the dark when we are constructing our corrected figure for the initial capital.

when one thinks it over; the fact that the machine may have produced some output in the past is irrelevant; the 'maintenance' work done in the present is not a contribution to current final output, but to the final output of future years.

Obsolescence of the kind described in Professor Hayek's example [of the firm which produces fashion goods, instals machinery which it plans to use for a limited period and then to scrap before the machinery is physically worn out] is true depreciation on our test. The fashion firm scraps its machinery in accordance with anticipations; it is not failure of foresight which makes the end-value less than the beginning value. But most problems of obsolescence do arise from imperfect foresight. The allowance for obsolescence which firms reckon among their costs is for the most part a reflection of their uncertainty about the value of their equipment at the end of the year; once this value is assumed known, the necessity for such obsolescence allowances disappears."

I have nothing to withdraw in the passage thus quoted, written thirty years ago. It will be noticed that the concept of *capital* implied is rigorously forward-looking.

XIV

THE ACCUMULATION OF CAPITAL

1. It will have been noticed that in Part II of this book we made hardly any use of a capital aggregate, however measured. There was indeed only one way in which we even appeared to make use of such an aggregate. This was when we allowed ourselves to assume that saving was a fixed fraction of profits—profits which were taken to be determined by the application of a market rate of interest (r) to a capital value (K). Such a capital value, we now see, must be a forward-looking value. It will however be remembered that it was only for the determination of the steady state path that such a rule was invoked; and in the steady state there is no forward-backward difference. Forward and backward measures —value at current prices and value at constant prices, which are the current prices—are identical. When we leave the steady state they cease to be identical; and precisely at that point the rule in question loses its convenience. When we work with a Take-out (Q) that is given exogenously, we can calculate the path of the economy without any reference to a capital aggregate. That is in fact what we did in our Traverse analysis.

It will nevertheless be useful, at the point we have now reached, to consider how the story would have run if it had been told in terms of capital aggregates; or at least to examine what would have happened to the aggregates in the course of the Traverse. This is an exercise that can be performed on our model, taking it quite strictly, with all its assumptions intact. Since the path of the economy was fully determined by our previous analysis, no difference can be made to our previous results by this re-statement. We shall merely be putting them in a different way, so as to make them more comparable with the results reached by others, and by the present author in other places.

2. I begin, as in Part II, with the Fixwage path—which turns out, in this place, to be more than usually instructive. For it enables us to set out the relations between the aggregates in a manner which is quite clear-cut. The Fixwage theory is more complete (and perhaps less paradoxical) than the Full Employment theory; so the latter will be better understood if Fixwage is taken first.

We set our usual problem. There is an 'invention' at time o, and we are concerned with its effects. We need not here assume that the economy was previously in a steady state; but we shall assume that the technique that is chosen for new processes after time o (chosen from the new technology) remains the dominant technique, for as far ahead as we shall go. As we know, there is a rise in the rate of interest at time o, but (since the wage is fixed) the higher rate remains unchanged thereafter. (In our usual notation, the rate of interest rises from r^* to r.)

All of the capital goods existing at time o belong to old processes. If these old processes continue to be carried through as planned, in spite of the rise in interest, their future net outputs will be unchanged (since the wage is fixed); so when they are discounted at the higher rate of interest, capital value must be reduced. Even if there are minor switches (or truncations) they can do no more than moderate the fall in capital value. There must thus in any case be a fall in capital value, from K_0^* (as we should naturally write it) to K_0.

The subsequent movement of capital value (K_T) can now be deduced, without lengthy calculation, from the rules that were established in Chapter III. The rate of interest is now equal to the rate of return on new processes (those started after time o), so the Social Accounting equation holds (as we there saw) without Discrepancy. The course of capital value will thus be given by the regular equation[1]

$$K_{T+1} - K_T = rK_T - Q_T$$

with the K_0, determined as explained, as initial condition. So there is just the initial fall, and then a regular rise—at a rate which may be described as the new (higher) rate of interest damped down by the Take-out.

For capital at cost, on the other hand, we are to value at constant prices, which may here be taken to be the prices ruling just before the 'invention' occurs. In view of the Fixwage assumption,

---

[1] I take the Social Accounting equation in the form appropriate to continuous time, thus suppressing the rQ which appeared in the 'week' formulae of Chapter III. (See above, p. 30.)

the only price that changes at time o is the rate of interest itself. Capital at cost is a backward-looking measure, so the Social Accounting equation may not hold for capital at cost without Discrepancy. If however it did hold without Discrepancy, we should have for capital at cost (C_T, as we may call it, in accordance with the notation of Chapter III)

$$C_{T+1} - C_T = r^*C_T - Q_T$$

with $C_0 = K_0^*$ as initial condition. Since r^* is the rate now being used for computation, r^* must take the place of r in the other formula. Though there is here no initial setback, the subsequent rate of growth is less, being describable as the *old* rate of interest damped down by the Take-out.

But now, what of the Discrepancy? As was shown in Chapter III, with a backward-looking measure Discrepancy arises at the termination of processes. There is a Discrepancy when the capital embodied in a process is valued at a rate of interest which is not that which belongs to the process (the yield of the process). In the present case, our computational rate of interest is that which ruled just before the 'invention', being therefore that which belonged to those which at that date were *modern* processes. On such processes, therefore, there is no discrepancy. But there may be a discrepancy (1) on still older processes, those which even before the present invention were already obsolescent (2) on the new processes started after time o. These, of course, raise quite separate questions.

The first discrepancy would certainly have to be allowed for, if we were measuring the capital invested in all processes consistently at cost—as, in the strict terms of the model, with all processes *mortal*, it would be perfectly possible to do. But, as was shown in the preceding chapter,[1] this is in application hardly practicable; for the beginnings of past processes (or what we should call those beginnings) are impossible to identify, and even if identifiable stretch so far back in time as to be practically irrelevant. We therefore concluded that the only cost measure which is usable is one that starts from a base date, and takes the *value of capital* at that base date as the base from which to reckon. If that method of valuation is applied to the present example, it will be seen that we do not need to attend to discrepancies on the older

---

[1] Above, p. 159.

processes, those which at the base date were already obsolescent. These discrepancies will already be absorbed in the K_0^*, which we have taken for our C_0. So they cause no trouble.

The other discrepancy also causes no trouble, so long as we confine attention to the calculation of capital at cost over a period that extends no further forward than the date when the first of the new processes, started at time o and after, comes to an end. That is to say, so long as we confine attention to the Early Phase of the Traverse. For discrepancy arises at the termination of processes, and during the Early Phase no new processes are being terminated.

So, *during the Early Phase*, the formula

$$C_{T+1} - C_T = r^* C_T - Q_T$$

does describe the course of capital at cost. And this, it will be noticed, is identically the same formula (with the same initial condition) as that which described the course of K_T^*, the *value of capital* on the reference path. All the time, during the Early Phase, capital at cost is what capital value would have been if the invention had not occurred.

So capital at cost, defined as we have been defining it, does seem to give a measure of capital which is unaffected by the 'inventions' that occur after its base date.[1] It does have this property *in a Fixwage model*. Not only in the short run, but also in the medium run, capital at cost (when properly reckoned) is invariant to technical change.

3. There are some further points, relating to the Fixwage path, which may be noticed before proceeding further.

According as capital is measured by value or at cost, there will be different meanings of the *rate of profit on capital*. The rate of profit on capital value is simply the rate of interest, or rate of return on modern processes; in a Fixwage model this changes when technology changes, but not otherwise. The rate of profit on capital at cost behaves quite differently. Since the latter is nearer

---

[1] The preceding argument will continue to hold even if there is a sequence of inventions after the base date, so long as we do not go beyond the point at which the first of the new processes, started after the base date, reaches its termination. Or, as we might say in more practical language, after the point at which the first of the *new* machines comes to be replaced.

to what business men, and statisticians, mean by profit on capital, we should notice what its properties are.

Assume, as before, that there is a single 'invention' at time o. Let π_T be the rate of profit, on capital at cost, at time T ($T \geqslant$ o). Then $\pi_T C_T = rK_T$. Initially, since $K_0 < C_0$, $\pi_0 < r$; the rate of profit on capital at cost is initially less than the rate of return on new processes. (That the obsolescent processes should drag down the average rate of profit is by no means surprising.) It will also usually[1] be true that $\pi_0 > r^*$; so there is some initial rise in π, but no more than a modest rise. Subsequently, however, since K_T has a higher growth rate than C_T, π_T will continue to increase; and the formulae seem to show that π_T will increase indefinitely.

But this is not so, because of the Discrepancy. It is a Discrepancy on new processes that has to be taken into account after the end of the Early Phase. In the Early Phase the capital invested in *fresh processes* (those begun at or after time o) is the same as it would have been on the reference path (the take-out being the same); the greater productivity of capital on the new-style processes does not yet affect the capital invested. In the Late Phase that ceases to be the case. Additional funds are now forthcoming from the completion of new-style processes; and these grow at a rate which depends on r, not on r^*. As time goes on, these funds, with their high growth rate, will become dominant. They do so, of course, only slowly; it takes much time before their dominance is established. But since the *ultimate* growth of C_T is the same as that of K_T, π_T will not increase indefinitely, but will tend to a limit. The limit, of course, is an asymptotic limit; but so, we have found, is the ultimate steady state itself, to which a Fixwage Traverse tends.

There remains the fact that the effect of the invention on the

---

[1] Suppose first that there are no minor switches. Then initial profit (rK_0) is the permanent annuity for which the *given* stream of net outputs (from the old processes) can be exchanged, at the rate of interest r; whether this is raised or lowered when r rises, depends on whether the exchange is mainly a matter of lending or of borrowing. If the old processes have what we have regarded as the normal form (an initial investment hump and subsequent utilization period of longer duration than the hump), most of the exchange will be lending (reinvestment of depreciation allowances). Thus profit will be raised, and the rate of profit in the sense of π_0 will be raised. If there are minor switches, it will of course be raised *a fortiori*.

Cf. the discussion of what is in substance the same point, in my *Value and Capital*, p. 188.

rate of profit, in the sense of π_T, is greatly dependent on T, the time of adjustment that is allowed. The initial effect is small; the ultimate effect, dimly perceivable in the distance, may be very large. We cannot allow ourselves, when we are working in terms of capital at cost, to think of a single effect of the invention on the rate of profit. To work in value terms is here much simpler; but that does not show that to work in cost terms is wrong.

4. I now turn to the Full Employment path, where the picture changes. For it is the value measure which here gets into the deeper water. The cost measure also encounters additional difficulties; but with it, if care is taken, rather more can be done.

On the Full Employment path, as we know, both wages and interest go on changing in the course of the Traverse; there are changes in capital value, due to these revaluations, going on all the time. There is not just a single revaluation (from K_0^* to K_0) as there was on the Fixwage path. It would be possible to calculate each revaluation, so as to present a sequence of capital values; but how much would it mean? The static expectations assumption, which we have allowed ourselves on some earlier occasions, is in the present application peculiarly hard to swallow. A sequence of capital values, in which each term is calculated on assumptions that are belied by later elements in the sequence, does not look like being worth the trouble of writing it down.

There is indeed an alternative—the sequence which is based on correct expectations, expectations of the wages and interest which in the course of the Traverse will be realized. But the place of this is in optimum theory; and that is not the kind of theory with which in this book we are concerned. In positive economics we must not endow our actors with perfect foresight; for to do so would abolish Time, which is our subject.

So, on the Full Employment path, not much can be done with capital value. Capital at cost, however, looks more promising. For with capital at cost we are valuing at base prices (now including wages as well as interest) which during the sequence are to be kept unchanged. We can avoid optimology, and yet have a sequence (C_T) that is self-consistent.

5. In order to calculate the course of capital at cost in a Full Employment Traverse, we can still make use of the rules of

Chapter III. The Social Accounting Equation will still hold, without Discrepancy (for the reasons previously given, which remain valid) during the Early Phase of the Traverse. Thus

$$C_{T+1} - C_T = r^*C_T - Q_T$$

or so it appears. We may still allow ourselves the initial condition $C_0 = K_0^*$; the old processes, valued at old wages and interest, still have the same capital value. All, therefore, seems as before; but there is a complication—a serious complication.

When the wage is variable, what is left for take-out depends on the wage; $Q_T = B_T - w_T A_T$. But for the calculation of capital at cost, on the principle to which we have come, the wage must be kept constant, at w_0; so what should appear in the formula is not the true take-out (Q_T) but the take-out adjusted for the change in wages. What we should write is therefore

$$C_{T+1} - C_T = r^*C_T - (B_T - w_0 A_T)$$
$$= r^*C_T - Q_T - (w_T - w_0)A_T.$$

If Q_T is given, as we have hitherto supposed, the course of capital at cost (*even* capital at cost) is not independent of the movement of wages.

This is important; but the nature of its importance should not be misunderstood. The concept of capital at cost (including the adjustment just indicated) is precisely what, in the last chapter, we advised the statistican to try to measure; for something of that character is the best, in the way of a volume measure, that he can hope to provide. We need not reject the measure because of the property just discovered. The measure is unscathed; but we do have to be very careful how we use it.

In a Fixwage system (we found) capital at cost behaves in the same way as capital value would have behaved in the absence of the technical change; $C_T = K_T^*$. On a Full Employment path, we now find, that ceases to be true. For the one, we have

$$C_{T+1} - C_T = r^*C_T - (B_T - w_0 A_T)$$

for the other

$$K_{T+1}^* - K_T^* = r^*K_T^* - (B_T^* - w_0 A_T)$$

for A_T and A_T^* are the same. Thus if we write $C_T = K_T^* - D_T$,

$$D_{T+1} - D_T = r^*D_T + (B_T - B_T^*)$$

with $D_0 = 0$. So D_T is the sum of the differences of final output, between actual path and reference path, between time o and time T, accumulated at the computational rate of interest. If $h > 1$, all of these differences will be positive; if $h < 1$, they will first be negative and then positive.[1] The correction can just as well be thought of as necessitated by the *actual* course of output, as by the actual movement of wages.

When the matter is looked at in this light, we see that it was possible to avoid a correction in the Fixwage case, simply because of our assumption of unchanged take-out—that Q_T is the same along actual as along reference path, being unaffected (over the length of time considered) by the change in productivity. How convenient an assumption for calculation this is we have learned from experience. But of course *in general* it cannot be maintained. There is in general no reason (whether the wage is fixed or variable) why the behaviour of capital at cost should be the same after an improvement in productivity, as it would have been if the improvement had not occurred. It must be expected that technical improvement will have a feed-back effect on quantity of capital, even though quantity of capital is measured in volume terms. By using a volume measure, we avoid the immediate re-valuation; but we cannot hope to avoid the effect of the change in the course of output, when that occurs.

More than this, however, is involved. Saving (or net investment), as measured in the prices of its own period, and then deflated by a price-index to a base period, does not measure the increment of capital at cost. This is very important; it may well be one of the main things that cause trouble.

By working in terms of take-out, we have avoided the necessity of measuring saving; we have avoided saving, because we have avoided profits. On the Fixwage path, we had profit as rK_T; but on the Full Employment path (when that is not in a steady state) K_T itself becomes a somewhat nebulous quantity. Let us cut the knot (as we did in sect. 3 of this chapter) by writing profit $\pi_T C_T$—

---

[1] See Chapter IX above. For the explicit calculation of D_T, it is simplest to take the first difference of the D-equation, for the first difference of the right-hand side is $x_T - x_T^*$, which we know—by equation (12.2) in Appendix—is $(\alpha - 1)G^T - \beta u^T$. The second-order difference equation is easily solved, since not only D_0 but also D_1 is zero. But it does not seem worth while to print the algebra.

without worrying too much how π_T is determined. We can then put

$$\text{Total saving} = \pi_T C_T - Q_T = S_T \quad \text{(say)}$$

(for saving out of wages has already been allowed for in Q_T itself). For the increment of capital at cost, we have (as before)

$$
\begin{aligned}
C_{T+1} - C_T &= r^* C_T - Q_T - (w_T - w_0) A_T \\
&= S_T - (\pi_T - r^*) C_T - (w_T - w_0) A_T
\end{aligned}
$$

so that there are these *two* adjustments to be made before we can pass from saving to 'accumulation'.

In a steady state, with constant wages, each of the two adjustments will vanish, so that equality between saving and accumulation (in the cost sense) will be preserved. Out of the steady state, adjustments are in principle required on both counts. Neither profit rate nor wage rate will correspond with those of the base date, those at which we ought to be valuing. Though we have found these discrepancies by working at our model, there seems no reason why they should not have quite general validity.

It is indeed possible, as many contemporary economists have discovered, to construct a 'pseudo' steady state in which the 'rate of technical progress' is constant. If this means that π_T is constant, we have only to take a base which incorporates that same rate of technical progress, so as to make $r^* = \pi_T$, and the first correction becomes unnecessary. If we also measure labour supply in 'efficiency units', supposing that the number of efficiency units per worker is continually increasing, wage per worker may be rising, while wage per efficiency unit remains unchanged; the second correction is then unnecessary. This, in some ways, is very convenient; but its convenience does not, I think, extend very far. It enables us to do easy exercises on the comparison of steady states, interpreted as 'pseudo' steady states; but it gives no help on the Traverse from one such steady state to another. If we are always to be in a steady state, even a 'pseudo' steady state, it is only one steady state that we must always be in; we can never get from one to another.

The economist may imagine that he is in a steady state; the statistician is untempted by such imaginations. The true increment in real capital at cost, if properly calculated by the statistician, is likely to differ from the apparent increment (saving, deflated for price-changes) by significant adjustments under each of the heads that have just been mentioned. It is the adjustment for wages which is likely to be the more important. In a progressive economy, with wages rising, the increment of capital at cost is almost certainly much lower than appears from social accounting statistics. A great deal of saving is needed to prevent the volume of capital from declining. It should cause no surprise if it were found that there were happily progressive economies, with rising real incomes, in which the volume of capital was declining; the rise in real incomes would then seem to be 'due' to technical progress, and to technical progress alone. But that would not mean that the saving was unnecessary; it would be necessary, to keep the 'real' wage fund rising, so that full employment could be maintained with the rising real wages.

These may seem to be paradoxical statements; but are they so paradoxical? Do we not find ourselves nowadays, when we are thinking of quite practical forecasting, coming to think of the problem in something like these terms?

XV

THE PRODUCTION FUNCTION

1. I COME at last to the nub of the Controversy: the Production Function itself. Product as a function of Labour and Capital applied—a function that is unchanged with given technology, but changes when technology changes. So static a concept does not fit at all readily into our present line of thought; it does not belong to that line of thought, so I shall treat it rather briefly. There are however ways in which the work we have been doing can be made to throw some light upon it.

I have elsewhere[1] explained what I mean by static theory. Its characteristic is that 'the equilibrium of the current period is taken to be determined by current parameters only', so that the current period 'can be treated as self-contained'. The Production Function, as commonly used, is without doubt a static concept in this sense. 'Product', 'labour', 'capital' and 'technology' are from its point of view all *current* concepts.

How is 'capital' to be made a current concept? The forward- and backward-looking measures of capital, which we have been distinguishing, are time-oriented; into a static model they will not fit. The 'capital' that is to figure in the production function must be neither forward- nor backward-looking; it must live in the present and belong to the present. Now if capital (against what we have learned to think of as its essence) is to be kept in the present, it must be interpreted as *physical capital*; and it had better be interpreted as physical *fixed* capital—'machines'. (Working capital is inherently uncomfortable in a static model; so by most production function theorists it tends to be forgotten.) In order to remind ourselves that it is physical fixed capital which is here to be the meaning of 'capital', I shall henceforward call it not 'capital' but *equipment*.

'Product' also must be made a current concept. So no distinction can be made, in this static model, between investment and consumption; we are not entitled to ask what happens to anything when the current period is over. Investment goods are

[1] *Capital and Growth*, Ch. III, esp. p. 32.

goods that are acquired for one purpose, consumption goods are goods that are acquired for another. That is all the difference that there is between them—all the difference that shows. Similarly in a static model there is no depreciation and no obsolescence. So 'product' is gross product—consumption *plus* gross investment.

Product, then, is made by labour and equipment. The equipment, of course, is heterogeneous. This has often been thought to be a difficulty, but I do not think it is. Heterogeneity of labour is a much more formidable difficulty, but—as is common practice, a practice that has been followed in this book—I shall assume it away. I shall also assume that the product is homogeneous.

2. We may now proceed by stages. First of all, take the Equipment to be given. (As long as it is given, it does not matter that it is heterogeneous.)

Some of the Equipment will be specific, requiring a particular complement of labour to work it; some less specific, so that it can be operated more or less intensively. Only on the second kind of Equipment does labour have a definite marginal product; all we can say about the first is that the marginal product lies between the whole product and zero. Equilibrium requires that the marginal product should be equal in all uses. This is attained (with homogeneous product[1]) if the wage of labour is equal in all uses. The wage will then be equal to the marginal product—with the understanding that on a specific machine this can mean no more than that the wage must not swallow up the whole product if the machine is to stay in production. Thus with given Equipment we have a definite marginal productivity curve of labour, and an equilibrium wage that is equal to marginal product.

The share of Equipment in the total product will then be determined as a rent—'quasi-rent' as Marshall would have called it. It is nevertheless true, under these same assumptions, that Equipment also is getting its marginal product—for the following reason.

The change in Equipment, needed for the determination of a marginal product, can at this stage be no more than a *virtual* change. It is not anything which does happen; it is something we

---

[1] With homogeneous product there is no opportunity for monopolistic distortions. There may be for monopsonistic; but it is not a strong assumption, with homogeneous labour, that these do not occur.

suppose to happen by an ideal experiment. Along the marginal productivity curve of Equipment, Equipment varies—without changing its character. This can only happen, if the machines are heterogeneous, if the quantity of each machine is increased in the same proportion; the equipment 'bundle' will then have constant composition. So on this particular path, Equipment is made homogeneous, and labour and product we have already made homogeneous. The conditions for a production function in the regular form thus appear to be established. And such a production function (too much tied down to be able to generate large-scale economies) can hardly fail to exhibit constant returns to scale. If it does so, it will follow that Equipment is getting its marginal product—by Euler's Theorem on the homogeneous function of the first degree. No more need be said.

It will be noticed that in this construction we need make no assumption about the units in which Equipment is measured. So long as the rule about constant proportions is maintained, any unit can be taken. If the unit were doubled in size, its marginal product would be halved; the share of Equipment, in the total product, would remain as before. The static production function is intact.

It will also be noticed that this is a production function which (in Marshall's sense) is 'short-period'. This is what it should be. We get into endless trouble if we try to repeat the construction for anything analogous to the 'long-period' of Marshall. That, I have become convinced, is not the way the Production Function should be used.

3. We do much better to proceed directly to a sequence—dealing with it as well as it can be, by a static method. We then see at once that in the subsequent period there will be a change in Equipment, new machines being added and old machines discarded. This change, *in general*, will be a different change from the virtual change that we previously considered. The machines will not be keeping their old proportions; so the increment in Equipment is a *different factor* from the initial stock. Thus, for the analysis of growth—even of the first steps of growth—we need (at the least) a three-factor production function. Product must now be a function of Labour, Old Equipment, and New Equipment.

There is indeed a special case in which Old Equipment and New Equipment are the same. It is a case with which we are very familiar—the Steady State. The Steady State is the only state where a two-factor production function will fit. But it is not a useful construction, even for the analysis of steady states, which, to be interesting, must be a comparative analysis. The Equipment which figures in one steady state and that which figures in another will not (in interesting comparisons) be the same Factor.

For an economy which is not in a steady state, New Equipment and Old Equipment will be different. They will be different even if, as between our two successive periods, there is no change in technology. For the new machines may be supposed to be adjusted to that *modern* technology, while some proportion (at least) of the Old Machines will not be. Even with no *present* change in technology, we still need the three-factor Function.

Even in terms of the three-factor Function, labour will still be getting its marginal product, for the preceding argument continues to hold. It is much more tricky to prove that New Equipment will be getting its marginal product. There may be some senses in which that is true, but I shall not investigate the matter, for I do not think we need it. The distribution of the earnings of Equipment between Old and New is not a particularly interesting question. It is enough to consider the effect of the New Equipment—the appearance, and then the growth, of New Equipment —on the earnings of labour, and on the relative share of labour in the total product.

We know very well that with a two-factor production function (under constant returns to scale) an increase in the supply of factor A must raise the marginal productivity curve of factor B; so with unchanged supply of factor B the earnings of factor B must rise. The condition for the relative share of B to rise is that the elasticity of substitution between A and B should be less than 1. When we pass to the case of three factors, it is more convenient to work with the reciprocal of my old elasticity of substitution, which I have elsewhere[1] suggested might be called the elasticity

---

[1] 'Elasticity of substitution again: substitutes and complements' (*Oxford Economic Papers*, Nov. 1970). In this article I have set out the algebra of the three-factor case in detail—in what is (I hope) at last a satisfactory form.

All that is necessary for the present purpose is to observe that (with x for quantity of product and a_1, a_2, a_3 for quantities of the factors) the elasticity of complementarity between factor 1 and factor 2, being the reciprocal of the old

of complementarity. A rise in the supply of A must then raise the marginal productivity of B and C, taken together; but it may not raise that of B (or that of C) when it is taken alone. It is possible that all elasticities of complementarity between pairs of factors are positive; if that is the case, but only if that is the case, the increase in A will increase the earnings of B and of C. If the elasticity of complementarity between A and B is greater than 1, the relative share of B in the total product will be raised; if it is positive but less than 1, the earnings of B will rise, but its relative share will decline; if it is negative (and it can be negative) the earnings of B will decline. This last is the case when A and B are strong substitutes. It is not possible that more than one of the three pairs (AB, AC, BC) should be strong substitutes; either all are complements, or one pair are strong substitutes. The possibility of strong substitution, in this sense, is the additional thing which has to be allowed for in the case of three factors.

We here take New Equipment to be factor A, and labour to be factor B. What has just been shown is that even in static theory, when that is properly interpreted, the whole range of alternatives is open. It is possible (1) that the new equipment may be strongly complementary with labour, so that its appearance raises labour's relative share, or (2) that it may be weakly complementary, so that the earnings of labour increase, though the relative share of labour declines, or (3) that it may substitute labour, in such a way that its appearance causes the earnings of labour to decline. Now this is just what we have found by our neo-Austrian method. For suppose that we were analysing an economy which was in the middle of a Traverse from one technology to another; and that we take as the current period, for static analysis, a single 'year'—

Theory of Wages elasticity of substitution, is defined as $(x\, x_{12})/(x_1\, x_2)$—using suffixes for partial derivatives. We know from Euler that

$$-a_1 x_{11} = a_2 x_{12} + a_3 x_{13}$$

and similarly for x_{22} and x_{33}. The usual maximization condition shows that x_{11}, x_{22}, x_{33} are all negative. It follows at once that not more than one of x_{12}, x_{13}, x_{23} can be negative; so that not more than one of the elasticities of complementarity ($c_{12} \dots$) can be negative.

The condition for k_2 (the relative share of factor 2) to increase when a_1 increases is simply that $\partial k_2/\partial a_1 > 0$. $k_2 = a_2 x_2/x$; so that with a_2 constant, this requires that

$$(\partial/\partial a_1)(x_2/x) = (x_{12}/x) - (x_1\, x_2/x^2) > 0$$

whence $c_{12} > 1$.

such that there is no change in technology to that year from the year preceding, nor from that year to the year after. Statically considered, there is no change in technology; but there has been a change in the past, and the economy is not yet fully adjusted to it. There will then (we know) be years, in the course of a Traverse which is strongly forward-biased, when the appearance of New Equipment will result in a fall in (real) wages, though there will also be years when its appearance has a favourable effect. This is consistent with what we find if we proceed by Production Function—or what we should find if we used that analysis correctly.

Though the results which are got by the two approaches are consistent, it may reasonably be claimed that the neo-Austrian approach is richer; it gives us a deeper understanding. This is not only because it offers some comprehension of the whole of a process of adaptation—not just snapshots of stages, which is all we can get from the static method. Still more important is the inability of the static method to relate the process of growth to saving and investment. It does not work in terms of saving and investment; for it works with Equipment, not with Capital; it is negligent of Capital in any accounting sense, so it is at the best no more than a part of a coherent growth model.

This is the explanation of that particular difference between 'schools' which is generally found so puzzling. According to Saving-Investment theories (and ours is in this respect a Saving-Investment theory) real wages depend on saving; in Production Function theories no such effect appears. The reason is that Production Function theories treat New Equipment as an independent variable; in their New Equipment (magnitude and composition) the effect of saving is concealed. Many other things also are concealed; so New Equipment, the increment of Equipment, is among the least suitable of all macro-economic magnitudes to be treated as an independent variable.[1] That is really what is wrong with the Production Function.

4. There is still one question, associated with the Production Function, which remains to be considered; it is a question which the reader will no doubt feel it is incumbent on me to try to answer. Is anything left, after what has been said in this book, of that old classification of invention-bias, that which I introduced

[1] I say 'among the least suitable', for it has a rival—the quantity of money.

in 1932, the 'Hicks' classification[1] as in numerous articles it has been called? Can it be brought into relation with the classification used in this book—the forward- and backward-biases over which we have taken so much trouble? It was shown, in Chapter VI above, that there is a relation beetwen our new classification and the 'Harrod' classification. If a change in technique is unbiased, in our sense, if saving is a constant proportion of profits (or of total income), and if there is full employment of a labour supply that is increasing at a constant growth rate, there will be a long-run tendency to a new equilibrium in which the rate of interest is the same as it was before the technical change, and in which distribution, in the sense of (rK/wA) is the same as before. From one steady state to another the Harrod condition is satisfied, for a change in technique which exhibits (our) lack of bias. That is how the Harrod classification fits in.

The 'Hicks' classification can hardly have the same reference, for when it was put forward the steady state, with constant growth rate, had not come into use.[2] It can have nothing to do with an equilibrium that is reached by saving, after what we can now see to be a long process of saving. If there is any sense in it, it must refer to a much shorter run.

It can hardly refer to the shortest of short runs—the Preparatory Phase, as we have called it[3]—the stage at which final output is still the output of old processes, so that, unless there is change in take-out (and there seems, at that stage, little reason why there should be), the real wage should be unchanged. It must refer to the stage after that, which is the first in which the bias has an influence. A strong forward bias (we have found) will at that stage, full employment being maintained, lead to a fall in wages; so it does correspond with what would have been called a strongly labour-saving invention, which would result, according to the old theory, in a fall in labour's *absolute* share. When there is no more than a weak bias, there will at the same stage be a rise in wages, and probably also in profits—again conformably. What does not seem to be marked out in the same manner is anything which corresponds to 'Hicks-neutrality'. We have not said, and on present

[1] *Theory of Wages* (1932), Ch. 6. The text is reprinted in the 1962 edition.
[2] The attempt at a growth theory which was made in Chapters 9 and 10 of *Theory of Wages* appeared more dismal than it need have done because of the lack of any steady state, other than the stationary state, with which to work.
[3] Above, p. 90.

principles we cannot say, that if there is no bias, distribution between labour and capital will at that same stage be unchanged. For at that stage the system is not in a steady state; and on our principles it is only in a steady state that distribution is unambiguous. Only in the steady state can we unambiguously determine the size of profits. Out of the steady state the profit that is allocated to a particular period depends on expectations, such as are in practice expressed by conventions about depreciation; there is no such convention that is unambiguously right. So we cannot expect to find that relative shares are determined by the real characteristics of processes, such as the model of this book has tried to take into account.

A reminder that the Distribution of Income is not, in the short-run, a well-founded economic concept is perhaps not the least important point which has emerged from our enquiry.

APPENDIX

THE MATHEMATICS OF TRAVERSE

1. THERE were several occasions, in Part II of this book, when I advanced propositions which were not intuitively obvious, though I hope they will have seemed to 'make sense'. Proofs can be given and this is the place to give them.

It is not my intention to give in this Appendix a continuous mathematical treatment, which can be read, in place of the text of Part II, by those who prefer such a version. The Appendix is complementary to the text, not a substitute for it. It will nevertheless be convenient to begin with a summary of the assumptions that underlie the analysis of Chapters VII–XI. This is chiefly for reference in what follows.

2. The model has been reduced to bare bones. There is just one original factor (labour) and one final product. A *technique* (a_t, b_t) is a process, of unit size, extending from $t = 0$ to $t = \Omega$, by which a stream of labour inputs (a) is converted into a stream of homogeneous outputs (b). We begin from a steady state, in which wage (w) and rate of interest (r) are constant, and in which just one such technique is used; it is a condition of equilibrium, in that steady state, that the rate of interest should equal the rate of return on the technique. The *ex-ante* capitalized value of the process, at wage w and rate of interest r, must therefore be zero;

$$k_0 = \sum_0^\Omega q_t R^{-t} = 0, \qquad (2.1)$$

where $\qquad q_t = b_t - wa_t \quad$ and $\quad R = 1 + r.$

Then at a certain date (called $T = 0$) a new technique is introduced, which at the old steady state rate of wages has a higher rate of return. This new technique is adopted for new processes, begun in week 0 and subsequently; but meanwhile old processes are continued, as long as it is profitable to continue them. We have to determine the path of the economy from $T = 0$ onwards. We do so by comparing this *actual* path with a reference path—that which would have been followed if the technical change had not occurred, so that the old steady state had continued. Magnitudes which refer to the old technique, to the old steady state, or to the reference path, will henceforward be starred.

3. x_T then denotes the number of starts of unit processes, on the actual path, in week T; x_T^* the corresponding number of starts of (old) processes on the reference path. Then on the reference path, where old processes alone are used, the employment of labour $= A_T^* = \sum_0^\Omega x_{T-t}^* a_t^*$; output $= B_T^* = \sum_0^\Omega x_{T-t}^* b_t^*$; while net output (or take-out) $= Q_T^* = B_t^* - w A_T^* = \sum_0^\Omega x_{T-t}^* q_t^*$. Along the actual path, for $0 < T < \Omega$, $A_T = \sum_0^T x_{T-t} a_t + \sum_{T+1}^\Omega x_{T-t}^* a_T^*$; and similarly for B_T and Q_T.

Since the reference path is a steady state, $x_T^* = x_0^* G^T$, where $G = 1 + g$, and g is the steady state growth rate. The reference path remains fixed in all subsequent discussion; x_0^* is simply a scale factor, so we shall often allow ourselves to set it equal to unity.

The actual path is calculated (i) as a Fixwage path (ii) as a Full Employment path. On the Fixwage path w is constant, so $x(T)$ is determined from $Q_T = Q_T^*$; on the Full Employment path, $x(T)$ is determined from $A_T = A_T^*$, while w_T (now variable) is then determined from $Q_T = Q_T^*$.

4. *The Standard Assumptions.* To make the problem more tractable, it is assumed (in Chapters VII–X and in sects. 5–17 following)

(i) that each technique has a Simple Profile, with a Constructional Period, lasting m weeks, and a Utilizational Period, lasting $\Omega - m$ weeks. In the former, there is no output, but input is at a constant rate, which we will (for the moment) express as a_0 per week. In the latter, input is at the constant rate a_1, while output is also at a constant rate, which it will again do no harm to write equal to unity.

(ii) that the durations (m and Ω) are the same in old and new techniques, though the input-coefficients (a_0 and a_1) are of course different.

(iii) that Ω is an integral multiple of m.

With these assumptions, it can be proved that it is permissible to simplify by taking the constructional period as unit period (*m weeks* equals one *year*). The proof is the same for Fixwage path as for Full Employment path. I set it out for the Full Employment path.

5. *The construction period as unit period.* We are to determine $x(T)$ from the Full Employment condition $A_T = A_T^* = A_0^* G^T$. Since employment on processes started before time 0 is the same on actual path as on reference path, it is sufficient to compare employment on processes started after time 0—*fresh* processes. We can then distinguish

(i) a Preparatory Phase (PP) during which all labour employed on fresh processes is constructional labour; it lasts for m weeks, from week 0 to week $m - 1$.

(ii) an Early Phase (EP), lasting from m to Ω, when both constructional and utilizational labour are employed on *fresh* processes, though there is still some labour not employed on such processes.

(iii) a Late Phase (LP) when all labour is employed on fresh processes.

The condition $A_T = A_T^*$ thus takes three forms:

(PP) $$a_0 \sum_0^T x_t = a_0^* \sum_0^T x_t^* \qquad (5.1)$$

(EP) $$a_0 \sum_{T-m+1}^T x_t + a_1 \sum_0^{T-m} x_t = a_0^* \sum_{T-m+1}^T x_t^* + a_1^* \sum_0^{T-m} x_t^*$$

(LP) $$a_0 \sum_{T-m+1}^T x_t + a_1 \sum_{T-\Omega+1}^{T-m} x_t = A_T^*.$$

These equations hold for any T within their respective stretches, so we may take first differences:

(PP) $$a_0 x_T = a_0^* x_T^* \qquad (5.2)$$
(EP) $$a_0 x_T - (a_0 - a_1)x_{T-m} = a_0^* x_T^* - (a_0^* - a_1^*)x_{T-m}^*$$
(LP) $$a_0 x_T - (a_0 - a_1)x_{T-m} + a_1 x_{T-\Omega} = A_T^* - A_{T-1}^* = gA_{T-1}^*.$$

Now write y_T for x_T/x_T^*, and remember that $x_T^* = G^T$. Dividing by G^T,

(PP) $$a_0 y_T = a_0^* \qquad (5.3)$$
(EP) $$a_0 y_T - (a_0 - a_1)G^{-m}y_{T-m} = a_0^* - (a_0^* - a_1^*)G^{-m}$$
(LP) $$a_0 y_T - (a_0 - a_1)G^{-m}y_{T-m} + a_1 G^{-\Omega}y_{T-\Omega} = gA_0^* G^{-1}.$$

In all forms of (5.3) the right-hand side is a constant. Thus in (PP) y is constant; and in (EP) y_T is linearly dependent on y_{T-m}. Thus from m to $2m$, y is constant; again from $2m$ to $3m$; and so on. With Ω an integral multiple of m, the same will hold in (LP). Thus we may take the 'year' of m weeks as our unit period; and confine attention to the determination of y in successive 'years'.

This is what we shall do in all later work on the Standard Case. Within the 'year', since y_T is constant, x_T simply follows the reference path. So we may now interpret x_T to mean the total number of starts within the year, and re-write equations (5.1) putting $m = 1$, and letting the utilizational period last for n years. Then

(PP) $$a_0 x_0 = a_0^* x_0^* \qquad (5.4)$$

(EP) $$a_0 x_T + a_1 \sum_0^{T-1} x_t = a_0^* x_T^* + a_1^* \sum_0^{T-1} x_t^*$$

(LP) $$a_0 x_T + a_1 \sum_{T-n}^{T-1} x_t = A_T^* = A_0^* G^T$$

with the (EP) equation holding for $T = 1, \ldots, n$, the (LP) for $T > n$. This is the form which we shall use in sects. 6–17 following.

It is evident that the Fixwage equation Q_T can be treated in exactly the same way, giving equations for x_T which are the same as (5.4) except that q's are written in place of a's.

6. *Steady State comparisons.* When the Profile takes the form to which we have now come

	year 0	year 1 to n
Input	a_0	a_1
Output	0	1
Net output	$q_0 = - wa_0$	$q_1 = 1 - wa_1$

the equilibrium condition ($k_0 = 0$) is much simplified. For now

$$k_0 = \sum_0^n q_t R^{-t} = - wa_0 + (1 - wa_1) \sum_1^n R^{-t},$$

so that if we put $(1/r_n)$ for $\sum_1^n R^{-t}$, we have, from $k_0 = 0$,

$$(1/w) = a_0 r_n + a_1. \qquad (6.1)$$

The equilibrium condition can thus be expressed as equality between value and cost, r_n being interpreted as the *gross* rate of return. It is obvious that $(1/r_n)$ diminishes with r, so that r_n increases (monotonically) with r, being equal to $(1/n)$ when $r = 0$. And further, since $\sum_1^\infty R^{-t} = (1/r)$, $r_n > r$.

In a steady state,

$$B_T = \sum_0^n x_{T-t} b_t = \sum_1^n x_{T-t} = x_0 \left(\sum_1^n G^{-t} \right) G^T.$$

Thus if we define g_n (the gross rate of growth), analogously with r_n, so that $(1/g_n) = \sum_1^n G^{-t}$, we have $B_T = x_0 (1/g_n) G^T$. In the same way,

$$A_T = \sum_0^n x_{T-t} a_t = a_0 x_T + a_1 \sum_1^n x_{T-t} = x_0 (a_0 + a_1/g_n) G^T.$$

Thus for *steady state productivity*,

$$(B_T/A_T) = 1/(a_0 g_n + a_1), \qquad (6.2)$$

which is a constant, as it should be.

On the reference path, where $Q_T^* = B_T^* - wA_T^*$, Q_T^* cannot be positive unless $(1/w)(B_T^*/A_T^*) > 1$. So it follows, from (6.1) and (6.2), that $r_n^* > g_n^*$, whence $r^* > g^*$. Since the new technique is more profitable than the old, $r > r^*$; so $r > r^* > g^*$; and (under standard assumptions) $r_n > r_n^* > g_n^*$.

g^* is also the growth rate of A_T^*; so that on the Full Employment path where $A_T = A_T^*$, g^* ($= g$) is also the growth rate of A_T. (Thus $g_n = g_n^*$.) The Full Employment path cannot reach a steady state unless at this given growth rate, so that in the steady state, if it is reached, (6.2) must be satisfied. Then the ratio of productivities,

$$(B_T/A_T) \mid (B_T^*/A_T^*) = (a_0^* g_n + a_1^*) \mid (a_0 g_n + a_1). \qquad (6.3)$$

Since g_n is a function of g, this ratio is a function of g; it is the Index of Improvement $I(g)$. The relation between $I(g)$ and the corresponding Index $I(r)$ is discussed in Chapter VI. We put $a_0^*/a_0 = h$; and $(a_1^*/a_1) = H$. On the Fixwage path $Q_T = Q_T^*$; Q_T^* has the given growth rate g^*, so Q_T must have this same growth rate. As will be shown in sect. 8, the Fixwage path cannot converge to a steady state with this growth rate; it does however converge (asymptotically) to a steady state with growth rate r.

7. *Convergence (Full Employment path).* I begin with the Full Employment path, proving that under standard assumptions, a sequence that is determined by our (LP) equation (5.4) will converge to a steady state, under one condition, which we shall assume, namely that $a_0 > a_1$.

It is immediately evident that

$$\text{(LP)} \qquad a_0 x_T + a_1 \sum_{T-n}^{T-1} x_t = A_0^* G^T$$

has an 'equilibrium' solution $x_T = \bar{x} G^T$, with $\bar{x}$ positive. Put $x_T = \bar{x} G^T + \xi_T$. Then

$$a_0 \xi_T + a_1 \sum_{1}^{n} \xi_{T-t} = 0 \qquad (7.1)$$

Taking the first difference (forward, as is here more convenient)

$$a_0 \xi_{T+1} = (a_0 - a_1)\xi_T + a_1 \xi_{T-n}. \qquad (7.2)$$

This is a difference equation which can be treated in various ways; it will be most instructive to proceed by the general method. Substituting $\xi_T = C\lambda^T$, we get the characteristic equation

$$a_0 \lambda^{n+1} = (a_0 - a_1)\lambda^n + a_1 \qquad (7.3)$$

of which $\lambda = 1$ is clearly a root, as it should be. It is easily verified that (7.3) has no repeated root, and that it has no root (other than 1) with modulus equal to 1. The solution of (7.2) is therefore of the form

$$\xi_T = C_0 + \sum_{r=1}^{r=n} \lambda_r^n, \qquad (7.4)$$

where 1, λ_r are the roots of (7.3).

Since none of the λ_r have modulus equal to 1, we have only to show that none has modulus > 1, and we have proved that $\xi_T \to C_0$. But if it were the case that some root had modulus > 1, it would follow from (7.4) that ξ_T would 'explode', increasing (or diminishing) without limit for large T. It is directly obvious from (7.2) that this cannot happen.

For it is shown by (7.2) that every ξ is a weighted average of two previous ξ's in the sequence. The initial ξ's have been determined by (PP) and (EP); so in (LP) they can be taken as given. ξ_{n+1} must lie between the greatest and least of these initial values; and so, by like reasoning, must each successive ξ that follows it. 'Explosion' is therefore excluded. It follows that ξ_T converges to C_0; and by (7.1) C_0 must be zero.

So, provided that $a_0 > a_1$, x_T converges to $\bar{x}G^T$. The condition does not seem unreasonable[1]; it should however be emphasized that it is a necessary, as well as sufficient, condition. For if it were the case that $a_0 < a_1$, (7.2) could be written

$$a_1\xi_{T-n} = a_0\xi_T + (a_1 - a_0)\xi_{T-1}$$

so that each ξ would be a weighted average of *later* ξ's in the sequence. Exactly the same argument as the preceding could then be used to show that the sequence must converge *backwards*. Earlier values must tend to be nearer together than later values. So the sequence must explode.

Since it is impossible that starts should be negative, what this means is that it *must* sometime become impossible, if $a_0 < a_1$, to complete the processes which have been begun.

8. *Convergence (Fixwage path)*. I proceed at once to the (LP) version of $Q_T = Q_T^*$, which may obviously be written

$$q_0 x_T + q_1 \sum_1^n x_{T-t} = Q_T^* = Q_0^* G^T.$$

As before, this has a solution $x_T = \bar{x}G^T$; but here this is *not* the solution to which the sequence converges. For the corresponding equation to (7.1)

$$q_0 \xi_T + q_1 \sum_1^n \xi_{T-t} = 0 \qquad (8.1)$$

[1] For discussion, see pp. 104–5 above.

has quite different properties from (7.1). For while a_0 is definitely positive, q_0 is definitely negative.

We have, however, the efficiency equation $k_0 = 0$ (since the technique is a dominant technique). Putting this in the form

$$q_0 + q_1 \sum_1^n R^{-t} = 0 \qquad (8.2)$$

it shows that CR^T is a solution of (8.1). Put $\xi_T = \eta_T R^T$. Then, from (8.1) and (8.2),

$$\eta_T = \left(\sum_1^n \eta_{T-t} R^{-t} \right) \Big/ \left(\sum_1^n R^{-t} \right)$$

of which a constant η is evidently a solution. But this again shows that each η is a weighted average of previous η's, with positive weights. So (by the argument of sect. 7, which will be found to apply[1]), η_T converges to a constant. How that constant is determined we shall be seeing in sect. 11. It obviously does not have to be zero.

It follows, finally, that

$$x_T R^{-T} = \bar{x}(G/R)^T + \eta_T.$$

As T increases $(G/R)^T$ tends to zero; so $x_T R^{-T}$ tends to the constant which we have identified. The ultimate equilibrium, of the path determined by $Q_T = Q_T^*$, is a steady state at growth rate r, the rate of return on the new technique. But it is only approached asymptotically.

No additional condition (such as $a_0 > a_1$) other than those included in the *standard* assumptions, is needed for this result.

(Chapter VIII)

9. *The Fixwage path (Early Phase).* Since the Early Phase of a path is determined by a first-order difference equation, there is no difficulty in working it out completely. We begin, as always, with the rate of starts (x_T). Once we have this, output (B_T) and employment (A_T) follow easily.

The (PP) and (EP) versions of $Q_T = Q_T^*$ are

$$q_0 x_0 = q_0^* x_0^* \quad \text{and} \quad q_0 x_T + q_1 \sum_0^{T-1} x_t = q_0^* x_0^* + q^* \sum_0^{T-1} x_t^*.$$

From the latter, taking the first difference,

$$q_0 x_T - (q_0 - q_1) x_{T-1} = q_0^* x_T^* - (q_0^* - q_1^*) x_{T-1}^*.$$

[1] For further detail, see sect. 20 below.

With Simple Profiles $q_0 = -wa_0$ and $q_1 = 1 - wa_1$; so

$$(q_0^*/q_0) = (a_0^*/a_0) = h, \quad \text{and} \quad q_1/(-q_0) = r_n,$$

the gross rate of return. Put $R_n = 1 + r_n$, according to our usual convention. The differenced equation may thus be re-written

$$-x_T + R_n x_{T-1} = h[-x_T^* + R_n^* x_{T-1}^*].$$

Now $x_T^* = x_0^* G^T$; and, as we have seen, since x_0^* is just a constant scale factor, it will do no harm if we set it equal to unity. Finally, therefore,

$$\text{(PP)} \quad x_0 = h \quad \text{and} \quad \text{(EP)} \quad -x_T + R_n x_{T-1} = h(R_n^* - G)G^{T-1}. \tag{9.1}$$

It is immediately evident that the solution of (9.1) is of the form

$$x_T = \alpha G^T + \beta R_n^T, \tag{9.2}$$

where α and β are constants. Substituting in (9.1 EP) we have

$$\alpha = h(R_n^* - G)/(R_n - G) = h(r_n^* - g)/(r_n - g),$$

while from (9.1 PP) $\alpha + \beta = h$.

As shown in sect. 6, $r_n > r_n^* > g$; it follows that α is positive and β is positive, while $R_n > G$. Thus x_T, which begins at h, thereafter steadily rises; and rises more rapidly than x_T^*, on the reference path.

10. The construction cost of the new machines, produced in year T, is $a_0 x_T$; that of the machines which *would have been* produced is $a_0^* x_T^*$. The difference, being the increment in gross investment, *measured at cost*, is proportional to

$$x_T - h x_T^* = \beta(R_n^T - G^T).$$

This is zero when $T = 0$ and thereafter steadily rises.

When, however, the same increment is taken in terms of output-capacity, it is

$$x_T - x_T^* = (\alpha - 1)G^T + \beta R_n^T = (h - 1)G^T + \beta(R_n^T - G^T).$$

Save when $h < 1$, this also increases steadily. But if $h < 1$ (the *strong forward bias*) $x_T - x_T^*$ is the sum of two terms, one negative and one positive. At $T = 0$, the negative dominates; but the positive term has the higher growth rate, so *in the end* it must win.

The increment in final output $(B_T - B_T^*)$ now follows at once. With Simple Profiles $b_0 = 0$, while $b_1 = 1$. So $B_T - B_T^*$ is simply the sum of the increments in output capacity $(x_t - x_t^*)$ up to $T - 1$. The implications of this are examined in the text of Chapter VIII.

The increment in employment $(A_T - A_T^*)$ is proportional to the increment in final output; so it behaves in the same way.

11. *The Late Phase of the Fixwage path.* I am unable to give an analysis of the Late Phase of the path in at all a comparable manner. We know (from sect. 8) that it converges to a steady state with a growth rate r; so that $x_T R^{-T}$ converges to a constant. Now it will be noticed that if the Early Phase could go on for ever, it would converge to a steady state with growth rate r_n; so $x_T R_n^{-T}$ would converge to a constant, which we have in fact identified as β. The corresponding constant for the Late Phase, the constant to which $x_T R^{-T}$ converges, I shall call β_1. We can determine β_1, in the manner which will be explained in the rest of this section.

It will be well, before beginning the enquiry (which is rather complex), to insist that there is an issue of principle involved. It is interesting to see whether the final steady state is entirely determined by the properties of the new technique (which do determine its growth rate), or whether its 'history' is still embodied in it. We shall in fact find that it does not escape from its history; the history is still reflected in the constant β_1.

We saw, in sect. 8, that the Fixwage path in its Late Phase is determined by

$$q_0 x_T + q_1 \sum_1^n x_{T-t} = q_0^* x_T^* + q_1^* \sum_1^n x_{T-t}^*$$

which we should now translate as

$$-x_T + r_n \sum_1^n x_{T-t} = h\left[-x_T^* + r_n^* \sum_1^n x_{T-t}^* \right]. \tag{11.1}$$

As before, this has a solution with growth rate g; when that is taken out, the remainder is the solution of a homogeneous equation, the characteristic equation of which is

$$f(\lambda) = \lambda^n - r_n \sum_1^n \lambda^{n-t} = 0. \tag{11.2}$$

Since $r_n > (1/n)$, this can again be shown to have no repeated roots. So the solution of (11.1) is of the form

$$x_T = \alpha_1 G^T + \sum_{r=1}^{r=n} \beta_r \lambda_r^T,$$

where the λ_r are the roots of (11.2).

Now $\lambda = R$ is a root of (11.2) and we know from sect. 8 that it is the dominant root. Put $\lambda_1 = R$. Then (since $R > G$) x_T converges to $\beta_1 R^T$, confirming that β_1 is the constant which we seek.

α_1 is determined, in the usual way, by substitution in (11.1); the β_r must be determined by initial conditions. These (for LP) are the already determined (EP) values of x_T. For $T = 0$ to n,

$$x_T = \alpha G^T + \beta R_n^T = \alpha_1 G^T + \sum_1^n \beta_r \lambda_r^T. \tag{11.3}$$

Now put $f(\lambda) = (\lambda - R)\phi(\lambda)$, where $\phi(\lambda) = \sum_1^n c_i \lambda^{n-t}$ with $c_1 = 1$. Form $\sum_1^n c_i x_{n-t}$. Since all λ except λ_1 satisfy $\phi(\lambda) = 0$, all terms in these λ's will vanish, leaving

$$\alpha\phi(G) + \beta\phi(R_n) = \alpha_1\phi(G) + \beta_1\phi(R). \tag{11.4}$$

From this, by mere algebra, β_1 can be calculated.

The algebra is simplified, if we write $(1/g_n)$ for $\sum_1^n G^{-t}$, so that g_n is the *gross rate of growth*, as defined in sect. 6. For we then find that

$$\alpha_1 = h(r_n^* - g_n)/(r_n - g_n)$$

so that
$$h - \alpha_1 = h(r_n - r_n^*)/(r_n - g_n).$$

Now
$$\alpha = h(r_n^* - g)/(r_n - g),$$

so
$$h - \alpha = \beta = h(r_n - r_n^*)/(r_n - g).$$

Thus
$$(h - \alpha_1)/\beta = (r_n - g)/(r_n - g_n)$$

and
$$(\alpha - \alpha_1/\beta = (g_n - g)/(r_n - g_n).$$

Accordingly, reverting to (11.4),

$$\beta_1\phi(R)(r_n - g_n) = \beta[(g_n - g)\phi(G) + (r_n - g_n)\phi(R_n)]. \tag{11.5}$$

All the terms in (11.5), except β and β_1, are clear of the parameters of the old technique; so we have shown that the ratio of β_1 to β is clear of those parameters. Now in Fig. 11 (above, p. 96) OE is log β while OL is log β_1. So what we have just shown is that EL is entirely determined by the parameters of the new technique. But OL is not so determined; for it still includes OE, which is in part a function of the old-technique parameters.

Calculation of the ϕ functions show that the ratio of β_1 to β is equal to that of $(r_n - g)/(r - g)$ (which is >1) to $(r_n - r)f'(R)$. This latter expression can be proved to lie between 0 and 1, since r_n lies between $(1 + r)/n$ and $(1/n) + r$. Thus $\beta_1 > \beta$, and L is above E, as drawn in Fig. 11.

(Chapter IX)

12. *The Early Phase of the Full Employment Path.* Here, from $A_T = A_T^*$, we have

(PP) $a_0 x_0 = a_0^* x_0^*$ (EP) $a_0 x_T + a_1 \sum_0^{T-1} x_t = a_0^* x_T^* + a_1^* \sum_0^{T-1} x_t^*$

and from the latter, taking the first difference,

$$a_0 x_T - (a_0 - a_1) x_{T-1} = a_0^* x_T^* - (a_0^* - a_1^*) x_{T-1}^*.$$

To put these in a form which is comparable with that used in sect. 9, we put $u = (a_1/a_0)$, with $U = 1 - u$; and similarly for u^* and U^*. As before, $x_0^* = 1$. So, comparably with (9.1),

(PP) $x_0 = h$ (EP) $x_T - U x_{T-1} = h(G - U^*) G^{T-1}$
$$= h(g + u^*) G^{T-1} \quad (12.1)$$

It is immediately apparent that the solution of (12.1) is of the form

$$x_T = \alpha G^T - \beta U^T, \qquad (12.2)$$

where α and β, which are of course to be distinguished from our former α and β, are suitable constants. Substituting in (12.1 EP), we find that

$$\alpha = h(G - U^*)/(G - U) = h(g + u^*)/(g + u),$$

while from (12.1 PP), $\alpha - \beta = h$.

It is obvious that since the a's are positive, $u > 0$; while we have found in sect. 7 that if the Traverse is to converge to an equilibrium, we must have $a_1 < a_0$, so that $U > 0$. I shall assume[1] that this condition is satisfied for both techniques; so that all of u, U, u^*, U^*, are between 0 and 1.

Here then as T increases, the second term in x_T continually diminishes, so that there is an apparent convergence to the path $x_T = \alpha G^T$, or $(x_T/x_T^*) = \alpha$. Now when α is written in full, as $(a_0^* g + a_1^*)/(a_0 g + a_1)$, we see that it is one of our family of *Indexes of Improvement*[2]; like the others, it is a mean between h and H. It is closely related to that which we called $I(g)$; but it is not the same as $I(g)$. For $I(g) = (a_0^* g_n + a_1^*)/(a_0 g_n + a_1)$, where g_n is the gross rate of growth. In the corresponding formula for α, the growth rate is *not* grossed up; and why this should be may be readily understood. What α determines is the 'pseudo-equilibrium' of the Early Phase, during which the question of replacing the new machines has not yet arisen. g is what g_n would be if the machines were immortal.

___

[1] See pp. 104–5 above.   [2] See Ch. VI and sect. 6 above.

Since $g_n > g$, α is nearer to H than is $I(g)$. With $r^* > g$, as we continue to assume,

$$h, I(r^*), I(g), \alpha, H$$

are in that order. So, in the case of a forward bias, $\alpha > h$ and $\beta > 0$; while, since $I(r^*) > 1$ (the change in technique is profitable) $\alpha > 1$. In the case of a backward bias, $\alpha < h$ and β is negative; and here it is not necessary that $\alpha > 1$. If $I(g) < 1$—and (as was shown in Chapter VI) this is a possibility that is not excluded in the case of a backward bias—then clearly $\alpha < 1$.

So the relative rate of starts (x_T/x_T^*) which always begins at h, *rises* towards α in the case of a forward bias; but *falls* towards α in the case of a backward bias. That is its course in the Early Phase.

13. We may now proceed in the usual way to calculate the course of final output, and hence of productivity (still in the Early Phase). The output coefficients being those of Simple Profiles, we have for final output

$$B_T - B_T^* = \sum_0^{T-1} (x_t - x_t^*) = (\alpha - 1) \sum_0^{T-1} G^t - \beta \sum_0^{T-1} U^t. \quad (13.1)$$

Now $A_T = A_T^*$, and B_T^*/A_T^* is constant; so (B_T/A_T) is proportional to (B_T/B_T^*); so to determine the course of productivity it is sufficient to calculate (B_T/B_T^*). Now, as shown in sect. 6, $B_T^* = (1/g_n)G^T$; so,

$$(B_T/B_T^*) - 1 = g_n\left[(\alpha - 1) \sum_1^T G^{-t} - \beta G^{-T} \sum_0^{T-1} U^t\right]. \quad (13.2)$$

Consider the first of these components, which in the *neutral* case ($\beta = 0$) will be the only component. The time-shape of its path is given by

$$g_n \sum_1^T G^{-t} = \left(\sum_1^T G^{-t}\right)\bigg/\left(\sum_1^n G^{-t}\right),$$

a *fraction* which increases with T, though at a diminishing rate, until at the end of the Early Phase ($T = n$) it equals unity. This is the path that is drawn for the neutral case on Fig. 12 (above, p. 102). In the neutral case $\alpha = I(g)$, for all the 'indexes' are equal; so at the end of the Early Phase productivity will have reached its equilibrium level.

For the more general character of the path, consider the increment in productivity from T to $T + 1$. Since A_T has growth rate g, productivity will be rising or falling according as $P_T = B_{T+1} - GB_T$ is positive or negative. $B_{T+1}^* - GB_T^* = 0$; so, from (13.1)

$$P_T = (B_{T+1} - B_{T+1}^*) - G(B_T - B_T^*)$$

$$= (\alpha - 1)\left[\sum_0^T G^t - G\sum_0^{T-1} G^t\right] - \beta\left[\sum_0^T U^t - G\sum_0^{T-1} U^t\right]$$

$$= (\alpha - 1) - \beta U^t + \beta(G - 1)\sum_0^{T-1} U^t$$

$$= (h - 1) + \beta(G - U)\sum_0^{T-1} U^t. \tag{13.3}$$

We know that $G > U$, and that $\sum U^t$ which begins at zero when $T = 0$, thereafter rises steadily, though at a diminishing rate. Thus from (13.3) the path of productivity can be read off directly.

If $h > 1$ and $\beta > 0$ (weak forward bias) it will always be true that $P_T > 0$, so productivity is steadily rising. If $h < 1$ while $\beta > 0$ (strong forward bias) P_T will be negative for $T = 0$, but is likely to become positive as T increases. For as T increases, $(G - U)\sum U^t$ will rise towards $(G - U)/(1 - U)$ which is > 1. So P_T is rising towards a limit which is $> (\alpha - 1)$; and we know that when $h < 1$ it is necessary that $\alpha > 1$, if the change in technique is to be profitable. Continuation of the Early Phase must therefore 'in the end' lead to rising productivity; but there is no guarantee that the rise must be reached before the end of the Early Phase.

If $\beta < 0$ (backward bias) it is necessary that $h > 1$. So P_T is positive when $T = 0$; but for large T it may become negative.

14. *The Late Phase of the Full Employment Path.* We have no trouble, in the case of the Full Employment path, with the calculation of the final equilibrium; for we know, from steady state theory, that in final equilibrium $(x_T/x_T^*) = (B_T/B_T^*) = I(g)$. The precise calculation of the path to that equilibrium is again a task that I have been unable to attempt.

We can however say something, of considerable interest, about the general nature of the path. For we can calculate the position reached at the end of the Early Phase. By comparing that with the final equilibrium, we can see what must happen in the Late Phase 'on the average'.

To do this most expeditiously, define u_n by $(1/u_n) = \sum_1^n U^{-t}$, analogously with $(1/g_n) = \sum_1^n G^{-t}$. Since $G > U$, $g_n > u_n$. From the definition of g_n, we have $G^n = g_n/(g_n - g)$; and in the same way $U^n = u_n/(u_n + u)$.

Now $I(g) = h(g_n + u^*)/(g_n + u)$; so

$$I(g) - h = h(u^* - u)/(g_n + u).$$

In the same way

$$\alpha - h = \beta = h(u^* - u)/(g + u).$$

So

$$(1/\beta)[I(g) - h] = (g + u)/(g_n + u)$$

and

$$\alpha - I(g) = \beta - [I(g) - h] = \beta(g_n - g)/(g_n + u)$$
$$= \beta g_n G^{-n}/(g_n + u).$$

With this preparation, the comparisons we are seeking to make follow easily.

Take first the rate of starts. At the end of the Early Phase, $(x_n/x_n^*) = \alpha - \beta(U/G)^n$. So

$$\frac{x_n}{x_n^*} - I(g) = \beta G^{-n}\left[\frac{g_n}{g_n + u} - U^n\right]$$

$$= \beta G^{-n}\left[\frac{g_n}{g_n + u} - \frac{u_n}{u_n + u}\right]$$

by the same transformation. Since $g_n > u_n$, the bracketed expression is positive. So if there is a forward bias ($\beta > 0$), the rate of starts at the end of the Early Phase will be above its equilibrium level; 'on the average' in the Late Phase it will have to slow down. If there is a backward bias, it will have to go up. In either case the Early Phase adjustment proves to have been overdone.

Since at the end of the Early Phase the 'fraction' of (13.2) is unity,

$$\frac{B_n}{B_n^*} = \alpha - \beta g_n G^{-n}\sum_0^{n-1} U^t = \alpha - \beta g_n G^{-n}(U^n/u_n),$$

so that

$$\frac{B_n}{B_n^*} - I(g) = \beta g_n G^{-n}\left[\frac{1}{g_n + u} - \frac{1}{u_n + u}\right],$$

where, again since $g_n > u_n$, the bracketed expression is clearly negative.

It follows that if there is a forward bias, productivity at the end of the Early Phase will be below its equilibrium level; while if there is a backward bias, it will be above. Thus even when there is the weakest of weak backward biases, there will be a fall in productivity at some stage in the process of equilibration; if not in the Early Phase, then later.

(Chapter X)

15. *Sequential changes in technique.* There is one more thing to be done in this Appendix before we leave the Standard Case. How much can be said about the effect (on the Full Employment path) of a second switch in technique superimposed on the first? I shall suppose that the second switch occurs within the Early Phase of the first switch, but not immediately after the first switch. Thus we begin, as before, with a steady state under an old technique, here called Technique [o]. At time o Technique [1] is introduced for new processes, in the manner with which we are accustomed. Then at time M (the beginning of year M) Technique [2] is introduced, which in its turn is used for processes started in year M and thereafter. I shall now use double stars for magnitudes which refer to technique [o], single stars for those which refer to technique [1], while those which refer to the latest technique [2] will, as usual, be left unstarred.

From $T = o$ to $T = M - 1$ (the First Lap, as we may call it) Technique [1] is dominant; so rates of start are given by our familiar formula (12.2), which should now be written

$$x_T^* = \alpha_{01}G^T - \beta_{01}U_1^t, \qquad (15.1)$$

U_1 being the U of Technique [1], while α_{01} and β_{01} are our usual α and β, marked as referring to the switch from [o] to [1].

In order to calculate the rates of start in the Second Lap (from $T = M$ onwards), we use the path which would have been followed if there had been no second switch, as our reference path. We have only to compare the starts which are *fresh* from the point of view of the Second Lap. Thus we have $a_0 x_M = a_0^* x_M^*$ as initial condition, and subsequently, taking the first difference (as usual)

$$a_0 x_T - (a_0 - a_1)x_{T-1} = a_0^* x_T^* - (a_0^* - a_1^*)x_{T-1}^*. \qquad (15.2)$$

Now the right-hand side of (15.2) is equal to the same expression with double stars (by comparison of the new reference path with the old reference path); thus it has growth rate g, as usual. So we see that the solution (for the Second Lap) must be of the usual form

$$x_T = \alpha'G^T - \beta'U_2^T,$$

where U_2 is the U of technique [2], and α' and β' are constants, to be determined.

We find, by direct substitution in (15.2), that

$$\alpha'(a_0 g + a_1) = \alpha_{01}(a_0^* g + a_1^*) = (a_0^{**}g + a_1^{**})$$

using (12.3); so α' is the regular α for a switch from [0] to [2], which may conformably be written α_{02}. (We note that $\alpha_{02} = \alpha_{01}\alpha_{12}$.)

To find β', we use the initial condition

$$a_0 x_M = a_0^* x_M^*, \quad \text{in the form} \quad x_M = h_{12} x_M^*. \tag{15.3}$$

Thus $\alpha_{02} G^M - \beta' U_2^M = h_{12}(\alpha_{01} G^M - \beta_{01} U_1^M),$

and $\beta' U_2^M = \alpha_{01}(\alpha_{12} - h_{12}) G^M + \beta_{01} h_{12} U_1^M$

$$= \alpha_{01} \beta_{12} G^M + \beta_{01} h_{12} U_1^M, \tag{15.4}$$

where β_{12} is the β for a direct switch from [1] to [2].

Thus β' is a compound of β_{01} and β_{12}, as we should expect. It will be noticed that (since $G > U_1$) the longer the deferment (M) the more important is the bias of the second switch.

16. Having established the rates of start, we may now proceed, in the usual manner, to calculate the behaviour of output, and of productivity. We shall, however, need a more compact notation.

Let D be an operator signifying divergence from the old (double-starred) reference path. Thus $DB_T = B_T - B_T^{**}$, $DB_T^* = B_T^* - B_T^{**}$, $Dx_t = x_t - x_t^{**}$, and so on.

Then, in the First Lap, before the second switch,

$$DB_T = DB_T^* = \sum_0^{T-1} Dx_t^*, \tag{16.1}$$

as in (13.1). But notice that in year M the second switch has not had time to affect output; so (16.1) holds for $T = M$ as well as for $T < M$. In the Second Lap, as soon as $T > M$,

$$DB_T = \sum_0^{M-1} Dx_t^* + \sum_M^{T-1} Dx_t = DB_M^* + \sum_M^{T-1} Dx_t. \tag{16.2}$$

As in sect. 13, the most interesting way of using these formulae is to calculate P_T, where $P_T > 0$ is the condition for productivity to be increasing from T to $T + 1$. Since $P_T^{**} = 0$,

$$P_T = DP_T = DB_{T+1} - GDB_T,$$

but this takes different forms according as $T < M$, $T = M$, or $T > M$.

For $T < M$, we can use (16.1) and find that P_T is given by (13.3) with appropriate change of notation. For $T = M$, DB_{T+1} is given by (16.2) but DB_T by (16.1). Let us therefore define P_M^* to be what P_M

would have been if there had been no second switch. So P_M^* is still given by (13.3). But

$$P_M - P_M^* = DB_{M+1} - DB_{M+1}^* = Dx_M - Dx_M^* \quad \text{by (16.2)}$$

$$= x_M - x_M^* = (h_{12} - 1)x_M^* \quad \text{by (15.3)}.$$

Now, for $T > M$,

$$P_T - P_M = DB_{T+1} - DB_{M+1} - G(DB_T - DB_M)$$

$$= \sum_{M+1}^{T} Dx_t - G \sum_{M}^{T-1} Dx_t \quad \text{(since } DB_M = DB_M^*\text{)}$$

$$= (\alpha_{02} - 1)\left[\sum_{M+1}^{T} G^t - G \sum_{M}^{T-1} G^t\right]$$

$$-\beta'\left[\sum_{M+1}^{T} U_2^t - G \sum_{M}^{T-1} U_2^t\right]$$

$$= \beta'(G - U_2) \sum_{M}^{T-1} U_2^t.$$

Thus, in the second lap,

$$P_T = P_M^* + (h_{12} - 1)x_M^* + \beta'(G - U_2) \sum_{M}^{T-1} U_2^t, \qquad (16.3)$$

where $\qquad P_M^* = (h_{01} - 1) + \beta_{01}(G - U_1) \sum_{0}^{M-1} U_1^t,$

from which the behaviour of productivity, with various (strong or weak) biasses, can be fairly easily read off.

17. Let us take the case explored in Chapter X. There is an initial switch, due to an 'autonomous' change in technology, and then a second switch, which is prompted by the change in wages induced by the first. If the initial switch is no more than weakly biased (in either direction) it must induce a rise in productivity, in its Early Phase, and hence, under any ordinary assumption about saving propensities, a rise in wages. Thus the second switch is induced by the rise in wages; hence, as shown in Chapter X, it must have a (relatively) strong forward bias.

On these assumptions, β_{12} is positive, and $h_{12} < 1$. So, referring to formula (15.4), we see that β' must be positive, so long as β_{01} is positive (or zero); and will usually be positive when β_{01} is negative, excepting when the second switch comes soon after the first (M is small). The second switch may then do no more than cancel out a part of the original backward bias. Delay in the second switch makes this less likely to happen (since $G > 1 > U_1$). Let us therefore take it that $\beta' > 0$.

Productivity, after $T = M$, will then behave in the regular strong forward biased manner, with a *relative* setback at $T = M$, which will persist until the relieving army (governed by β') comes to the rescue. Whether the setback is an absolute setback depends on the sign of P_M.

To investigate this, consider the case in which the initial switch is unbiased ($\beta_{01} = 0$ and so $h_{01} > 0$). Then $x_M^* = \alpha_{01} G^M = h_{01} G^M$. $P_M^* = (h_{01} - 1)$; so

$$P_M = (h_{01} - 1) + h_{01}(h_{12} - 1)G^M.$$

If M were zero (so that the second switch was immediate) this would reduce to $h_{01}h_{12} - 1 = h_{02} - 1$, as it should do. So productivity may still rise, even though $h_{12} < 1$, so long as h_{01} is sufficiently greater than 1 to offset. But as M increases, the negative term increases; so delay in the second switch increases the chance of an absolute setback at $T = M$.

It can be shown that if the initial switch is forward-biased ($\beta_{01} > 0$) this effect of delay will be intensified; but if the initial switch is backward biased, it will be weakened.

(Chapter XI)

18. *Shortening and lengthening of the construction period. Full Employment Path.* W now lose the convenient assumption of equal durations, and must revert (for the moment) to working in 'weeks'. As in sect. 5, I use m for the length of the construction period, though we must here distinguish between an unstarred m for that of the new technique and starred m for the old. Here again there is a Preliminary Phase, in which all labour that is employed on fresh processes is constructional labour; but now it extends from 0 to m or m^*, whichever comes first. There is an Early Phase, in which both constructional and utilizational labour are employed on fresh processes; but now it begins from m or m^*, whichever comes later. In between there is an Intermediate Phase (IP), extending from m to m^* or from m^* to m. The (PP) and (EP) equations are as written in (5.1); but in (IP), when $m < m^*$, the left-hand side is the same as in (EP) while the right-hand side is as in (PP). When $m > m^*$, left and right are reversed.

As in sect. 5, we take first differences, so as to get equations corresponding to (5.2). For (IP)

$$(m < m^*) \qquad a_0 x_T - (a_0 - a_1)x_{T-m} = a_0^* x_T^* \qquad (18.1)$$
$$(m > m^*) \qquad a_0 x_T = a_0^* x^* - (a_0^* - a_1^*)x_{T-m}^*.$$

We again put $y_T = x_T/x_T^*$; but it will now be convenient to write G for the growth multiplier for m weeks, G^* for m^* weeks. Then with $(a_1/a_0) = 1 - u$, as usual,

$$(PP) \qquad\qquad y_T = h \qquad\qquad (18.2)$$
$$(IP, m < m^*) \qquad y_T - (U/G)y_{T-m} = h$$
$$(IP, m > m^*) \qquad y_T = h[1 - (U^*/G^*)]$$
$$(EP) \qquad y_T - (U/G)y_{T-m} = h[1 - (U^*/G^*)].$$

It will clearly be convenient, for the manipulation of these equations, to put $(U/G) = v$, $(U^*/G^*) = v^*$.

In all forms of (18.2) the right-hand side is a constant; so, as in the Standard Case, y_T will be constant over suitable stretches. In every stretch, the value of y_T reflects what it was at $T - m$; that at y_{T-2m}; and so on. The initial conditions of these sequences are however different according as the sequence begins with (PP) or with one of the forms of (IP). If, as in the text of Chapter XI, we make m one 'year', there is one form that belongs to the 'January' or 'December', going back to (IP), and one for the rest of the 'year', going back to (PP). With *rest of year* values, we have, for year T,

$$y_T = \alpha - \beta v^T$$

with $\alpha = h(1 - v^*)/(1 - v)$, derived from (EP), while from (PP) $\alpha - \beta = h$. Thus 'rest of year' values are substantially the same as in the Standard Case; there is just the difference that v^* is (U^*/G^*) not (U^*/G). It is this which gives the first growth effect, a gain (with shortening) or a loss (with lengthening). That is all that happens, to the rate of starts, in the 'rest of the year'.

The January values (for shortening)

$$y_{T\,\mathrm{Jan}} = \alpha - (\beta_{\mathrm{Jan}})v^T$$

have the same α, but a (β_{Jan}) that is derived from (IP $m < m^*$). This gives

$$y_{1\,\mathrm{Jan}} = h(1 + v) = \alpha - (\beta_{\mathrm{Jan}})v;$$

so that, generally,

$$y_{T\,\mathrm{Jan}} = \alpha - (\alpha - h - hv)v^{T-1} = \alpha - \beta v^{T-1} + hv^T.$$

It is immediately apparent that $y_{T \text{ Jan}} > y_{T-1}$; while, from

$$y_T - y_{T-1} = \beta(1 - v)v^{T-1} = h(v - v^*)v^{T-1},$$

we see that $y_{T \text{ Jan}} - y_T = hv^{T-1}v^*,$

which is clearly positive. So there is a *special* January gain, which is equal to hv^T when measured backwards, and to $hv^{T-1}v^*$ when measured forwards. Since $v < 1$, the *special* gain diminishes as time goes on.

The December values (for lengthening) are

$$y_{T \text{ Dec}} = \alpha - (\beta_{\text{Dec}})v^T,$$

where (from IP $m > m^*$)

$$\alpha - (\beta_{\text{Dec}}) = h(1 - v^*) = \alpha(1 - v).$$

So $\beta_{\text{Dec}} = \alpha v,$ and $y_{T \text{ Dec}} = \alpha(1 - v^{T+1}).$

We then have

$$y_{T \text{ Dec}} - y_{T+1} = -hv^{T+1}, \quad \text{and} \quad y_{T \text{ Dec}} - y_T = -hv^T v^*,$$

so that there is a *special* December loss, to match the *special* January gain in the other case. But it is interesting to notice that in this case of lengthening the special value y_{Dec} always rises with T, whatever the bias. The lowest y is always that of December year o.

We may now proceed to determine final output, in the usual way, by comparing output from fresh processes. In (PP) there is no output from fresh processes, on either path. In (IP) there is no fresh output from the longer process, but there is from the shorter. So there is here another *special* gain from shortening, loss from lengthening. In (EP) the increment in $B - B^*$ at time T

$$= x_{T-m} - x_{T-m}^* = [y_{T-m} - (G/G^*)]x_{T-m}^*.$$

The deduction of (G/G^*) instead of 1 (as in the Standard Case) gives a second growth effect (again a gain from shortening, loss from lengthening). By summing, as usual, the total effect on output can be worked out.

19. *Shortening and lengthening (Fixwage path).* The (IP) equations corresponding to (18.1) are here

$(m < m^*)$ $q_0 x_T - (q_0 - q_1)x_{T-m} = q_0^* x_T^*$

$(m > m^*)$ $q_0 x_T = q_0^* x_T^* - (q_0^* - q_1^*)x_{T-m}^*$

From these, together with the usual (PP) and (EP) equations, we have

—putting q's in terms of R_n and h, and then putting $R_n/G = V$, $R_n^*/G^* = V^*$,

(PP) $$y_T = h$$

(IP $m < m^*$) $$y_T - Vy_{T-m} = h$$

(IP, $m > m^*$) $$y_T = h(1 - V^*)$$

(EP) $$y_T - Vy_{T-m} = h(1 - V^*)$$

corresponding to (18.2).

Now the reference path is a steady state under the old technique. For it to engender a positive surplus, we must have $R^* > G^*$ (both being reckoned with the construction period of that old technique as time-unit). The gross rate of return must be greater than the net rate, so $R_n^* > R^* > G^*$, and $V^* > 1$. We see at once that the (IP, $m > m^*$) equation yields a negative rate of starts, which is impossible. Thus it is impossible for the construction period to be lengthened, when the real wage is fixed, unless some *special* supply of saving (or other external finance) is forthcoming.

Next consider shortening. As in sect. 18, (IP) may be reckoned to be January of year 1. We then have, for non-Januaries,

$$y_T = \alpha + \beta V^T$$

where α incorporates a growth effect, similar to that of sect. 18, and $\alpha + \beta = h$, by (PP). For Januaries

$$y_{T \text{ Jan}} = \alpha + \beta_{\text{Jan}} V^T,$$

where β_{Jan} is given by

$$\alpha + \beta_{\text{Jan}} V = h(1 + V),$$

so that
$$y_{T \text{ Jan}} = \alpha(1 - V^{T-1}) + hV^{T-1} + hV^T.$$
$$= \alpha + \beta V^{T-1} + hV^T.$$

It is obvious that $y_{T \text{ Jan}} - y_{T-1} = hV^T$; and it may be shown, as in the last section, that $y_{T \text{ Jan}} - y_T = hV^*V^{T-1}$. Thus there is a *special* January gain, whether measured forward or backward, as in the Full Employment case. But here, since $V > 1$, the special gain will increase from year to year. Even the ratio $y_{T \text{ Jan}}/y_T$ will increase, though not beyond a finite limit.

(Chapter XII)

20. *Convergence (of the Full Employment path) more generally considered.* I now abandon the Simple Profile, and revert to the more general form that was considered in Part I. For the study of convergence, we may proceed directly to the (LP) equation

$$\sum_0^n a_t x_{T-t} = A_T^* = A_0^* G^T$$

as we should now write it. When the equilibrium solution is taken out, the remainders are given by the homogeneous equation

$$\sum_0^n a_t \xi_{T-t} = 0 \qquad (20.1)$$

in which all a's are non-negative (a_0 and a_n, at least, being positive). As usual we take the first difference, getting

$$a_0 \xi_{T+1} - (a_0 - a_1)\xi_T - (a_1 - a_2)\xi_{T-1} - \cdots - a_n \xi_{T-n} = 0$$

which we shall write

$$\xi_{T+1} = p_0 \xi_T + p_1 \xi_{T-1} + \cdots + p_n \xi_{T-n}, \qquad (20.2)$$

in which, it will be observed, $\sum p = 1$.

It is well known that a *sufficient* condition for a sequence such as (20.2) to converge to a constant is that all p's should be positive (so that $a_0 > a_1 > a_2 > \cdots > a_n$). For if this condition is satisfied, every ξ is a weighted average of previous ξ's in the sequence (with positive weights); it must therefore lie between the largest and smallest of initial values (as in sect. 7 above); so explosive solutions are excluded. It can also be shown, by consideration of the characteristic

$$\lambda^{n+1} = \sum_0^n p_t \lambda^{n-t} \qquad (20.3)$$

that cyclic solutions are excluded.[1] For if λ is a root with unit modulus, its conjugate must also be a root; so

$$1 = \lambda^{n+1} \bar{\lambda}^{n+1} = \left(\sum_0^n p_t \lambda^{n-t}\right)\left(\sum_0^n p_t \bar{\lambda}^{n-t}\right)$$

$$= \sum p_t^2 + \sum p_t p_{t'}(\lambda^t \bar{\lambda}^{t'} + \lambda^{t'} \bar{\lambda}^t)$$

and therefore, since $\sum p_t = 1$,

$$\sum p_t p_{t'}(\lambda^t - \lambda^{t'})(\bar{\lambda}^{t'} - \bar{\lambda}^t) = \sum p_t p_{t'}(\lambda^t - \lambda^{t'})^2 = 0, \qquad (20.4)$$

which is impossible if all p_t are positive, unless $\lambda = 1$ (as may be seen by taking $t - t' = 1$).

[1] Repeated roots are not necessarily excluded, but these make no difference to the argument.

If we know no more than that no p is negative (some positive), it is still the case that explosive solutions are excluded; but a cyclic solution may not be excluded. It is nevertheless clear that it will be excluded if *any* pair of successive p's are both positive; and it will also be excluded if p_0 is positive (since a_0 and a_n are positive, we are already committed to p_n positive). For it follows, from (20.4) that, if p_0 and p_n are both positive, a root with unit modulus must be such that $\lambda^n = 1$; but then, from (20.3), $\lambda - p_0 = \sum_1^n p_t \lambda^{n-t}$. Since the modulus of a sum is not greater than the sum of moduli, $|\lambda - p_0| \leqslant \sum_1^n p_t = 1 - p_0$; thus $\lambda + \bar{\lambda} \geqslant 2$, which is impossible unless $\lambda = 1$. So it is sufficient that p_0 (and p_n) should be positive, other p's non-negative. The Convergence of the Simple Profile is a special case of this proposition; what we have just proved is a little wider.

In economic application, however, it is of limited help. For we still require that the maximum application of labour should be in the first period (period o), 'year' or 'week' as we like to interpret it. A preparatory phase, during which the application of labour increases over time, seems still to be ruled out.

21. It can however be shown that the existence of such a phase is not *necessarily* inconsistent with convergence to equilibrium, though very often it will be.

Let us go back to (20.1) and take its characteristic equation

$$f(\lambda) = \sum_0^n a_t \lambda^{n-t} = 0 \qquad (21.1)$$

in which (for the present) I shall take n to be even. Since all a's are non-negative, it is directly evident that (21.1) can have no positive roots. Either, therefore, all its roots are complex, or there is an even number of negative roots. $f(\lambda)$ can therefore be factorized into real quadratic factors, by taking complex conjugates together, and pairs of negative roots together. So put

$$f(\lambda) = a_0 \Pi(\lambda^2 + c_i \lambda + d_i) \qquad (21.2)$$

where the c's and d's are real, and i runs from 1 to m, where $m = \frac{1}{2}n$.

The conditions for the roots of such a quadratic to have modulus < 1 are that $|d| < 1$ and that $|c| < 1 + |d|$. Here, if the roots of the quadratic are complex, $d > 0$; while if they are both real and negative, again $d > 0$; so always $d > 0$. If the roots are negative, $c > 0$; but if they are complex, c may have either sign. Thus the conditions on the individual quadratic reduce to

$$d < 1, \qquad |c| < 1 + d.$$

These conditions must hold for *all* the quadratics if the sequence is to converge.

If every $d < 1$, their product must be < 1. But the product of the d's is a_n/a_0; that this should be < 1 (so that $a_n < a_0$) is a *necessary* condition for convergence. So far as I can see, it is the one simple necessary condition. (It corresponds, of course, to the necessary condition on the Simple Profile with which we are familiar.)

It will on the other hand be observed that the convergence conditions will be satisfied, so long as all d are positive and < 1, even if all c are positive and fairly large (but all < 1). Suppose that every $c > \mu$, where $0 < \mu < 1$. Then, from (21.1) and (21.2), comparing the co-efficients of λ^{n-1}, $(a_1/a_0) = \sum c_i > m\mu$, so that $a_1 > a_0$ if $m > (1/\mu)$. Further, comparing the coefficients of λ^{n-2},

$$(a_2/a_0) = \sum c_i c_j + \sum d_i > \sum c_i c_j$$

Now since $(c_i - \mu)(c_j - \mu) > 0$, $c_i c_j > \mu(c_i + c_j) - \mu^2$, so that

$$\sum c_i c_j > (m-1)\mu \sum c_i - \tfrac{1}{2}m(m-1)\mu^2.$$

Thus $a_2 > a_1$ if $[(m-1)\mu - 1] \sum c_i > \tfrac{1}{2}m(m-1)\mu^2$, which will be satisfied if $(m-1)\mu > 1$, and if $\tfrac{1}{2}m(m-1)\mu^2 > m\mu$, or if $(m-1)\mu > 2$. These are sufficient to show that if μ is large enough, and $m (= \tfrac{1}{2}n)$ is large enough, sequences with increasing a's, at the beginning, are not ruled out.

It should however be noticed that we have similar information about small powers of λ. Comparing coefficients of λ^1 and λ^0, $(a_{n-1}/a_n) = \sum (c_i/d_i)$; and this, if all c's are positive, must be $> \sum c_i$ (for all d are between 0 and 1). So it is necessary, if all c are positive, that $(a_{n-1}/a_n) > (a_1/a_0)$. Thus a rising phase at the beginning of the sequence must be matched by a falling phase at the end.

It is clear, from the same argument, that if all c's are positive, $a_0 > a_1$ requires that the greatest $c < (1/m)$; so that if m is at all large, all c's must be very small. It seems safe to conclude that the non-increasing sequences, which were discussed in sect. 20, must usually be such that the c's are of various signs. (It is clearly impossible that all c's should be negative, since if that were so, a_1 and a_{n-1} would be negative.)

In all of this section I have assumed n even. If n is odd, there must be one real negative root in addition to those (if they exist) of which account has been taken. For convergence, this root must have modulus < 1. I shall not trouble to work through the analysis, taking account of this extra root, for it is easy to see that it would not be changed in any way which would affect the outcome.

22. *Convergence (Fixwage path).* No more is needed than an application of the same device as was used in sect. 8 above, in order to make a similar analysis of the Fixwage path. The (LP) equation

$$\sum_{0}^{n} q_t \xi_{T-t} = 0 \qquad (22.1)$$

which corresponds to (20.1), cannot be treated directly in the same way, since some of the q's must be negative. We know, however, from the efficiency equation that $\sum_{0}^{n} q_t R^{-t} = 0$, so that $\xi_T = C_1 R^T$ is a solution of (22.1). Put $\eta_T = \xi_T R^{-T}$, as in sect. 8. Then

$$\sum_{0}^{n} q_t R^{-t} \eta_{T-t} = 0. \qquad (22.2)$$

Now we know, as shown in Chapter II in the text, that

$$q_t = k_t - k_{t+1} R^{-1},$$

so that (22.2) may be re-written as

$$\sum_{0}^{n} (k_t R^{-t} - k_{t+1} R^{-t-1}) \eta_{T-t} = 0,$$

or as

$$\sum_{1}^{n} k_t R^{-t} \zeta_{T-t} = 0, \qquad (22.3)$$

where $\zeta_T = \eta_T - \eta_{T-1}$, and the term in $t = 0$ is omitted, since $k_0 = 0$.

By the Fundamental Theorem of Chapter II, all k_t $(t > 0)$ are positive; so (22.3) is an equation that is formally identical with (20.1) and has the same properties. There is assured convergence if the successive $k_t R^{-t}$ $(t > 0)$ are steadily diminishing. But $k_t R^{-t} - k_{t+1} R^{-t-1}$ $= q_t R^{-t}$; so what is required is that all q_t $(t > 0)$ should be positive. In the case of the Simple Profile, this condition is satisfied, without more ado. Where there is trouble is when the initial investment is spread over several periods, so that several initial q's are negative. It follows, from sect. 21, that even so convergence is not excluded; but it will have to be matched by a running-down at the end of the process if convergence is to be possible.

Such conditions as these will establish that the series of ζ's converges to a constant; but we require that the η's should converge to a constant, so that the ζ's must converge to zero. But if ζ_T converges to

C_2 (a non-zero constant), η_T must converge to $C_1 + C_2 T$. But then (from 22.2) $\sum_0^n q_t R^{-t}(T - t) = 0$ for large T, so that $\sum_0^n (t q_t R^{-t}) = 0$. But this is

$$\sum_0^n t(k_t R^{-t} - k_{t+1} R^{-t-1}) = \sum_1^n k_t R^{-t} = 0,$$

which, since all k_t $(t > 0)$ are positive, is impossible. So, under the conditions stated, η_T converges to C_1.

INDEX

INDEX

213

Truncation 19–22, 66–7, 83
Turnpike Theorem 10

von Neumann, J. 5–6, 10–11

Wage, as single non-intertemporal price-ratio 37; wage fund, 58–62, 101, 108–9

Walras, L. 7–8
Wicksell, K. 7, 133, 148

'Year', defined 84; proof that it may be taken as unit period (in standard case) 186–8